IMAGES
of America

THE MACHIAS BAY REGION

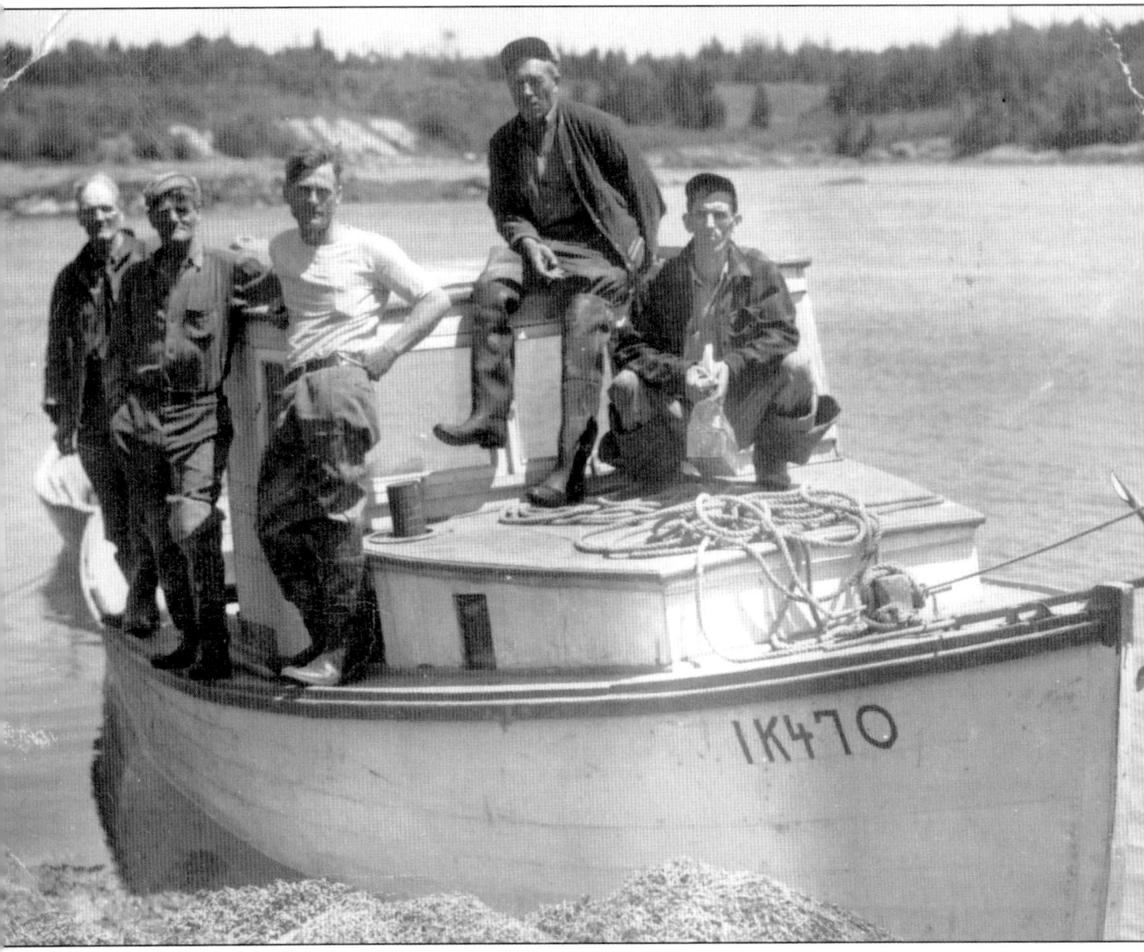

This Bucks Harbor crew poses for a photographer on June 26, 1948.

IMAGES
of America

THE MACHIAS BAY REGION

Jim and Jane Harnedy

ARCADIA
PUBLISHING

ISBN 978-0-7385-0501-5

Published by Arcadia Publishing
Charleston, South Carolina

Printed in the United States of America

Library of Congress Catalog Card Number: 2001086554

For all general information contact Arcadia Publishing at:
Telephone 843-853-2070
Fax 843-853-0044
E-mail sales@arcadiapublishing.com
For customer service and orders:
Toll-Free 1-888-313-2665

Visit us on the Internet at www.arcadiapublishing.com

Contents

ACKNOWLEDGMENTS

The authors wish to thank the following: Valdine Atwood of the Hannah Weston Chapter of the Daughters of the American Revolution (DAR), Theone Look Bagley, Victor Berry, Eleanor Black, A.M. Look Canning Company, Donald W. Look, Charlene Cates, Pauline Cates, Margaret Flaherty, Dr. James G. Flanagan, George Flynn, Harley Flynn, George Gaddis, Steve Gay, Gay Wreaths, Gary Hanscom, Helen's Restaurant, Flo Hanscom, Herb Hanscom, Flo's Wreaths, Richard Hayward, Ruth Leubecker, Wayne Lobey, Linda Lund, BBS Lobster, Donna Michaud, University of Maine at Machias, Norman Nelson, Marjorie Pinkham, Maxine Porter, Bill Prescott, Rev. Michael Sheridan, Tommy Smith, Clayton Vose, J. Scott Whitney, Washington Academy, Gwendelyn Wood, Vernon Wood, Pennell Worcester, Bob Wright of Roundabout Inc., and Michael W. Zimmermann.

Other *Images of America* titles by Jim Harnedy:
The Boothbay Harbor Region
Around Wiscasset
Best of Maine (Selections)

Also by Jim and Jane Harnedy:
A Handy Guide for Eucharistic Ministers, 2001 (Alba House)

INTRODUCTION

Before the arrival of Europeans to the Machias Bay Region, Native Americans of various tribes made an annual September pilgrimage to the shores of the Machias River at Clark's Point. Here have been found extensive clam heaps, providing evidence of their gatherings.

The first Europeans to set foot in the Machias Bay Region were most likely Norsemen. The Picture Rock at Clark's Point in Machiasport and the man-made Norse Pond at Cutler provide some evidence that Norsemen may well have had a settlement here as early as the 11th century.

The French explorer De Montz left the first tangible proof of discovery of the Machias River. There are records that document that some of De Montz's sailors established a trading post at Clark's Point, Machiasport, in 1605–1606.

An ill-fated trading post was established in the Machiasport area in 1733 by the Pilgrims, but the French who claimed the area sent a ship to confiscate the goods and take the occupants prisoners. Later, the French killed two of the Pilgrims, took four prisoners, confiscated all the goods, and burned the post.

Legend says that a Capt. Samuel Bellamey, an infamous pirate, was the next to settle in Machias. After he built a fortified settlement, he and his men took to the sea in their ship the *Whidah* in a quest to capture women for their new settlement. The ship was wrecked off Cape Cod. It is still unknown whether their rich treasures are buried along the banks of the Machias River or lie on a sand bar off Cape Cod.

In 1763, Machias was successfully settled by a group of pioneers from Scarborough who had seen their fields and forest lands devastated by drought and forest fires during the summers of 1761 and 1762. In Machias, they found an abundance of marsh hay, extensive forests, and a sheltered harbor.

In 1775, the Burnham Tavern was the meeting place of the settlement. Standing near the head of Main Street in Machias, this gambrel-roof building, built in 1770 by Job Burnham, was a hostel for weary travelers as well as the spot where the local men came to drink. The tavern also served as the home for the Burnham family.

When news of the battles of Lexington and Concord reached the local men at the Burnham Tavern, they decided to erect a liberty pole on the village green. The townspeople selected a tall tree from which they stripped branches, save a tuft at the top. After erection of the liberty pole, the local citizens pledged themselves to the defense of the colony.

Captain Jones, a trader, had been involved in trading with Machias since the early days of the settlement. In early June 1775, he arrived in Machias from Boston with two sloops, the *Unity* and the *Polly*. It is believed that Jones's mission was to move his family and possessions away from the activity leading up to the Revolutionary War to the safety of this remote outpost. He planned to trade supplies for lumber and sell the lumber to be used to build barracks for the British in Boston. To insure that Captain Jones would get a king's tender for the lumber, the *Margaretta*, under the command of Captain Moore, was sent as an escort. The local citizens were asked to vote whether or not to accept the supplies in trade for the lumber. They voted to accept the trade and also to protect Captain Jones and his crew and property. His two sloops were ordered to be docked at the local wharves.

All would have gone fine if Captain Moore of the *Margaretta* had not seen the liberty pole and demanded in the King's name that it be removed or he would fire upon the town. After numerous public and secret meetings, the men of Machias and local communities decided that the liberty pole would not come down. Instead, they would attempt to capture Moore and his crew while they were attending church.

In preparation for this action, Machias men requested volunteers from the surrounding villages to provide assistance. When Sunday came and Moore was in church, he observed through a window a group of armed men approaching and suspected what they were up to. He did not wait to find out. He bolted out through the window, ran down to his ship, and set sail down the river.

On June 12, 1775, a group of about 40 men aboard the *Unity* set out in pursuit of the *Margaretta* into Machias Bay. They caught up with the ship near Round Island, engaged its crew in battle, and defeated its crew in a battle that historians have called the "Lexington of the Sea." Captain Moore was wounded during the battle and died the next day.

History honors many Machias patriots of the Revolutionary War for their heroism. Col. Jeremiah O'Brien commanded the local patriots in their capture of the *Margaretta*. During July 1775, the *Machias Liberty*, commanded by O'Brien, and the *Falmouth Packet*, under Capt. Benajamin Foster, captured the *Diligence*, another British ship. Hannah Watts Weston, a bride of 17, and her sister-in-law Rebecca, 15, knew how little ammunition the local patriots had to launch their attach on the *Margaretta*. They collected all the powder, lead, and pewter they could find before setting out for Machias. Heavily laden, they started on a 16-mile trek through the woods from Chandler's River (now Jonesboro) on June 12, 1775. Although the young women arrived too late for their ammunition to be used in the capture of the *Margaretta*, the two were rewarded for their heroism.

The Burnham Tavern, which served as the gathering place for Machias patriots, also served as a hospital for the wounded from the *Margaretta* engagement. Since September 28, 1910, the Hannah Weston Chapter of the Daughters of the American Revolution (DAR) have taken on the responsibility for the tavern. Since coming under their jurisdiction, it has been operated as a local museum, with but one notable exception. During the summer of 1916, it was once again put into use for our country when it became headquarters for the Machias branch of the Surgical Dressing work. Here local women helped the World War I effort.

For more than two centuries, the Machias Bay Region has been the home to foresters, shipbuilders, fishermen, farmers, and tradesmen. Just as in the earliest days of our country when folks where called to patriotism, local men and women through the years have always heard the call to do their part for their country.

The photographs, postcards, and related memorabilia in this book chronicle life's unbroken continuity in the towns of the Machias Bay Region: Cutler, East Machias, Jonesboro, Machias, Machiasport, Marshfield, Whiting, and Whitneyville.

One

A Tour of the Region

The Machias Bay Region consists of a group of small homogeneous communities in the nation's easternmost county. Machias, the seat of Washington County, was successfully settled in 1763 by fire-ravaged Scarborough residents who were drawn to this coastal outpost by timber and salt marsh hay. Machiasport, just south of Machias, includes the historic fishing villages of Larrabee, Bucks Harbor, and Starboard. To the west of Machias are Jonesboro (originally Chandler River), Roque Bluffs, Marshfield, and Whitneyville. Jonesboro was the home of Hannah Weston, a Revolutionary War heroine. Roque Bluffs was a part of Jonesboro until 1891, when the community voted to become a separate township. A wealthy Boston businessman named H.P. Gardner, who owned a nearby island, asked that the town be named Roque Bluffs. Life in Marshfield during the late 1890s and early 1900s is beautifully described in Laura Beam's *A Maine Hamlet*, first published in 1957. Whitneyville, on the banks of the Machias River, saw the longest log drives in the east for decades. East of Machias are the towns of East Machias, Whiting, and Cutler. East Machias was settled in 1768 by members of the Foster family. The historic fishing villages of Whiting and Cutler round out the communities of the region.

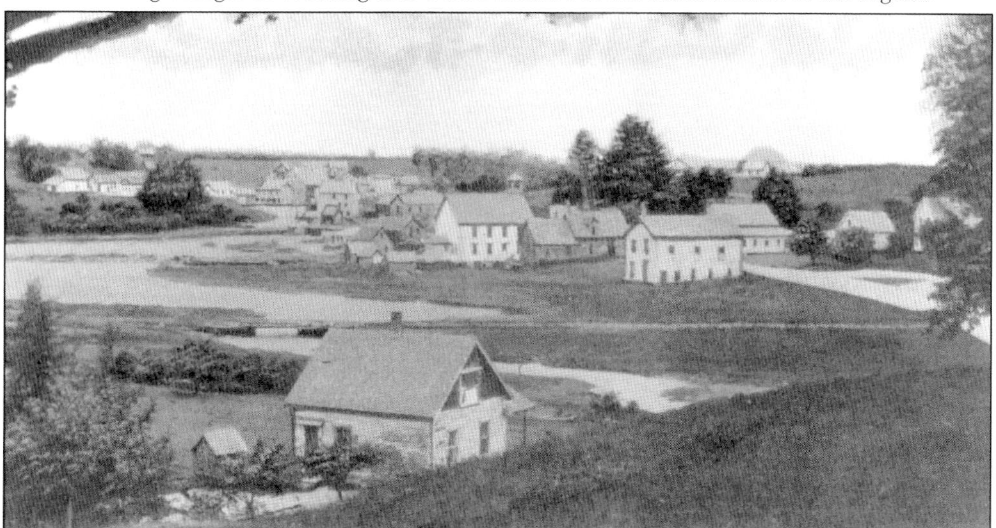

The historic township of Jonesboro was originally called Chandler River.

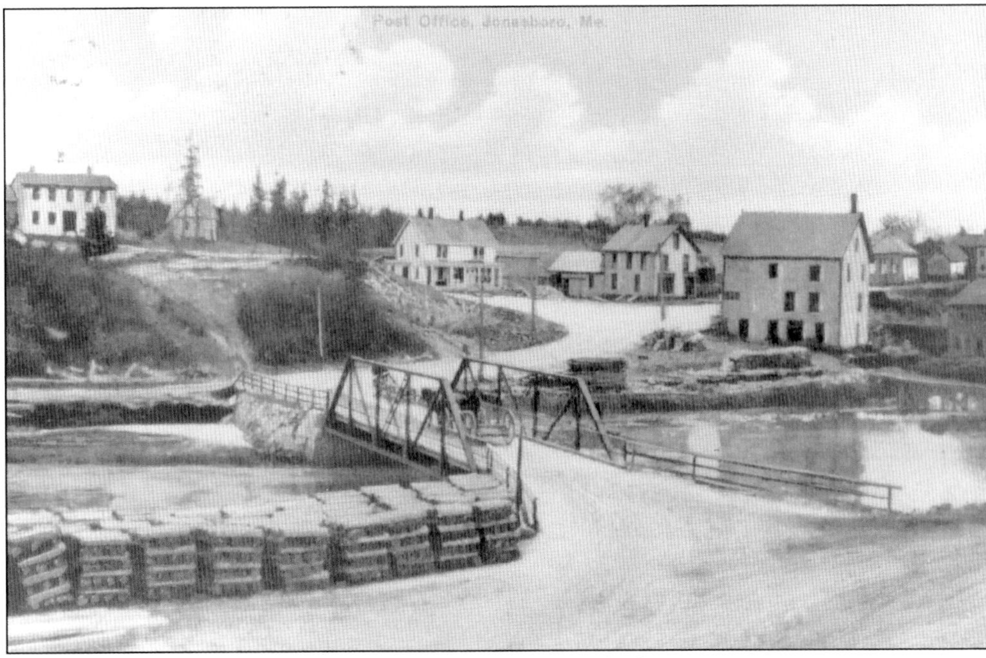

Shown in 1905, the Chandler River Bridge was built in the late 1890s.

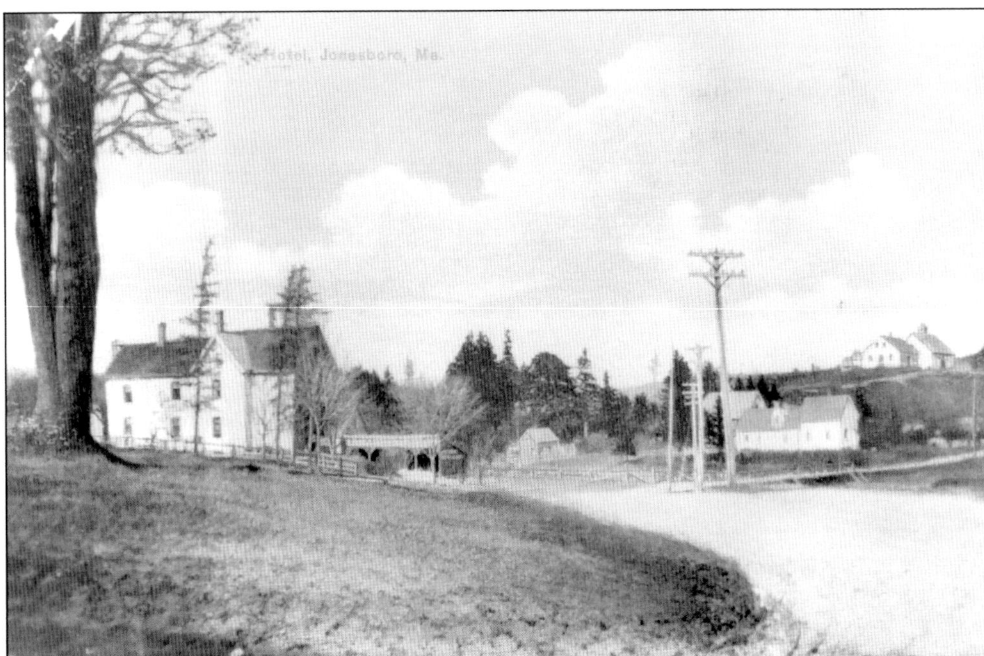

The landmark Jonesboro Hotel, shown *c.* 1905, was a welcome hostelry for weary DownEast travelers.

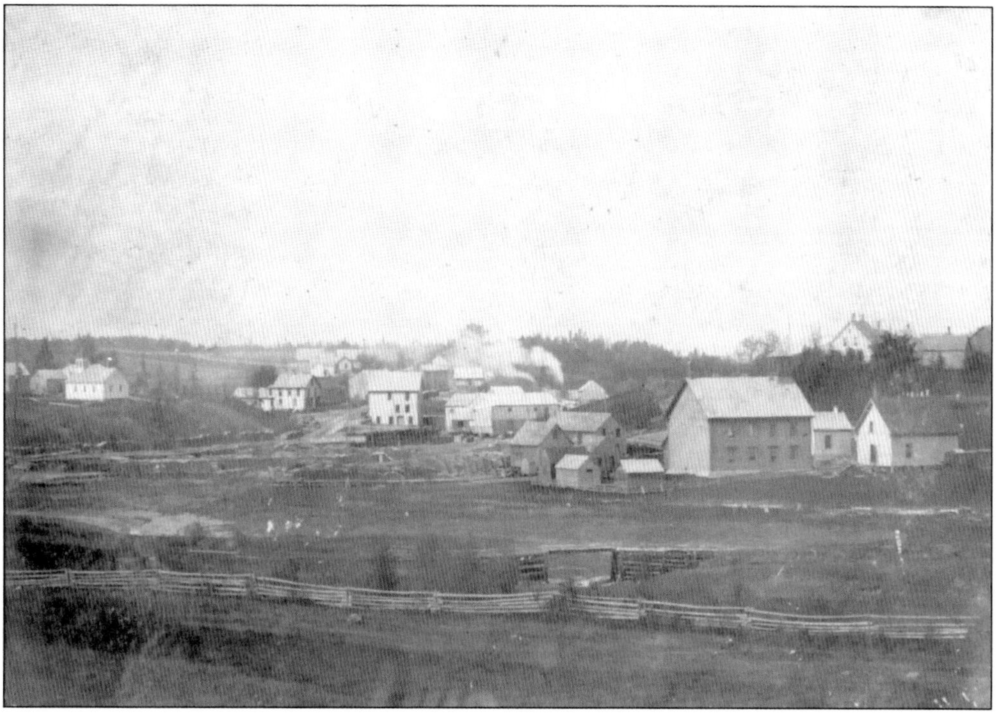

Jonesboro is seen here from a southwesterly position, *c.* 1890s. The photograph captures a number of homes and buildings in the community.

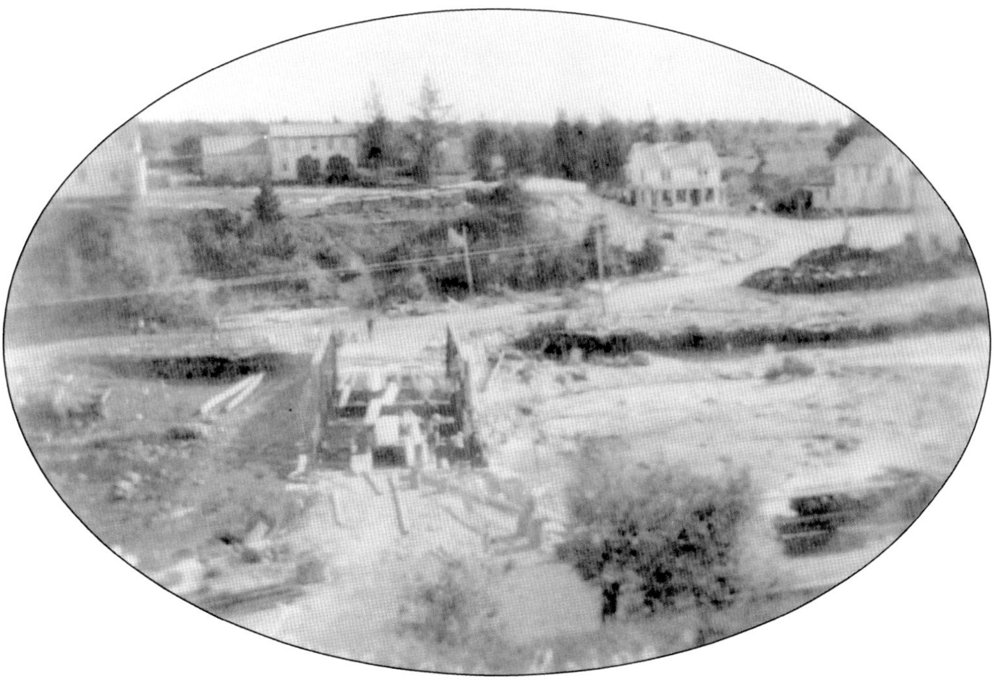

The Chandler River Bridge, shown during its construction in the 1890s, provided easier access north and south.

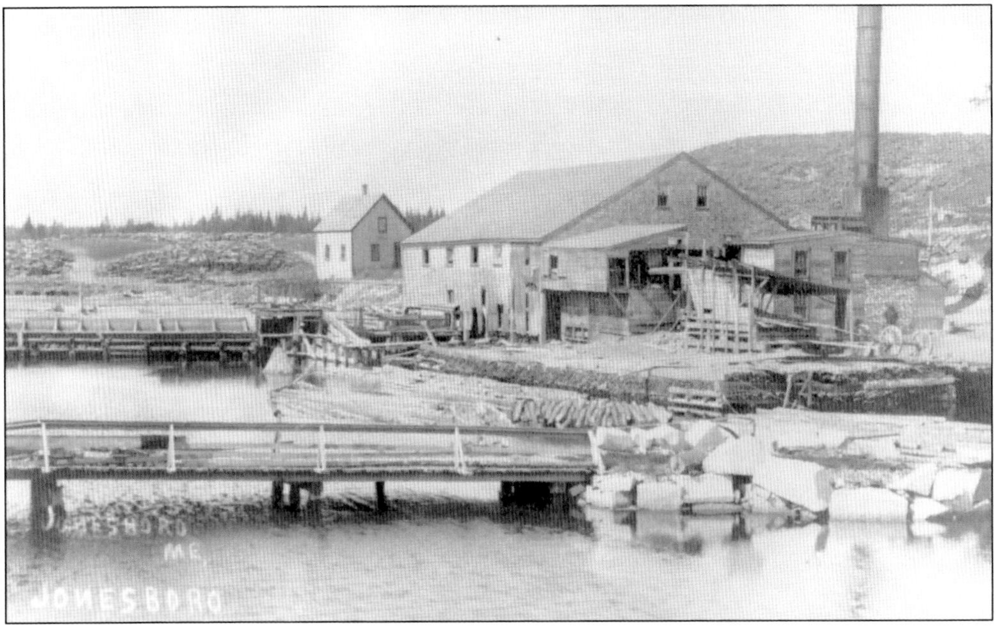

Lumber, seen at this sawmill on the Chandler River *c.* 1900, was still an important part of the economic life of Jonesboro during this time.

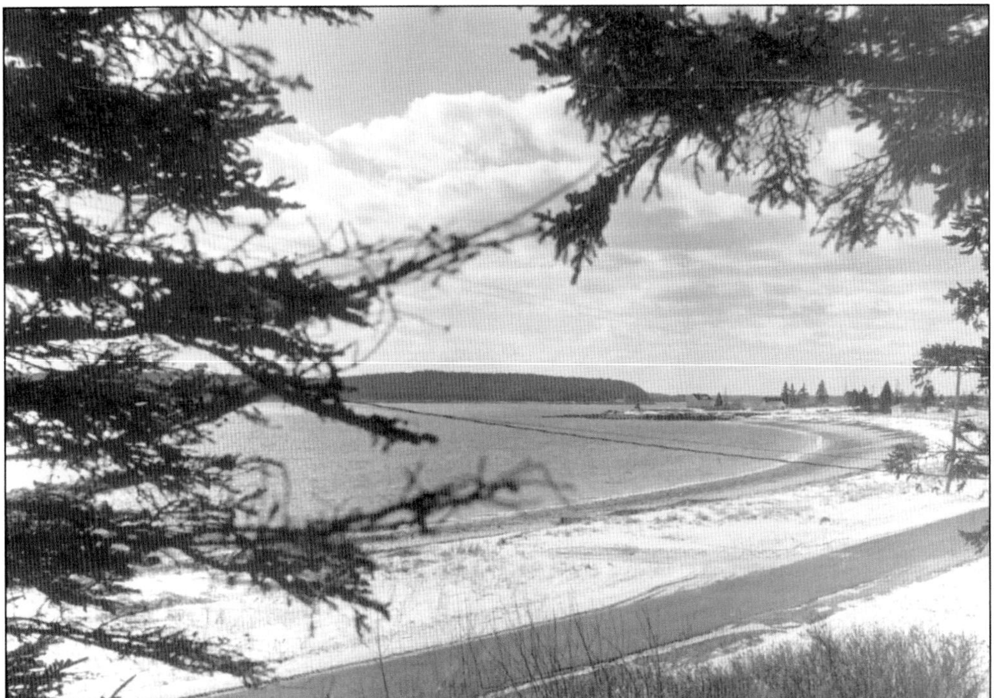

This beautiful beach at Roque Bluffs State Park and the freshwater beach on the opposite side of the road provided the perfect spot for swimming and picnicking.

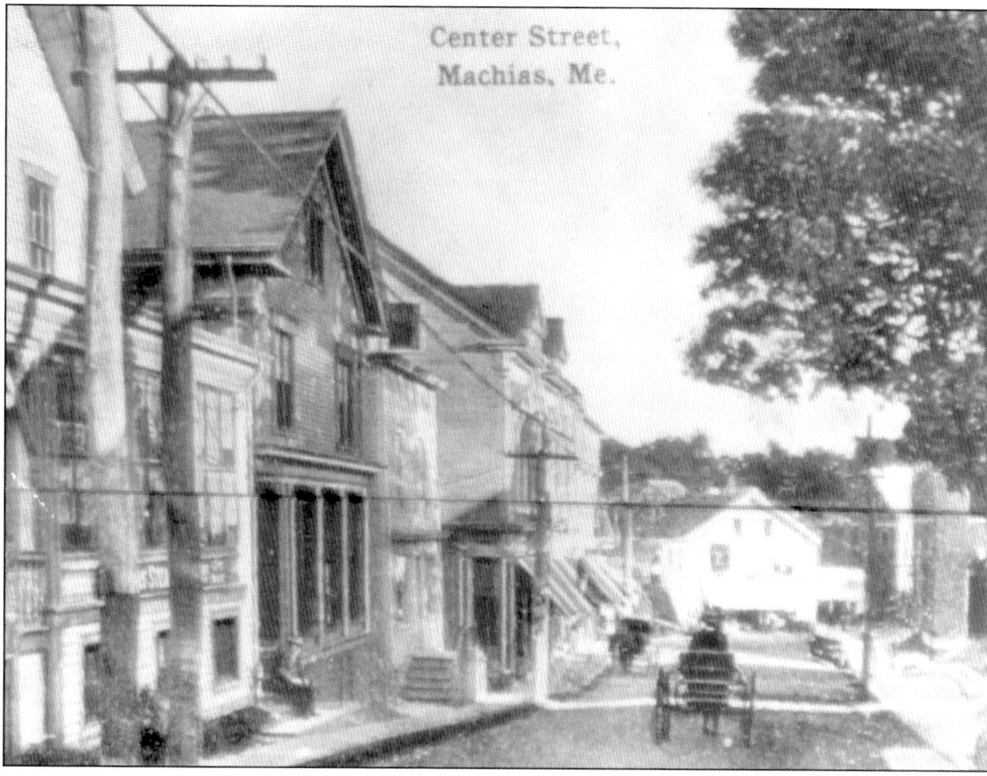

A bygone era is captured in this *c.* 1890 view of Center Street in Machias.

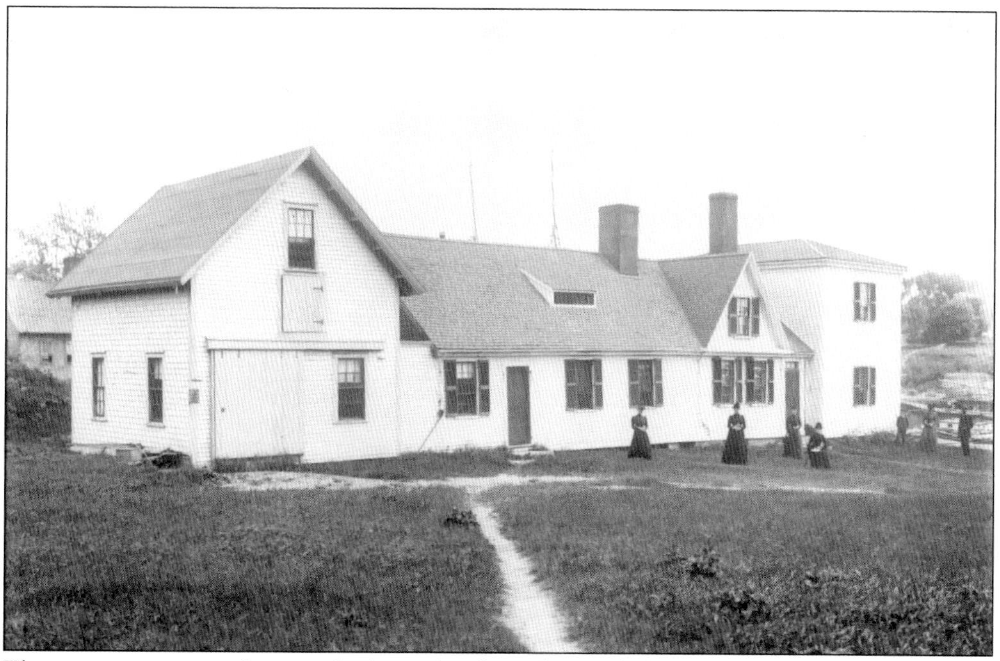

These women were photographed on the front lawn of the Foss House on Main Street, Machias, in the 1890s.

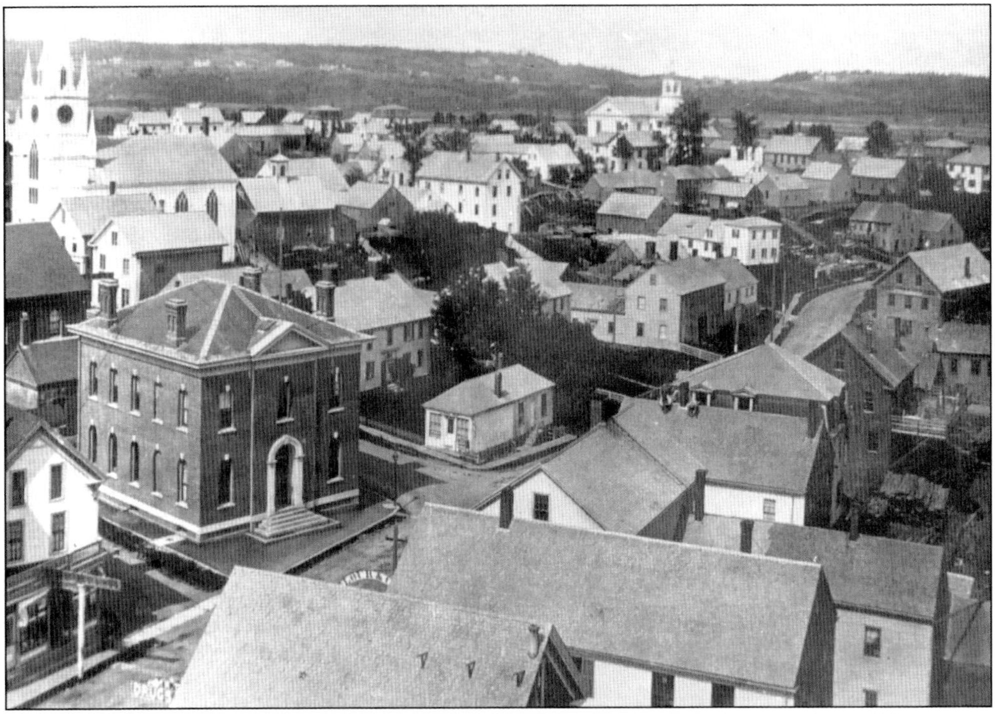

Many of the buildings seen in this photograph of downtown Machias in the 1920s remain as landmarks today, including the stately Centre Street Congregational Church in the upper left corner.

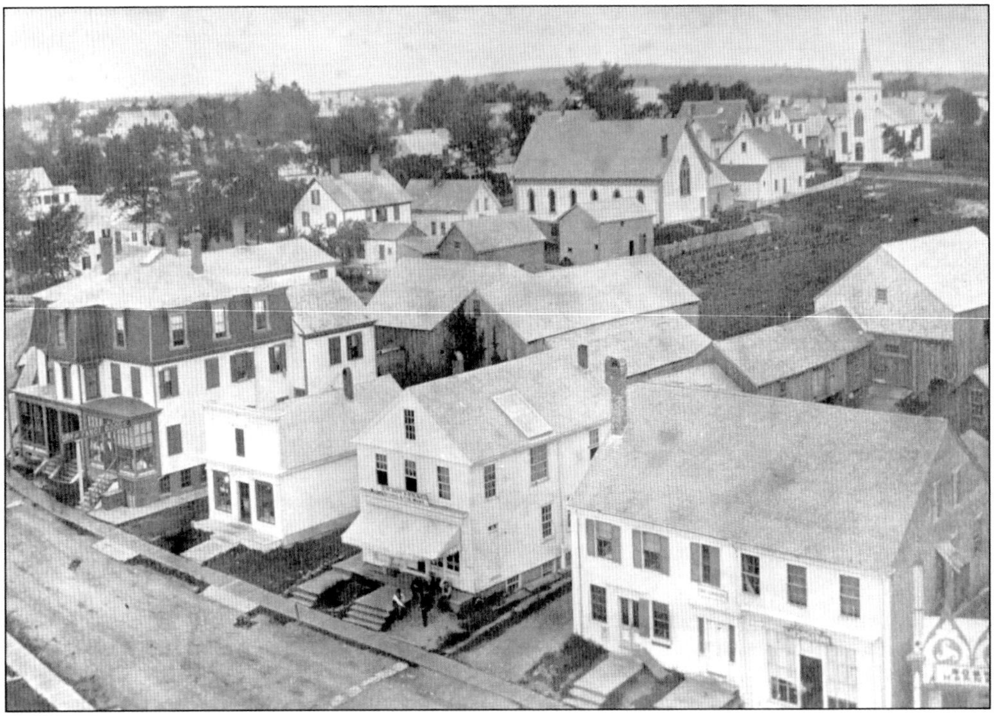

Wooden sidewalks were used along Main Street in Machias, *c.* 1890.

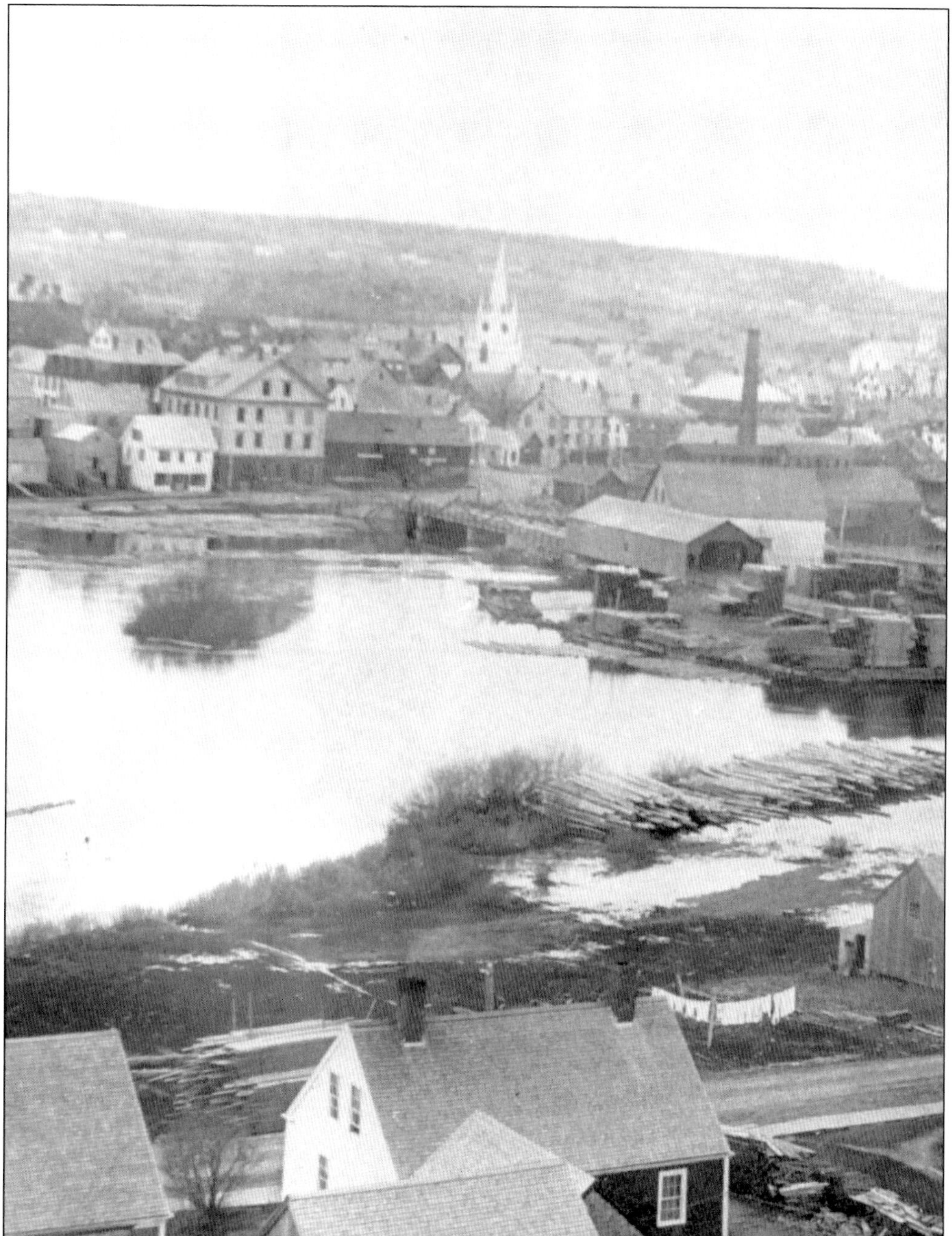

Several lumbermills were located by the old covered bridge at Machias, *c.* 1910. By this time, the industry had begun to wane.

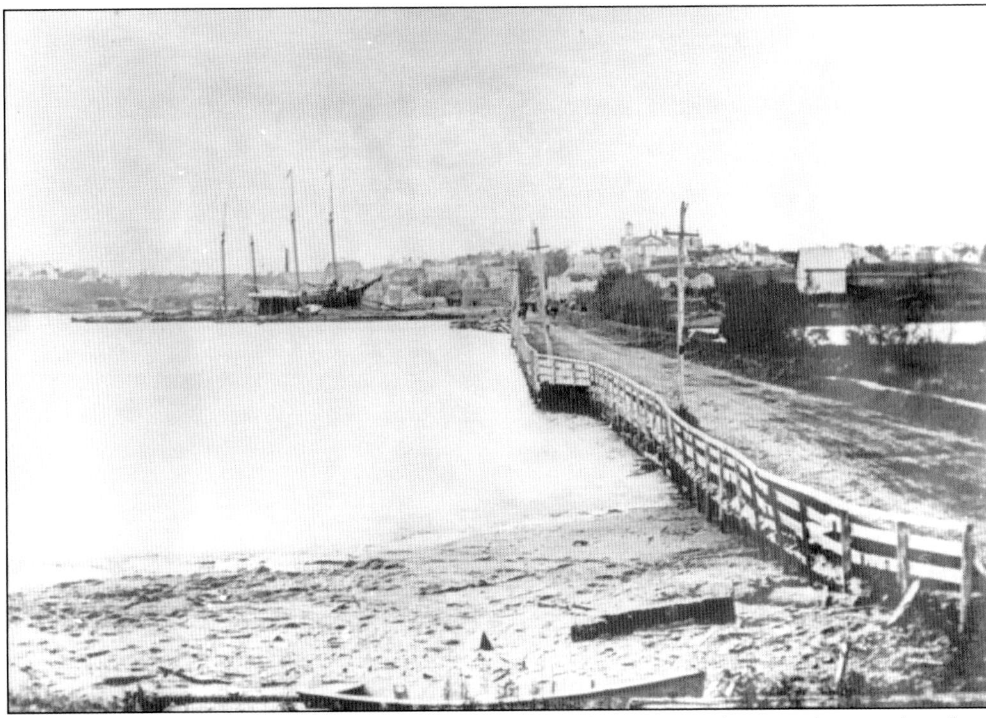

Schooners were tied up at the Machias wharves when this *c.* 1890 photograph was taken from across the dike.

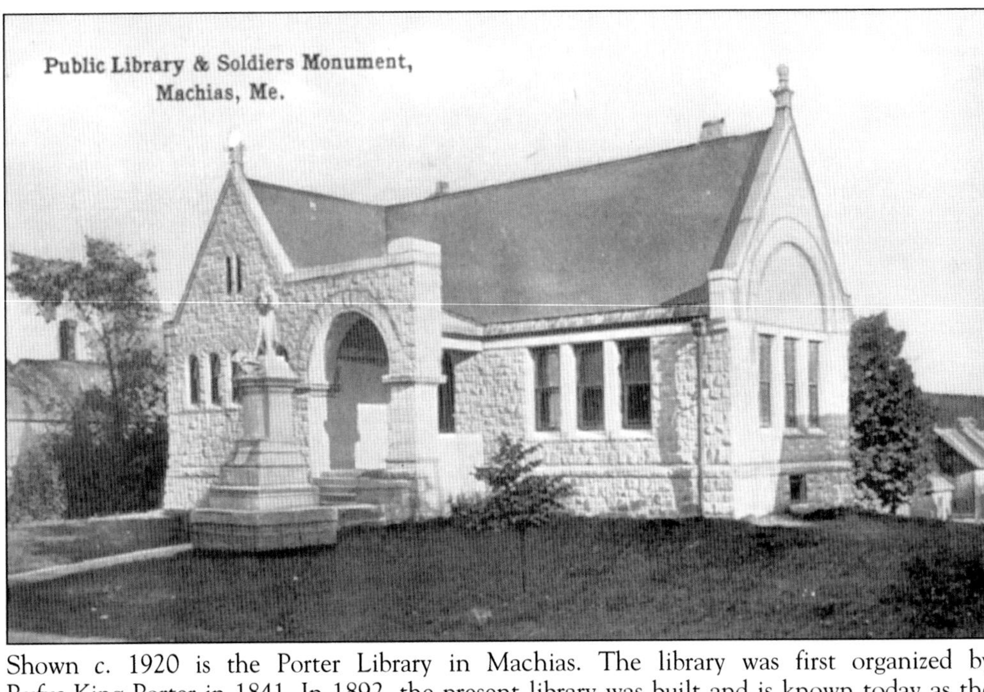

Shown *c.* 1920 is the Porter Library in Machias. The library was first organized by Rufus King Porter in 1841. In 1892, the present library was built and is known today as the Porter Memorial Library.

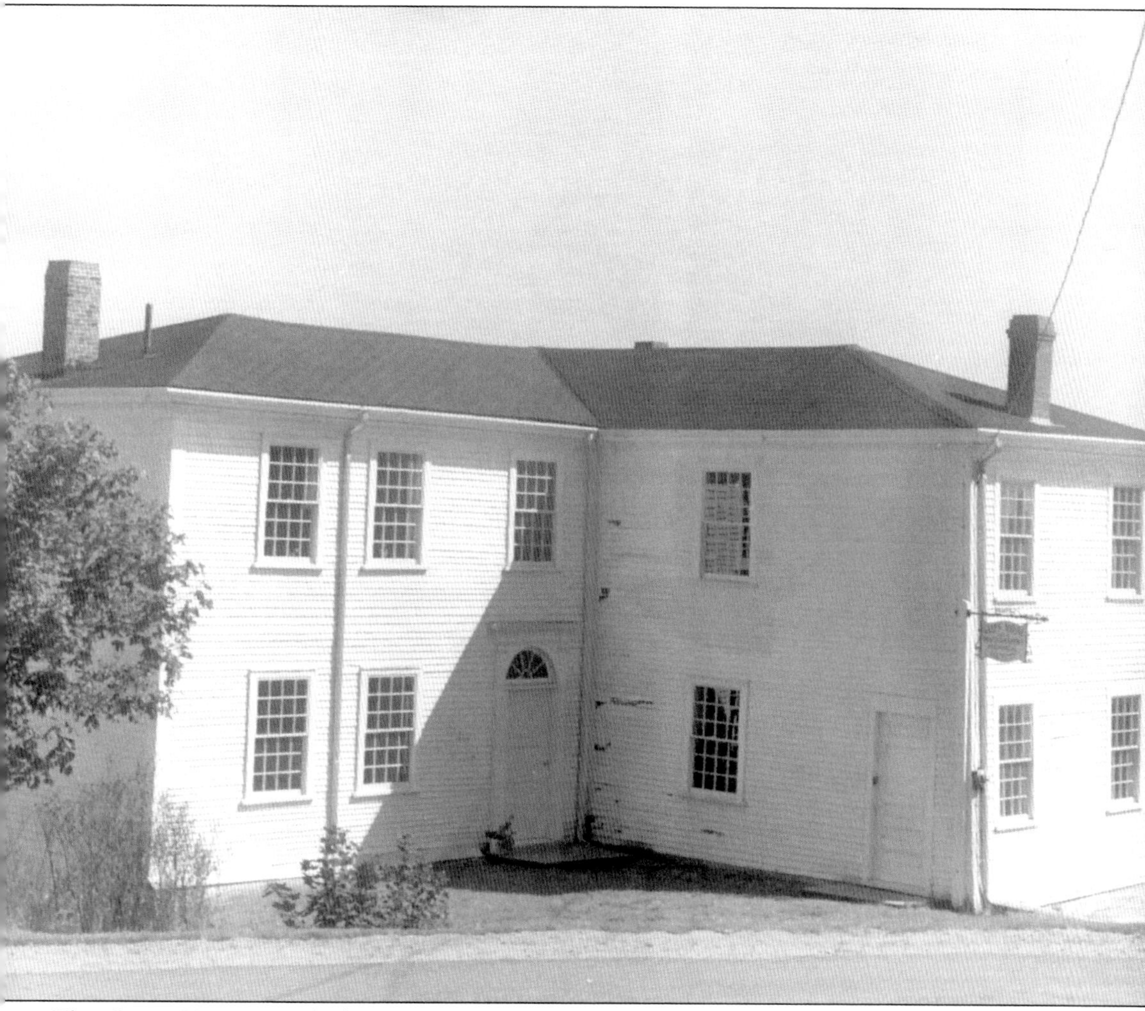

The Gates House was built *c.* 1807. Nathan Gates purchased the home, and his family occupied it for about 120 years. Since 1966, it has served as a museum and headquarters for the Machiasport Historical Society. In 1975, it was entered on the National Register of Historic Places.

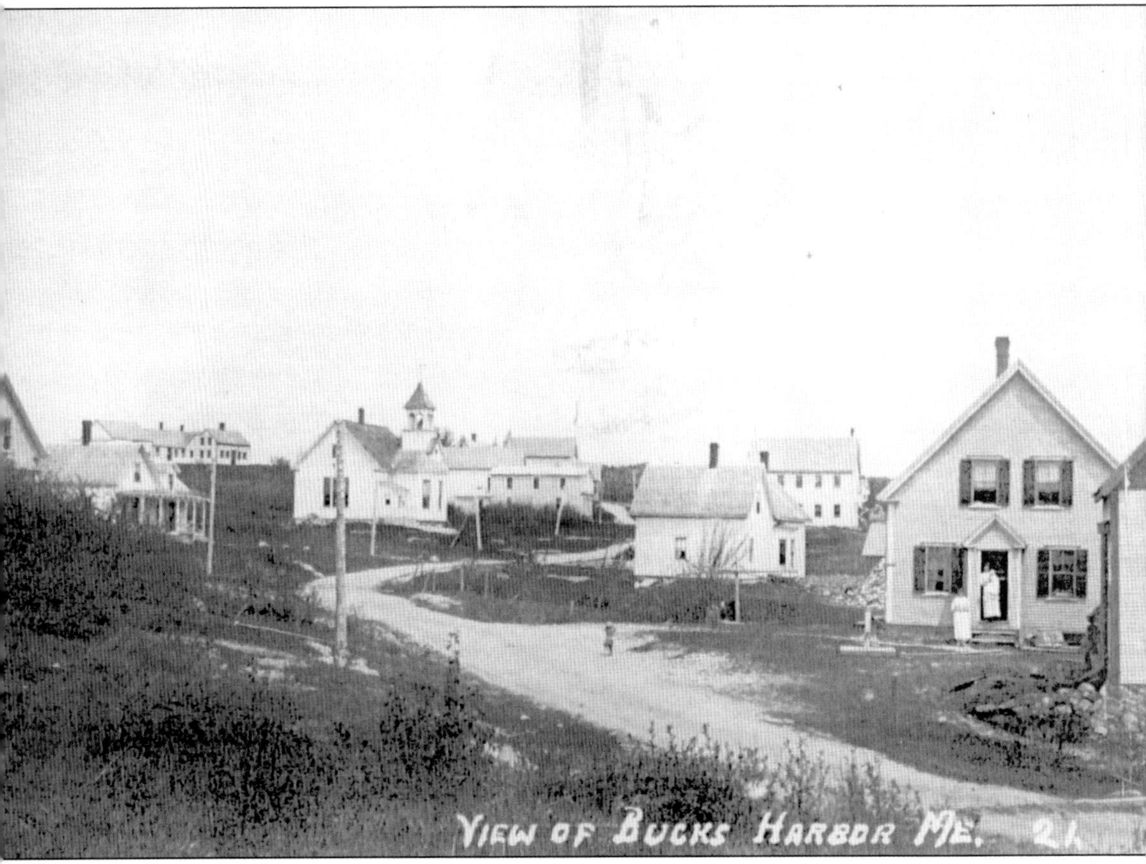

The Bucks Harbor community is shown c. 1920. On the right is Charlie Johnson's barn and home, with two women standing by the doorway. Next on the right is the home of Ella and Henry Emerson. The building beyond the Emersons' home is the Bucks Harbor School. The first home on the left is that of Alvah and Emily Hooper, and the next home is that of Gleason Colbeth. The home on the hill belonged to the George Colbeth family. Below that house is the original Bucks Harbor Baptist Church, and beyond it is a grain shed and Charlie Johnson's Variety Store.

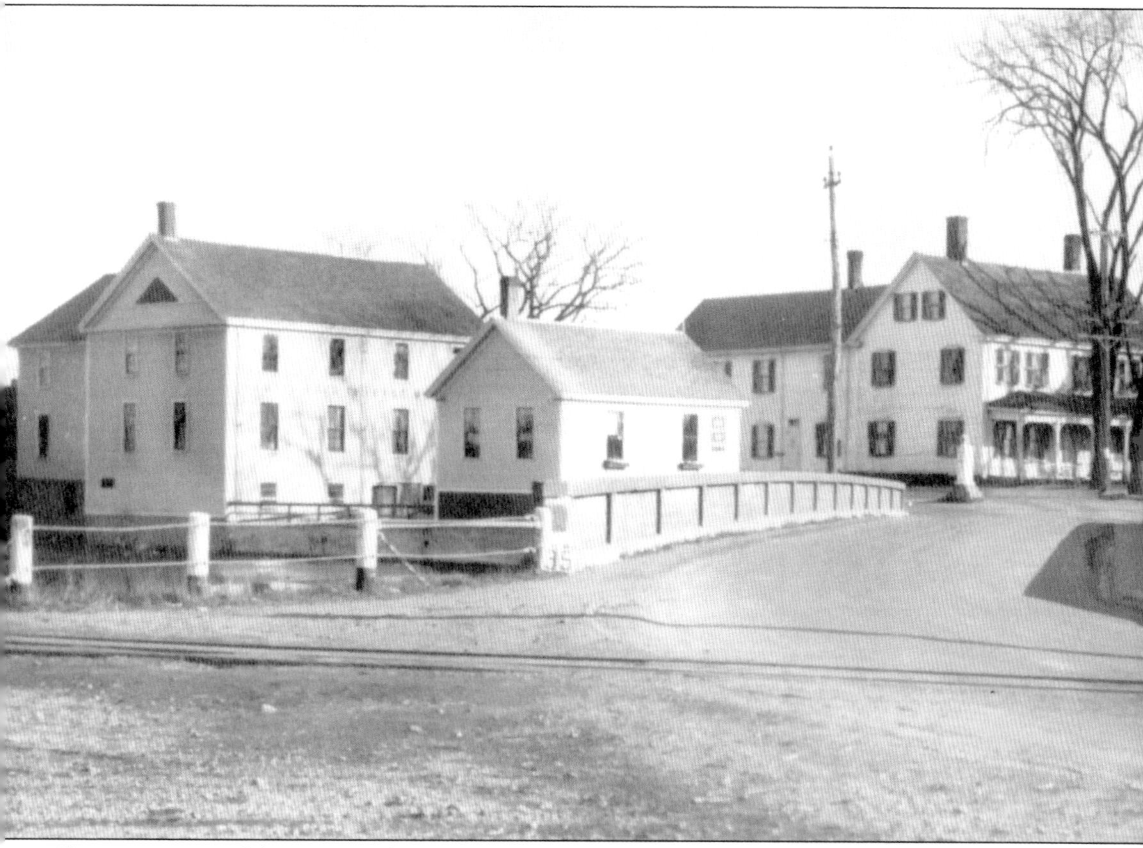

Shown is a view of the East Machias store and post office in the 1940s. Although the post office building no longer remains, the former store building is now used by Doug Campbell, where he builds custom furniture.

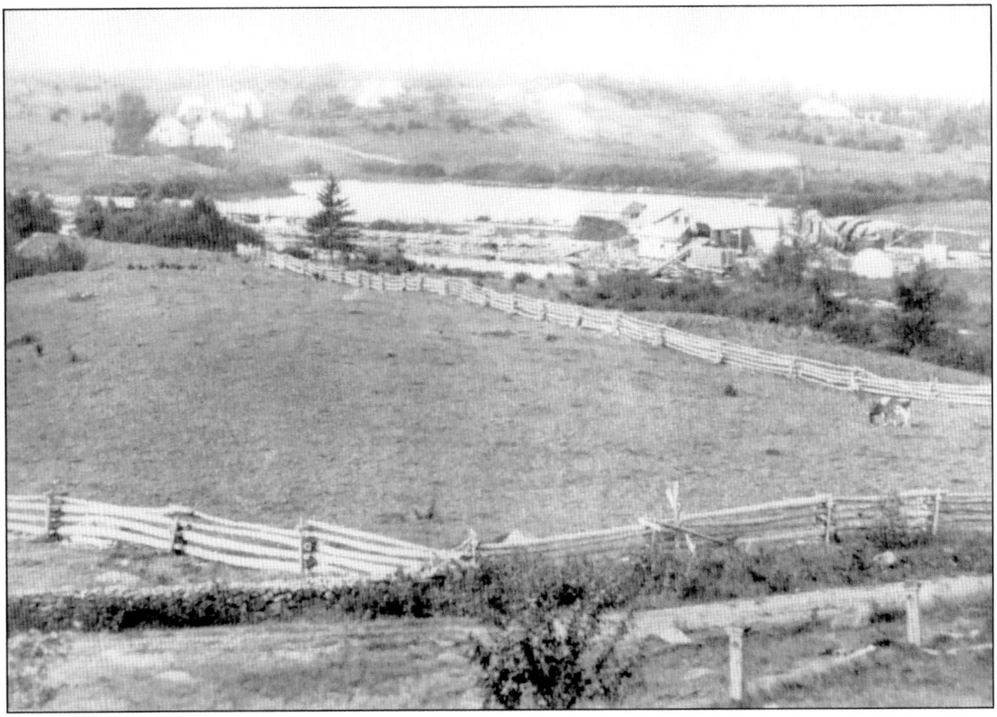

The Jacksonville Mill is shown *c.* 1900.

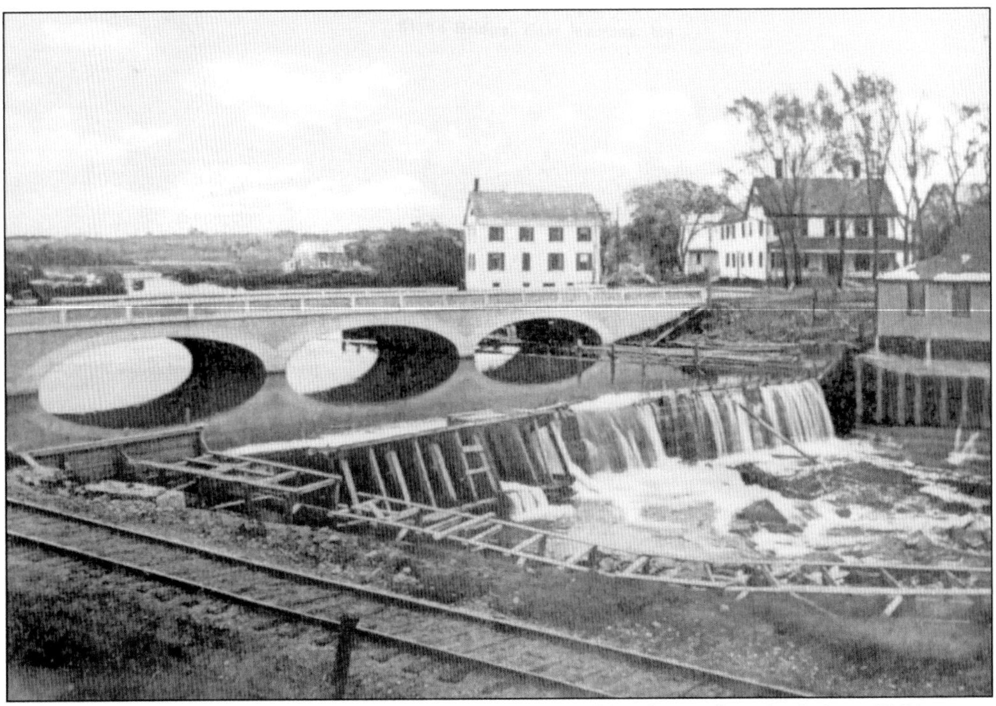

The East Machias store is seen across the Pope Memorial Bridge and to the left, *c.* 1910.

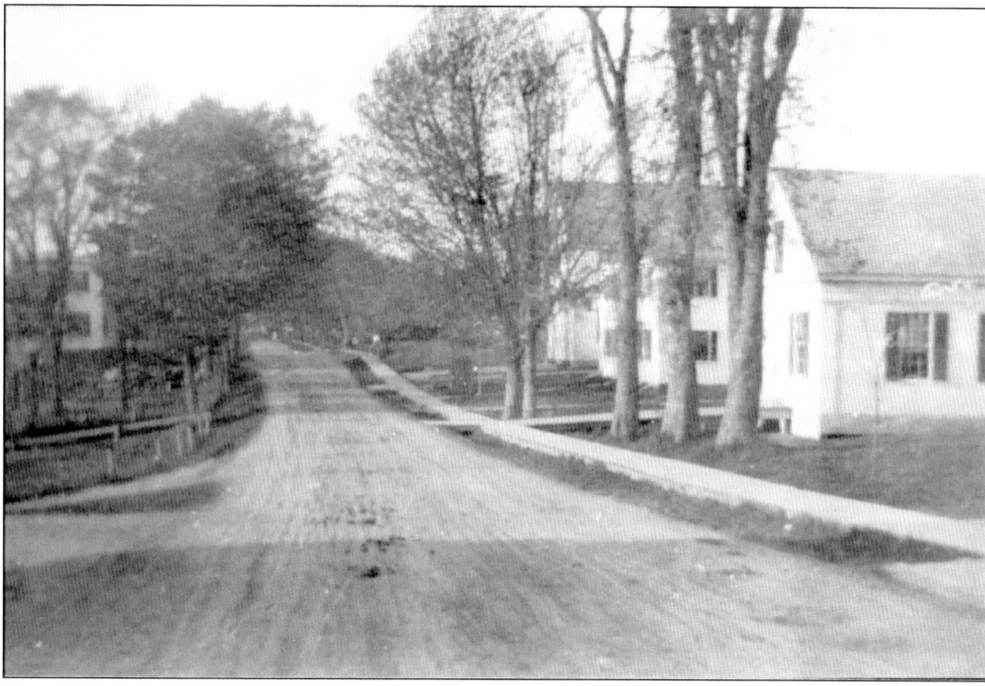

This view of High Street in East Machias was taken in the early 1930s.

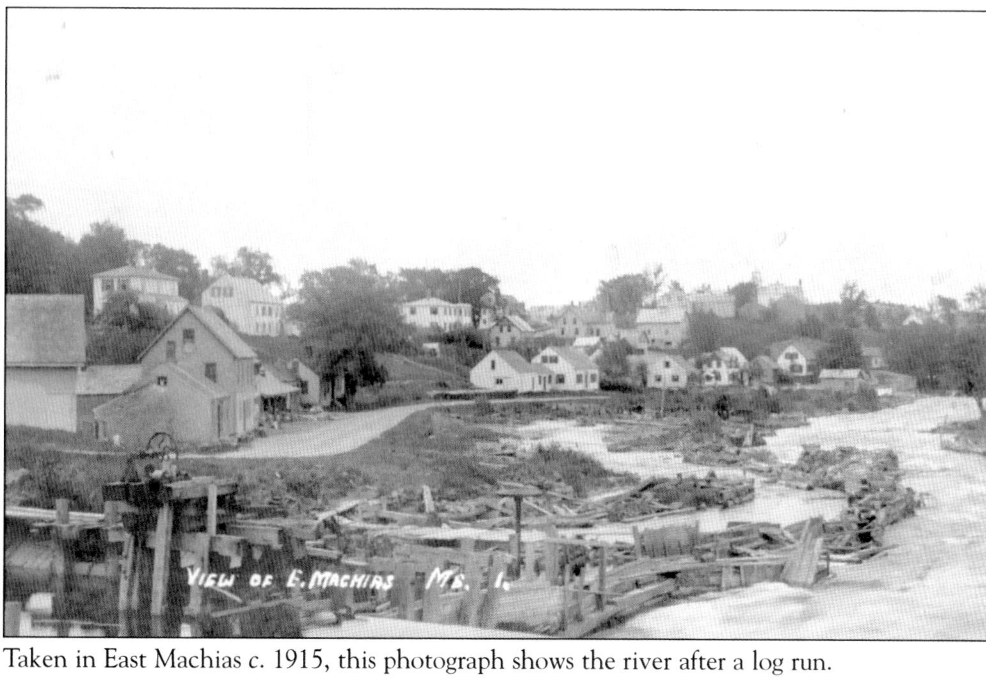

Taken in East Machias *c.* 1915, this photograph shows the river after a log run.

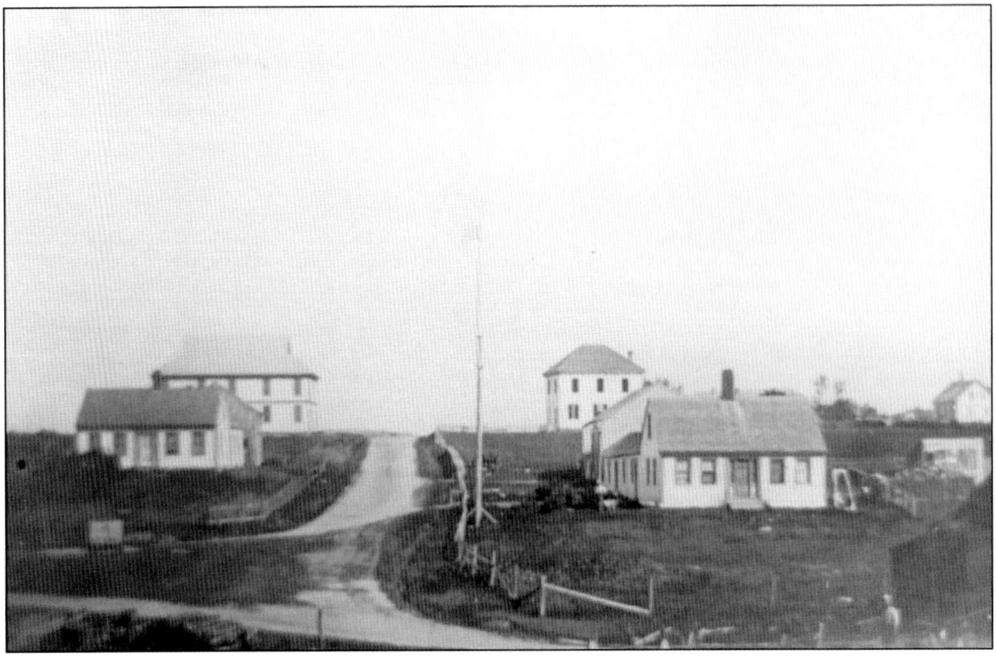

The Grange is on the left and the school on the right in this *c.* 1915 photograph of the road from Cutler to Lubec.

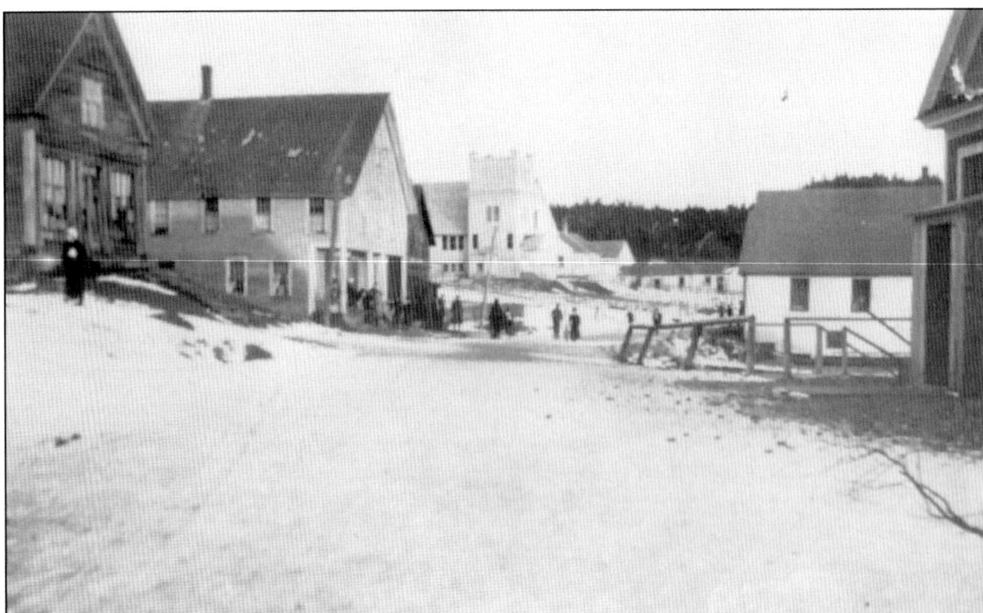

This is Cutler Harbor, *c.* 1920s. On the left are Wilder's store, Kelley's store, and the old post office, all of which burned in a 1945 fire.

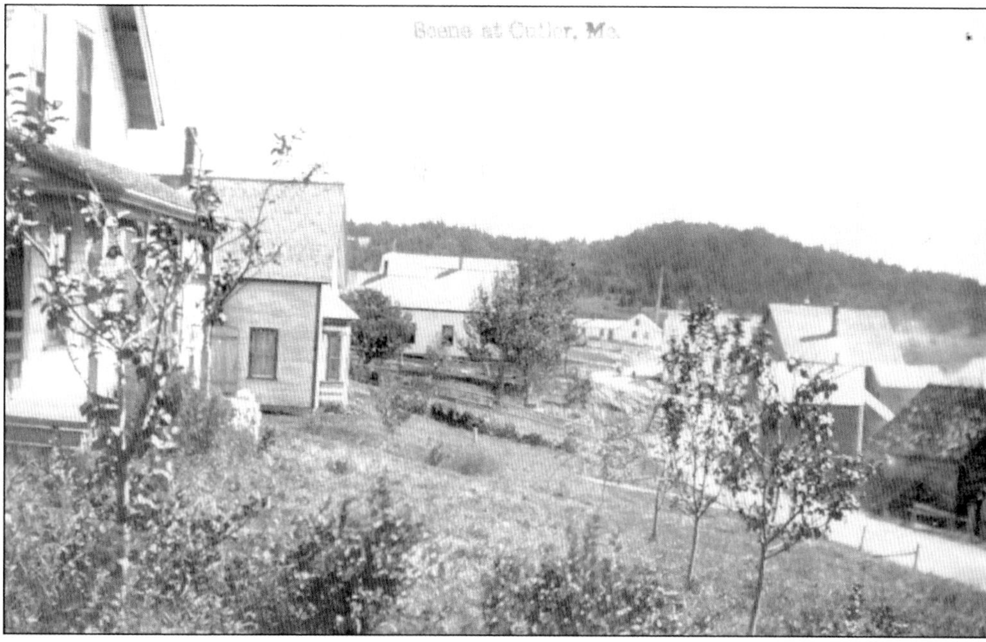

A pastoral summer setting is seen in Cutler Harbor, 1910.

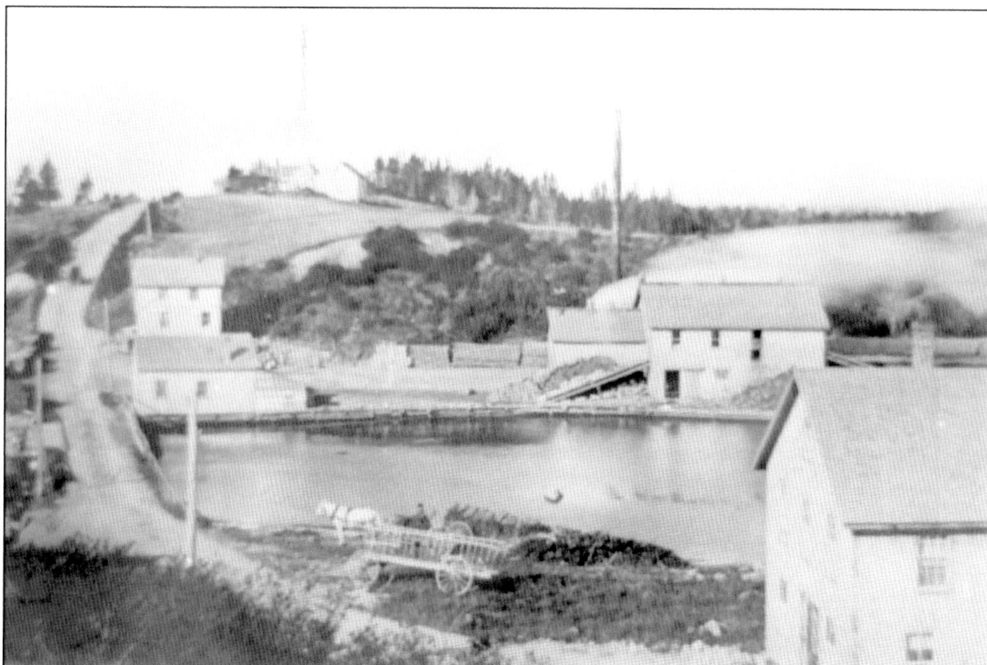

A man draws his hay wagon over Mills Turner Bridge in North Cutler, c. 1915.

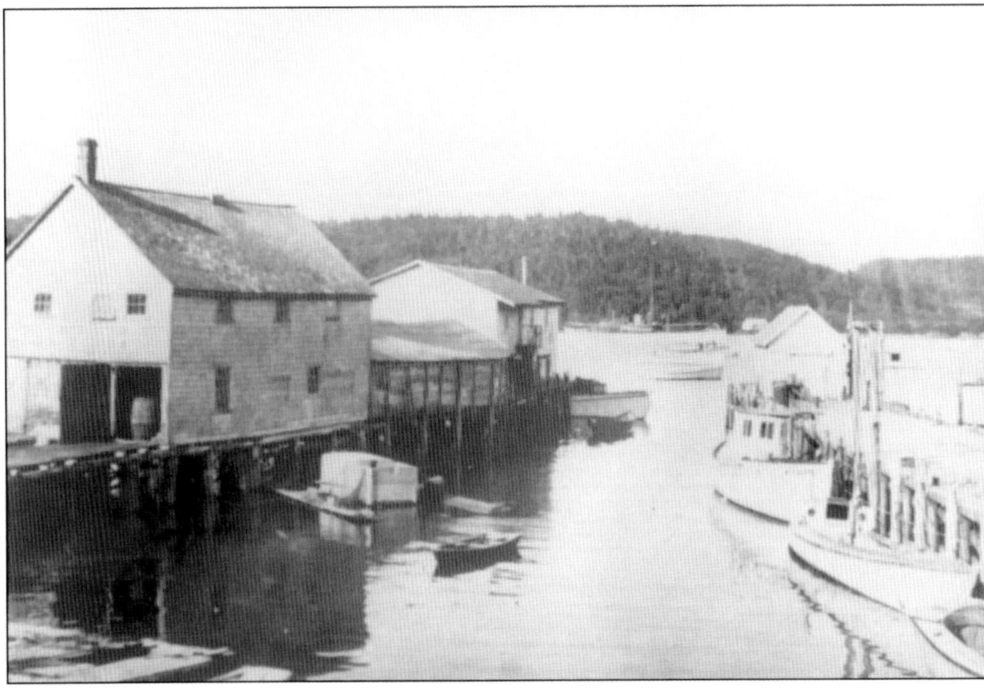

Steamboat Wharf in Cutler Harbor was photographed *c.* 1940s.

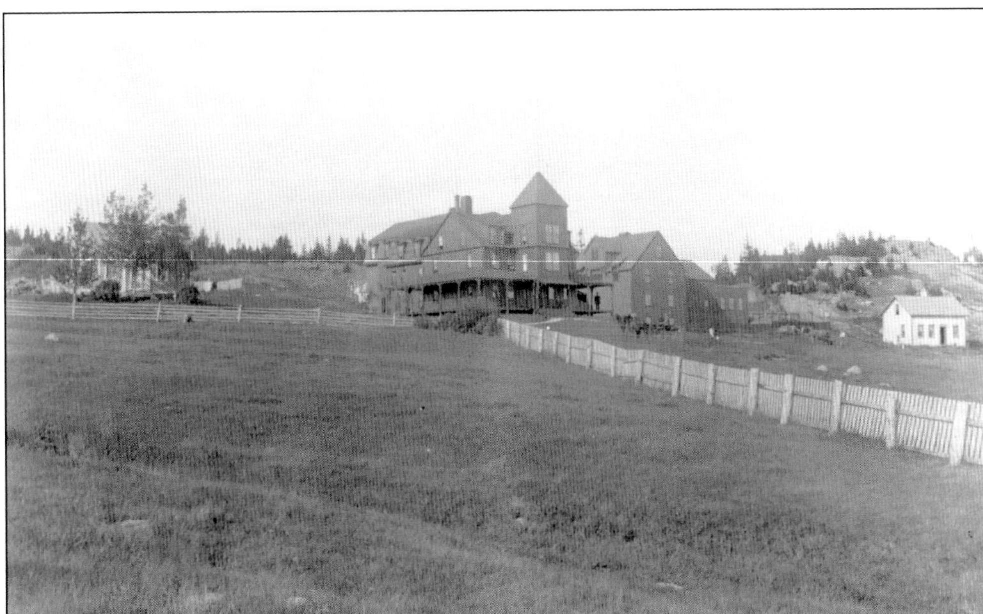

Little River Lodge was originally called the Hotel Cutler. To the left of the lodge is Alene Dennison's house, shown *c.* 1885.

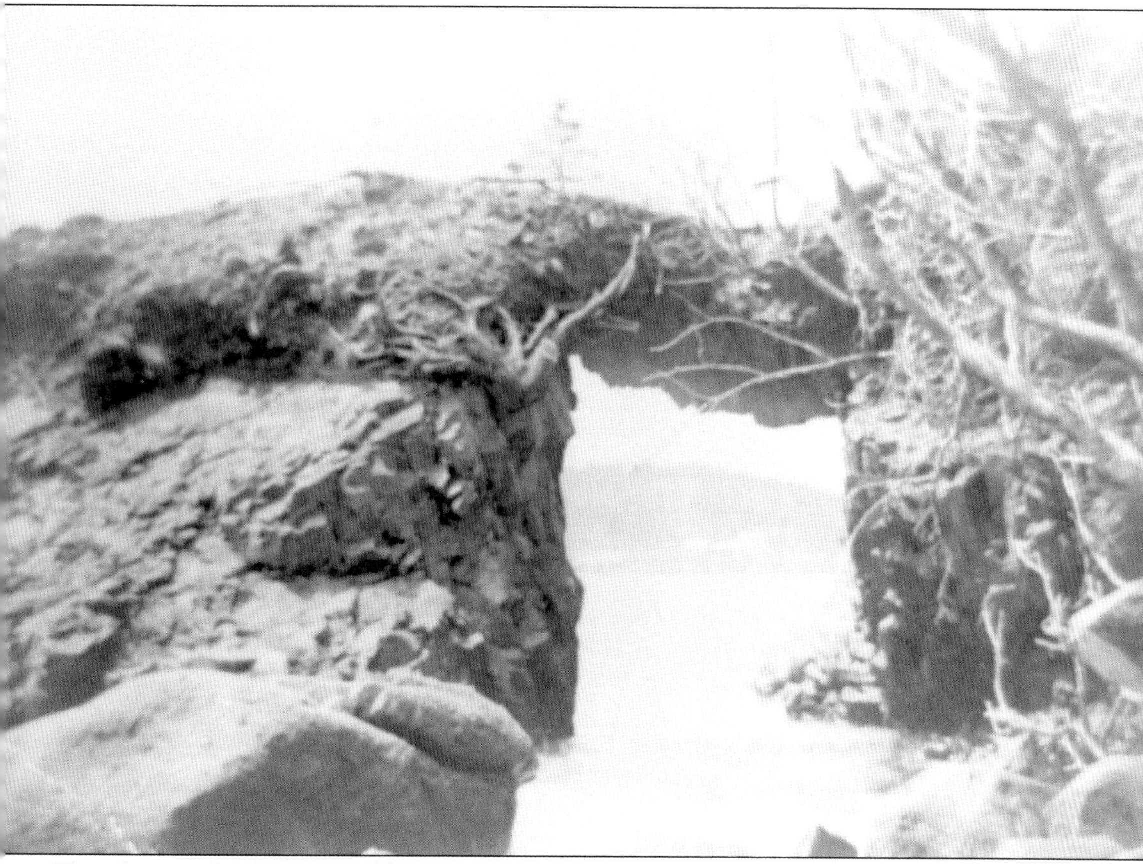
This photograph of the natural bridge in Cutler dates to 1910.

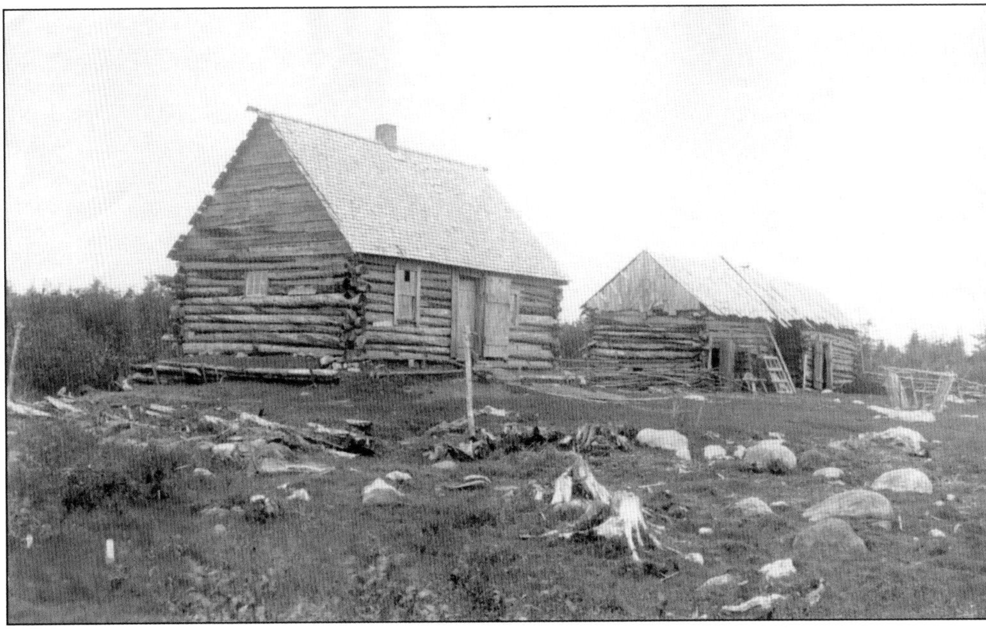

A log cabin and barn on the road from Cutler to Lubec are shown in 1885.

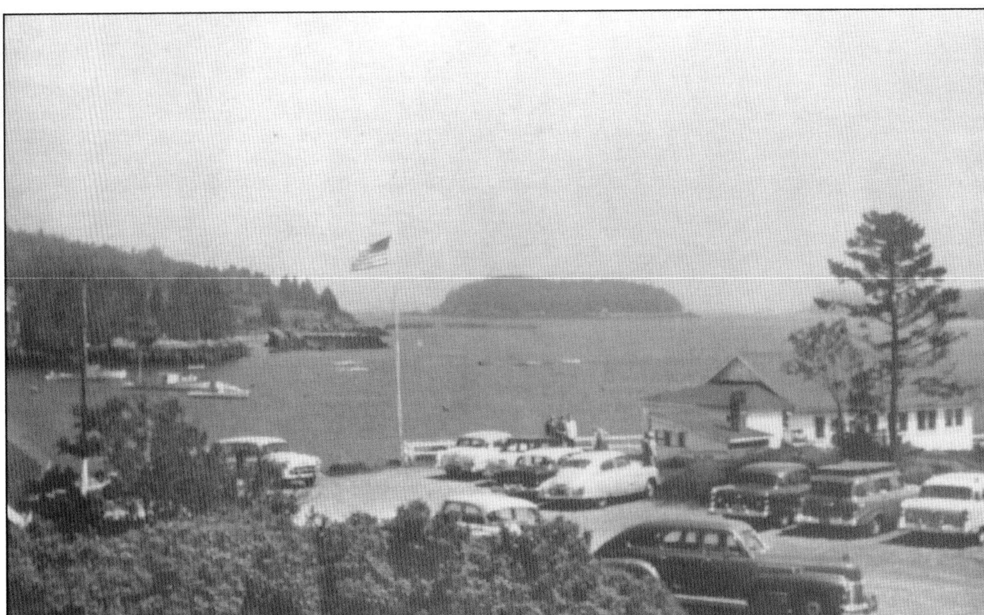

The Harborview Restaurant is shown here in the 1950s. It was built on the site of the old Cutler sardine factory, which burned in the 1930s.

Two

THE TIDES CONNECT US

From across the sea they came in ships as early as the 11th century. Deep water in the harbors and the abundance of timber and fish aided the settlers who used these resources.

Ships, brigs, and schooners were needed for trade, and the fine craftsmen of the region built them for years. The Ships Registry maintained by the Peabody Museum in Salem, Massachusetts, documents that considerable shipbuilding was carried on at Roque Island, in Paradise Cove on the westerly end of Shorey's Cove, as early as 1815. This registry identifies numerous ships built at Jonesboro during the 19th century.

Through the ages, the tides have always fed us. The extensive clam heaps found at Clark's Point, Machiasport, provide evidence that Native Americans had gathered there for centuries. As early as 1785, Machias settlers voted to regulate the fishing of alewives and salmon on the Machias River. Fishing remains a major industry of the region. The tides have not only provided us with our trades and work ethic but have also inspired us and connected us as a people.

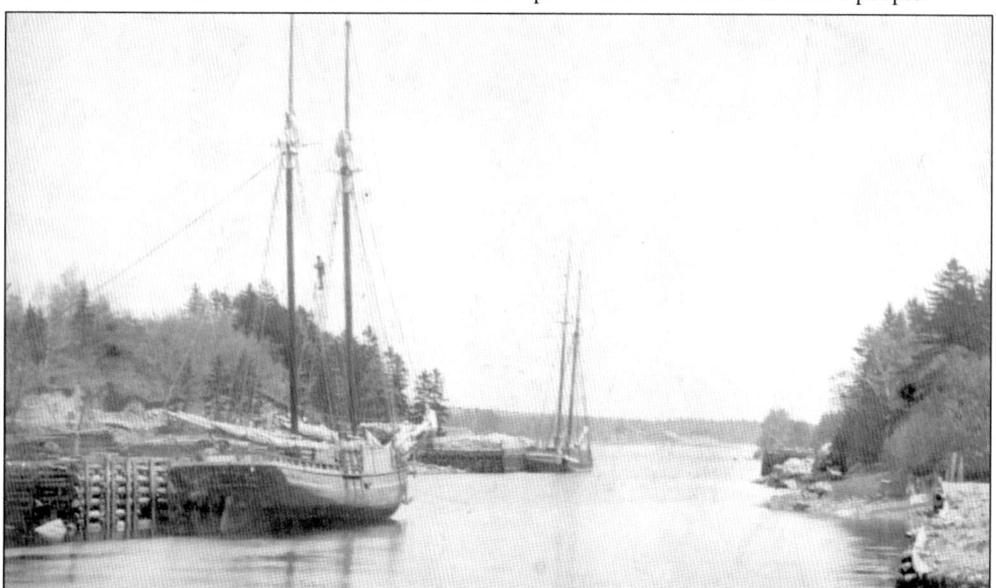

Rigging is being repaired on a two-masted ship on the Chandler River, Jonesboro, c. 1900.

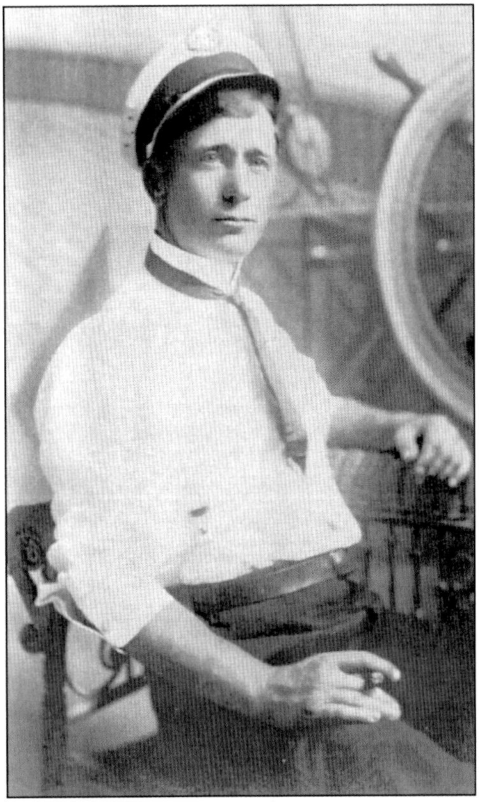

Capt. Fred Berry of Machiasport is at the helm of his ship c. 1917.

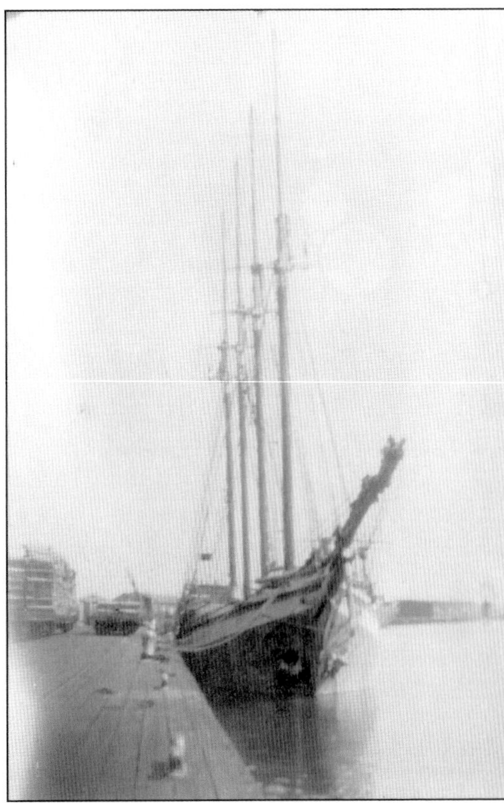

This vintage 1920 photograph shows a typical schooner of the type built in the Machias Bay Region.

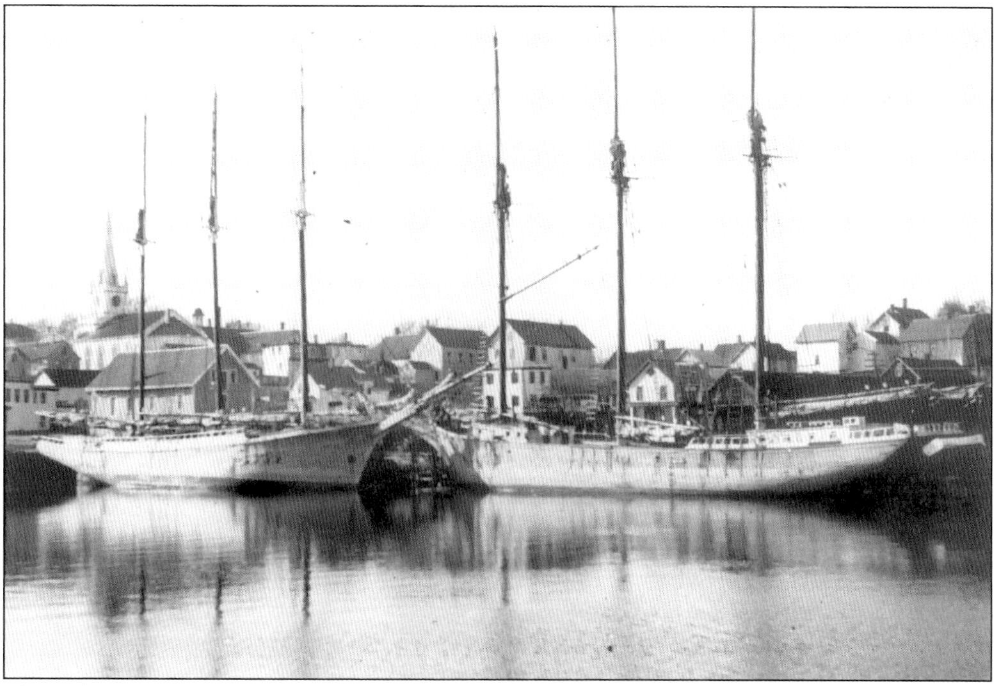

The *Rebecca R. Douglas* and the *Lucy Evelyn* are tied up at Machias, *c.* 1920s.

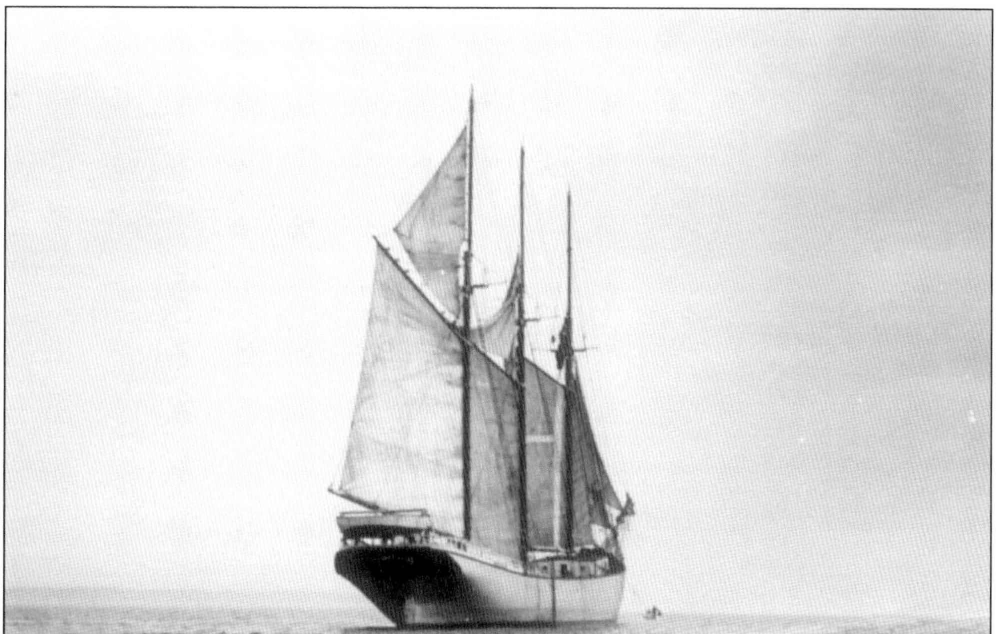

The *Lucy Evelyn* gets under way, setting the topsail. Built at the Harrington yard, the *Lucy Evelyn* was launched Thanksgiving Day 1917 for a Capt. Everett C. Lindsey at a cost of $64,000. Machias was the ship's home port.

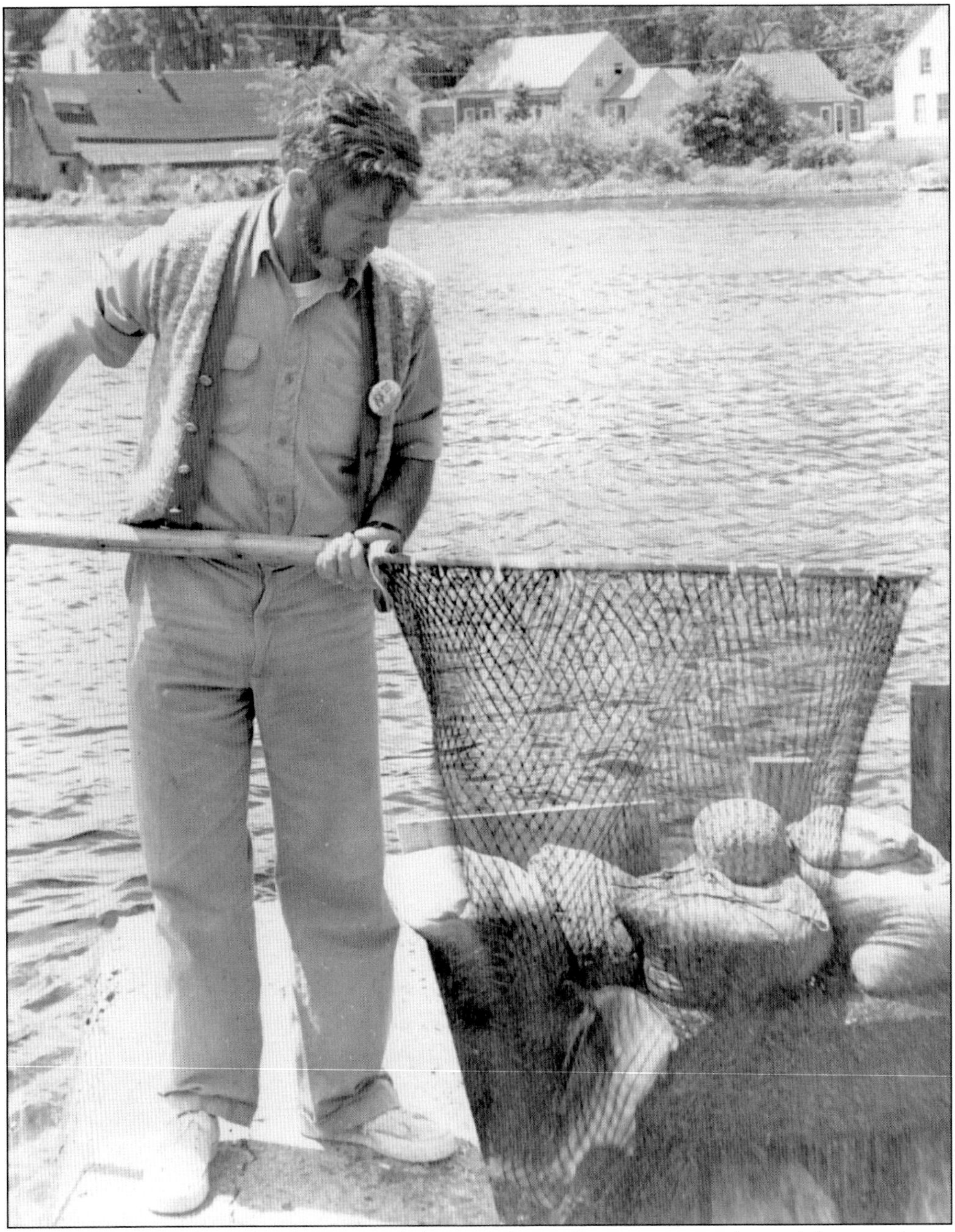

James Fletcher, biologist for the Maine Atlantic Salmon Commission, is shown lifting a salmon from the weir at the lower dam on the Machias River, *c.* 1960.

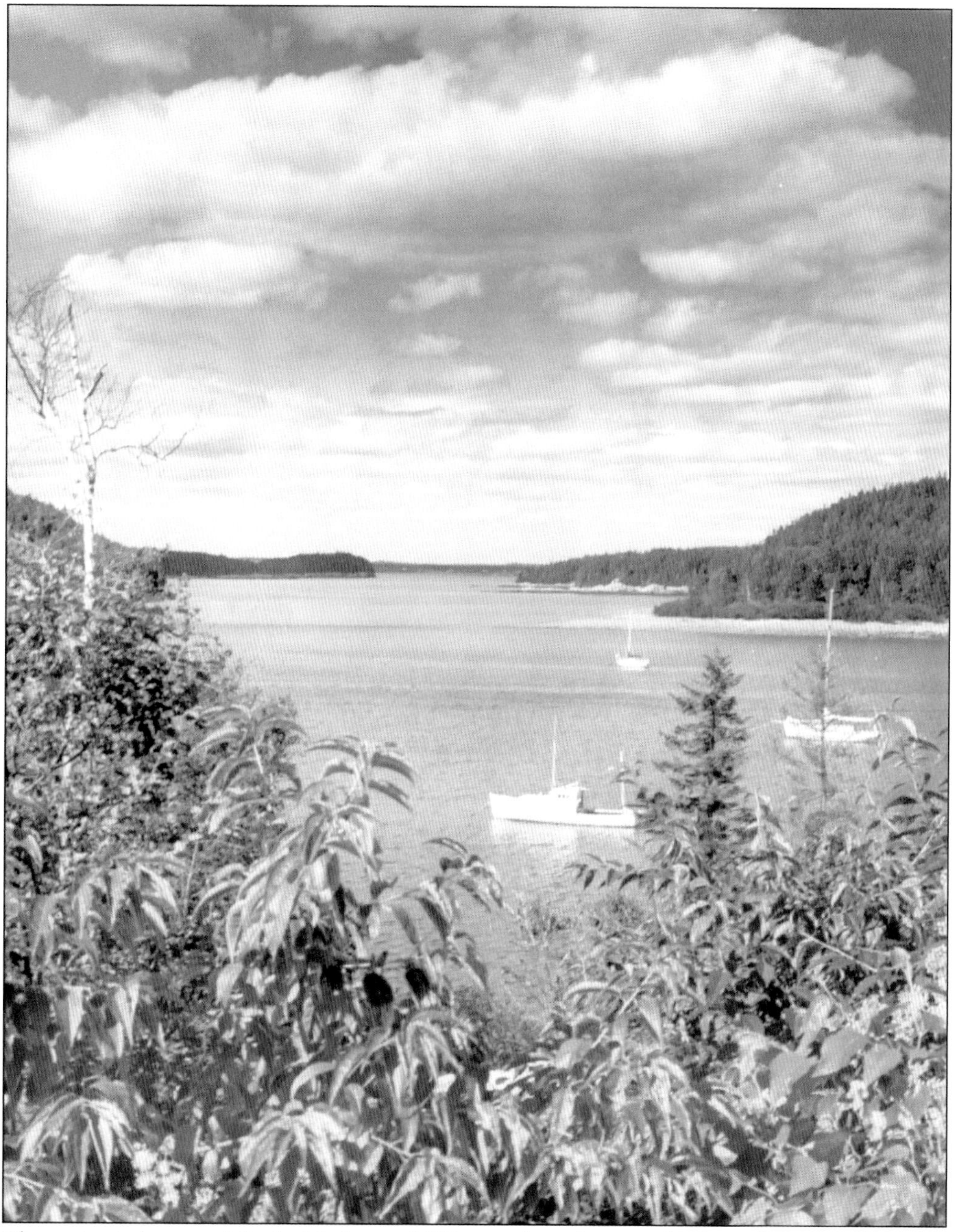

The majestic beauty of Bucks Harbor, *c.* 1950, is truly a photographer's, and visitor's, dream.

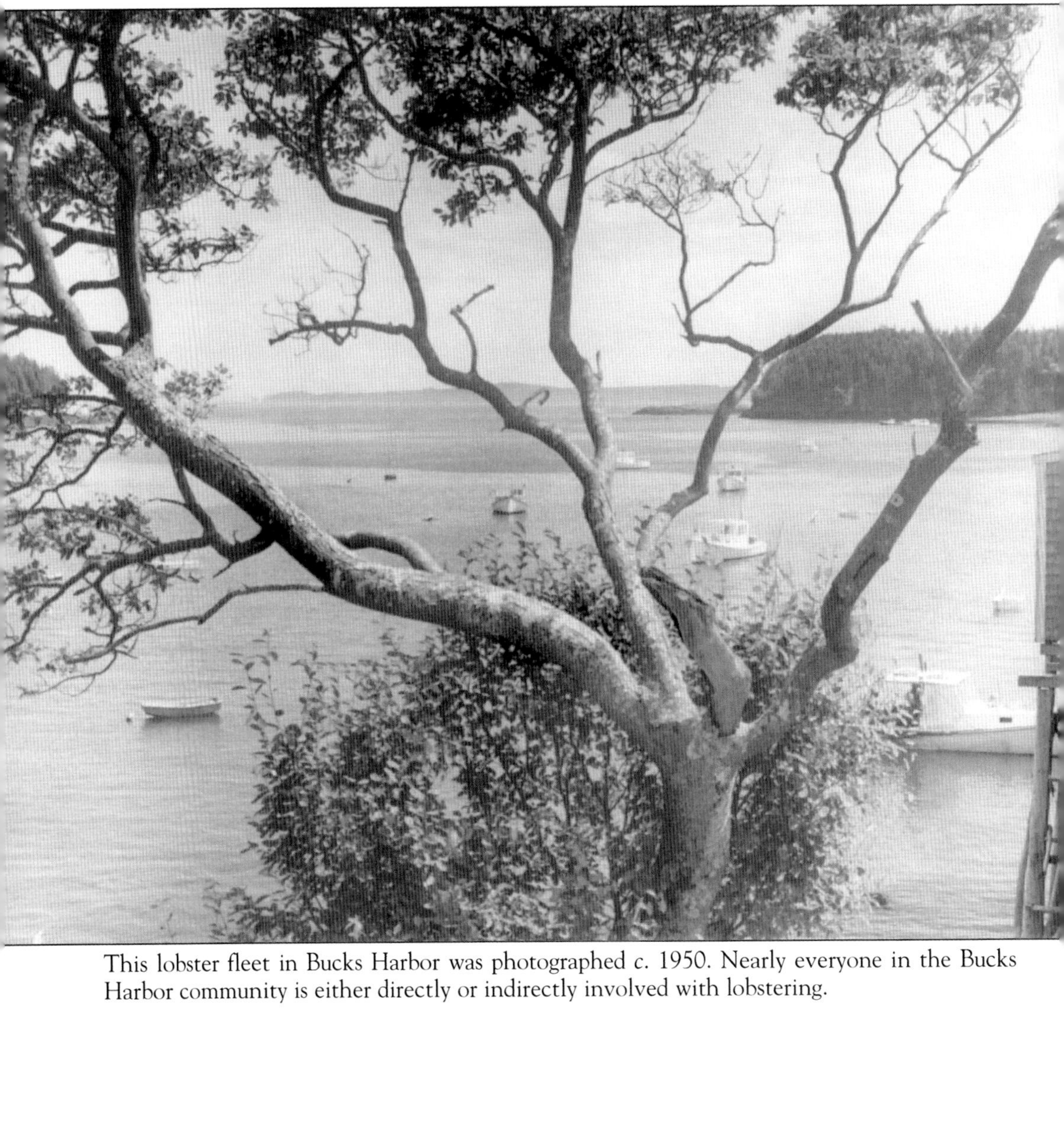

This lobster fleet in Bucks Harbor was photographed *c.* 1950. Nearly everyone in the Bucks Harbor community is either directly or indirectly involved with lobstering.

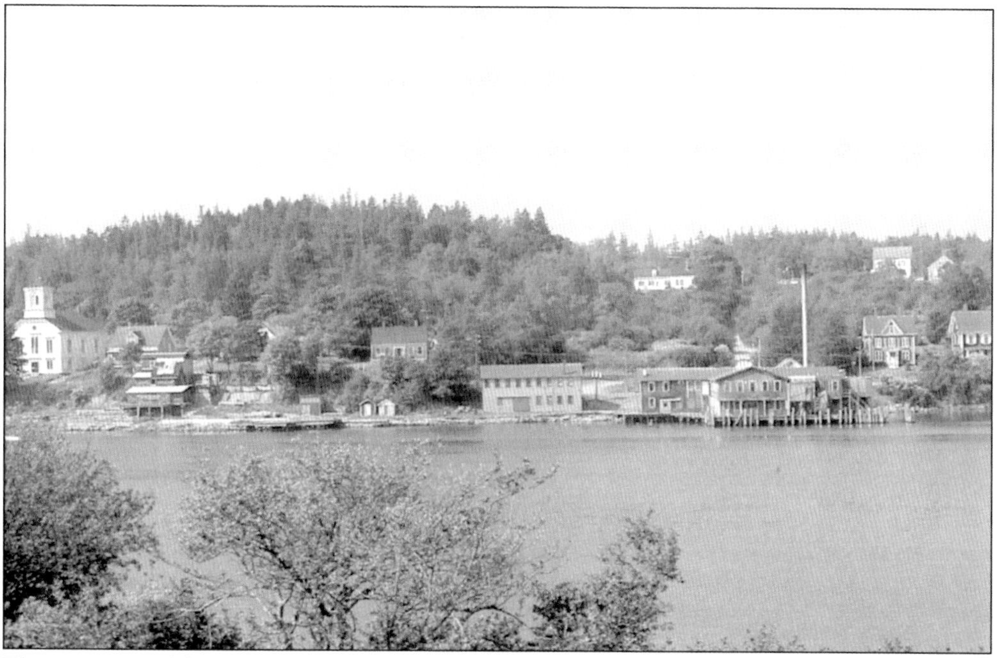

This is a view of the Machiasport Packing & Canning Company. For many years, sardines were packed and shipped from this venerable plant.

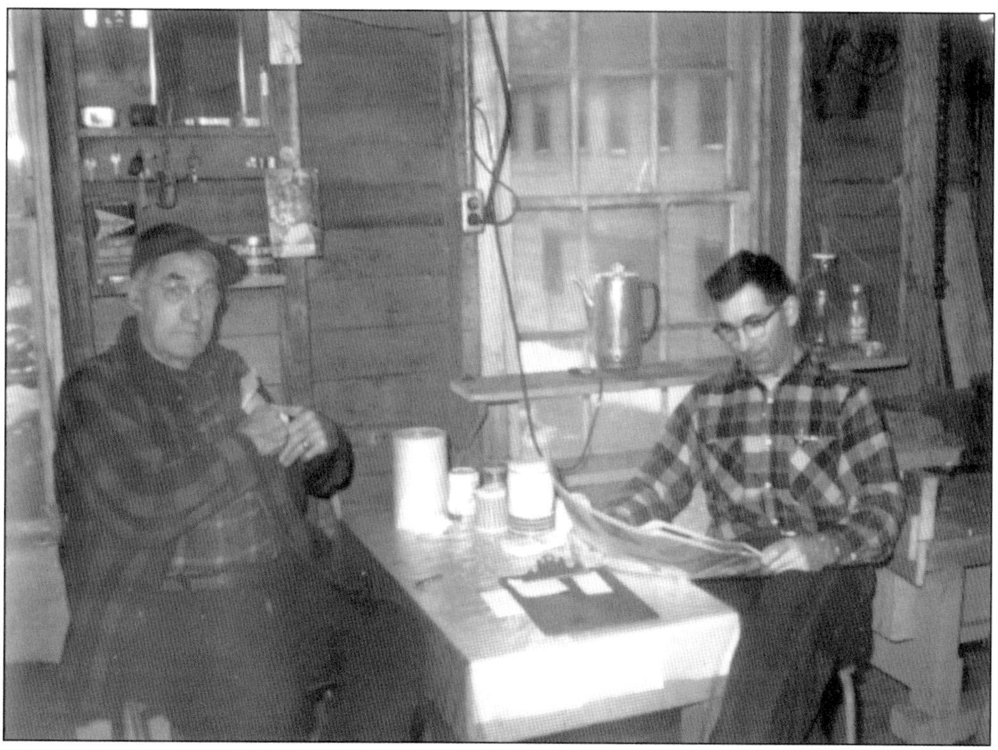

Capt. Eddie Pettegrew (left) visits with Clayton Vose, manager of the Machiasport Packing & Canning Company, *c.* 1964.

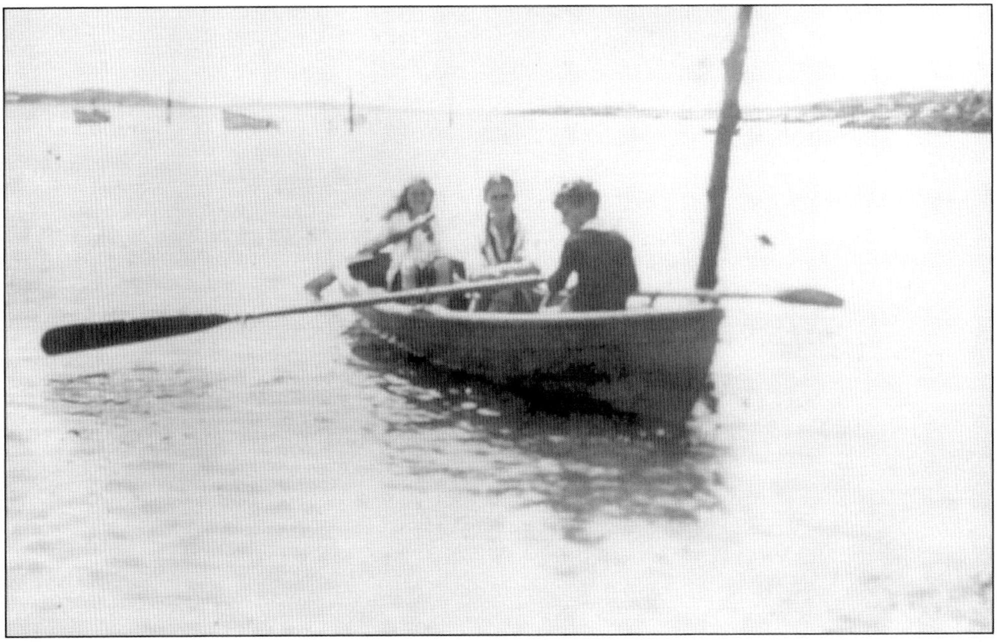

Checking out the waters off starboard in the summer of 1916 are Herbert Rose (rowing), Allison Rose, and Lucia Rose (handling the stern steering).

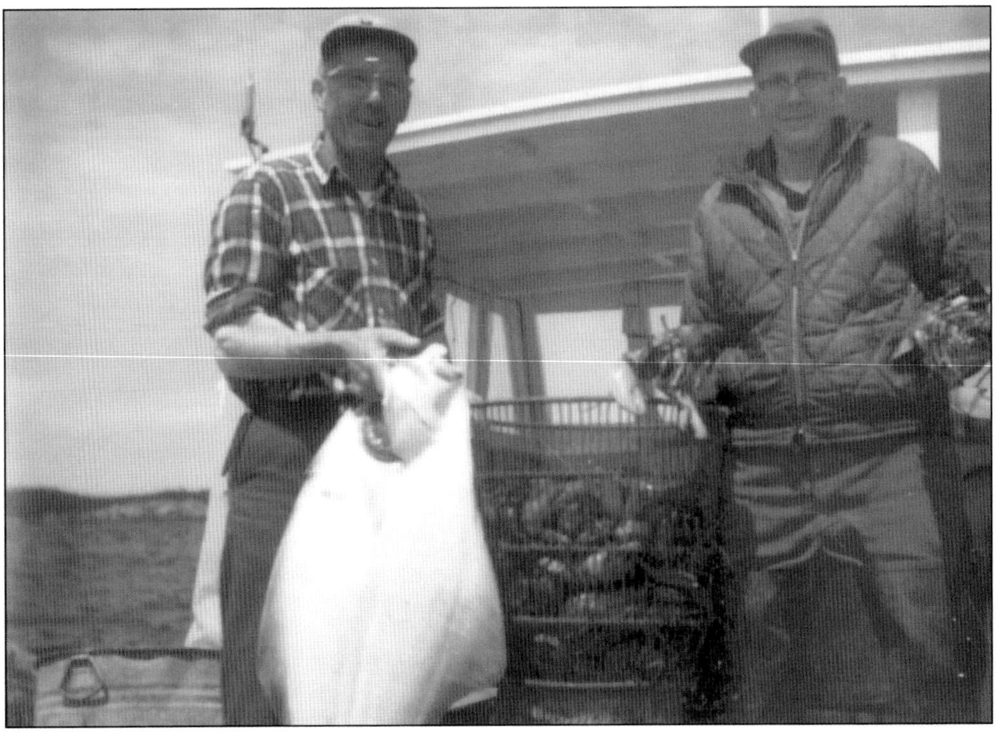

Bill Vose (left), with a nice halibut catch, and Simeon Dobbin, with some lobsters, pose on George Flynn's new lobster boat in Machias Bay in 1968.

Herbert Rose is lobster fishing in Bucks Harbor, c. 1960s.

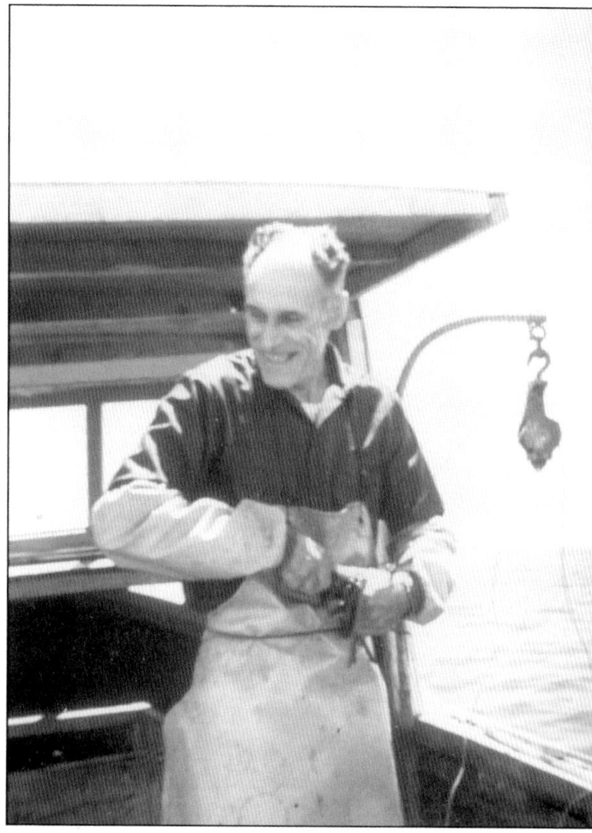

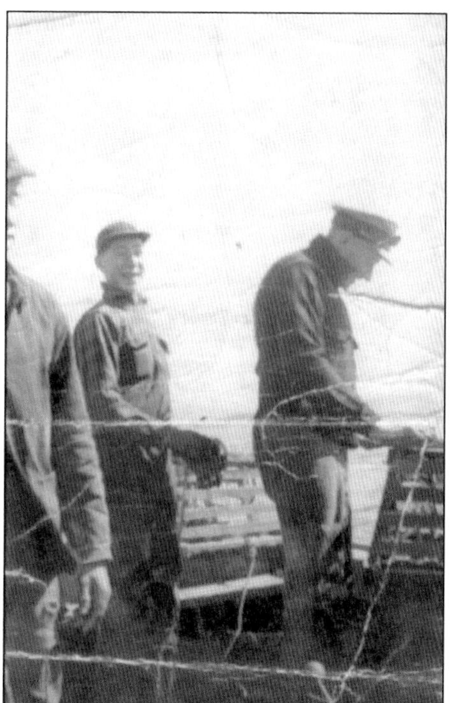

Irving Gilbert (left) and Loring Pettegrow are lobstering out of Bucks Harbor, c. 1940s.

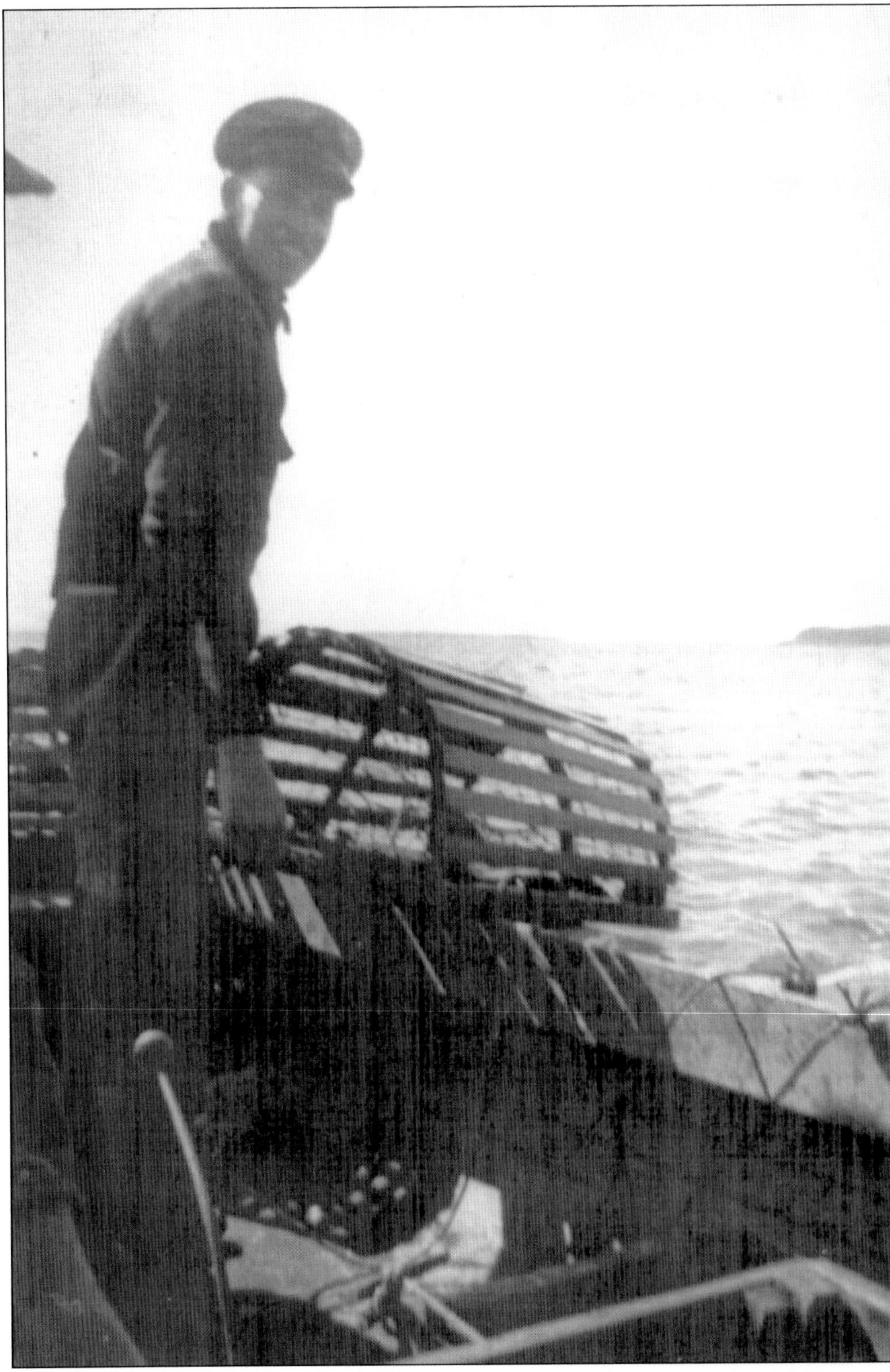

Loring Pettegrow is dropping a trap, c. 1940s.

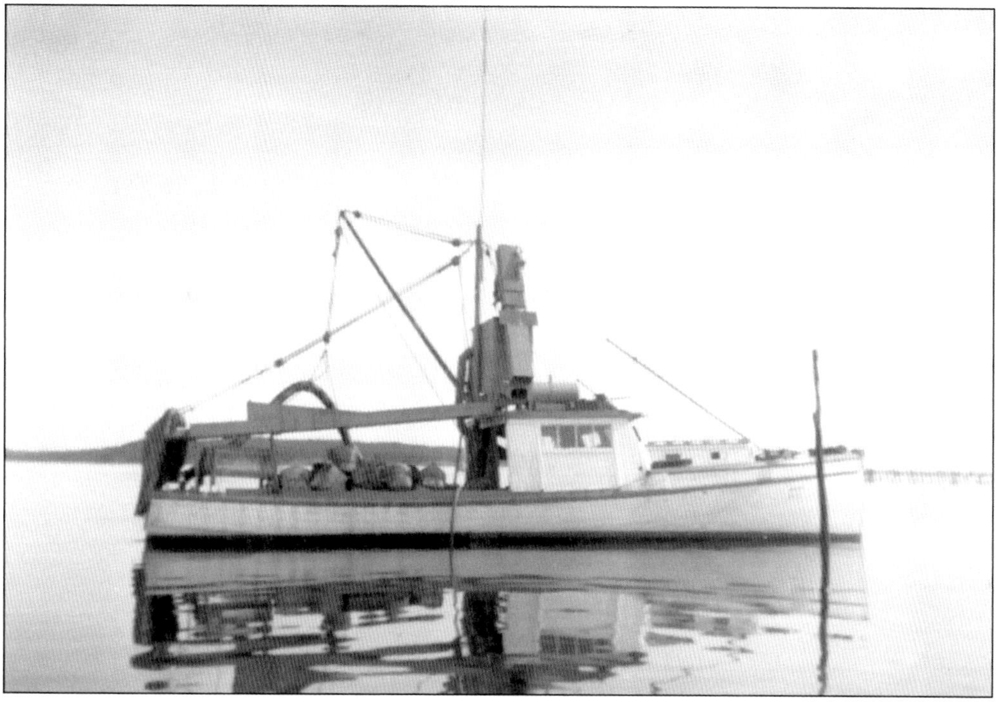

Sardines were an important commodity. They were packed and shipped from plants that dotted the Down East coastline through the 1960s. Shown is a sardine smack at Starboard in 1956.

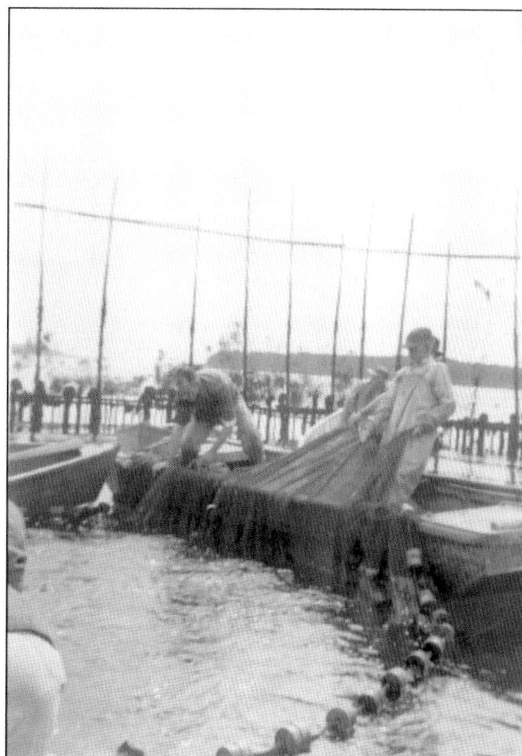

Shown from left to right are Herbert Rose, Ralph Sprague, and Jamie Sprague pulling a seine net full of sardines in 1956.

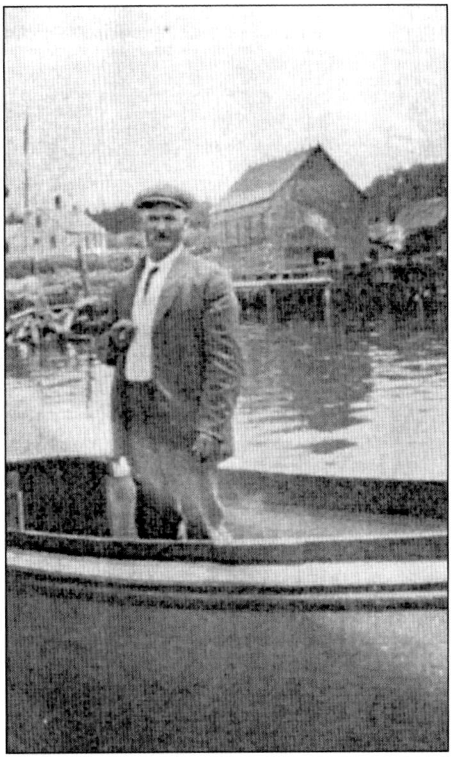

Charles Kenney poses aboard his boat in Bucks Harbor, *c.* 1920.

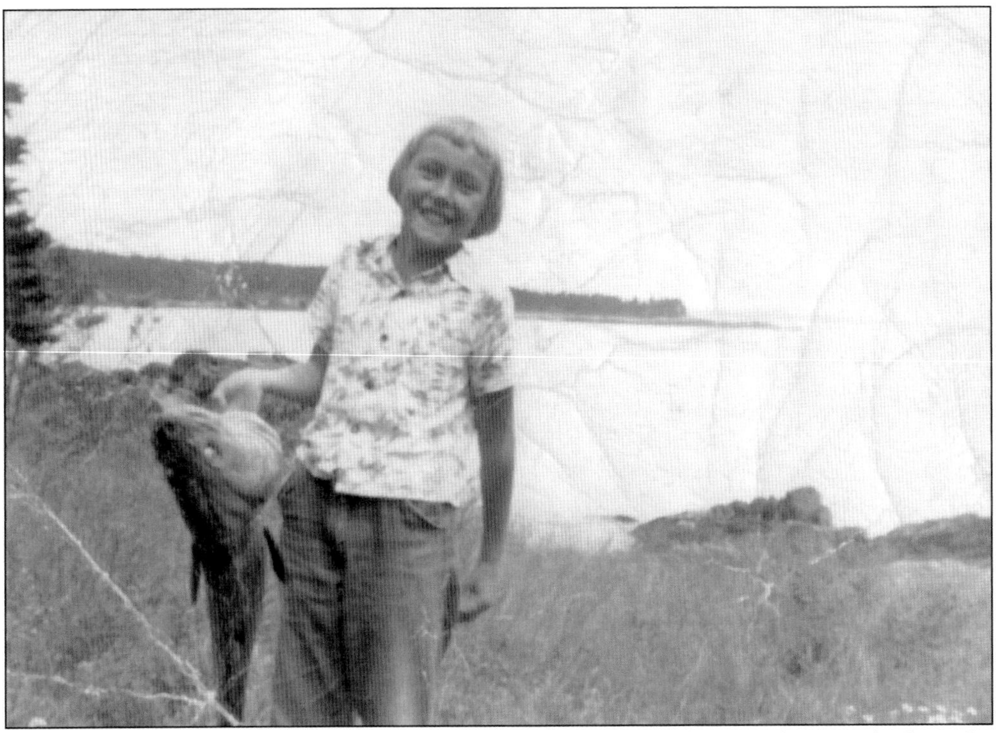

Linda Lund and a nice cod that she caught off Ingalls Island were photographed in the summer of 1950.

Willard M. Look was a pioneer in the development of big clam flats in the Cutler area. In 1918, he built a canning plant on the bayside in Whiting. It was called the East Machias Canning Company. This was the first canning company in America to process crabmeat and steamed clams. In 1938, the canning plant was renamed the A.M. Look Canning Company of East Machias.

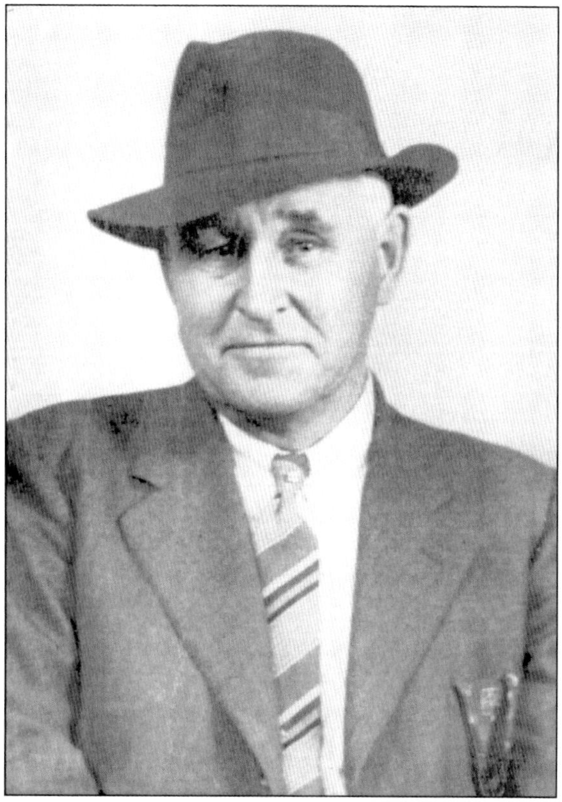

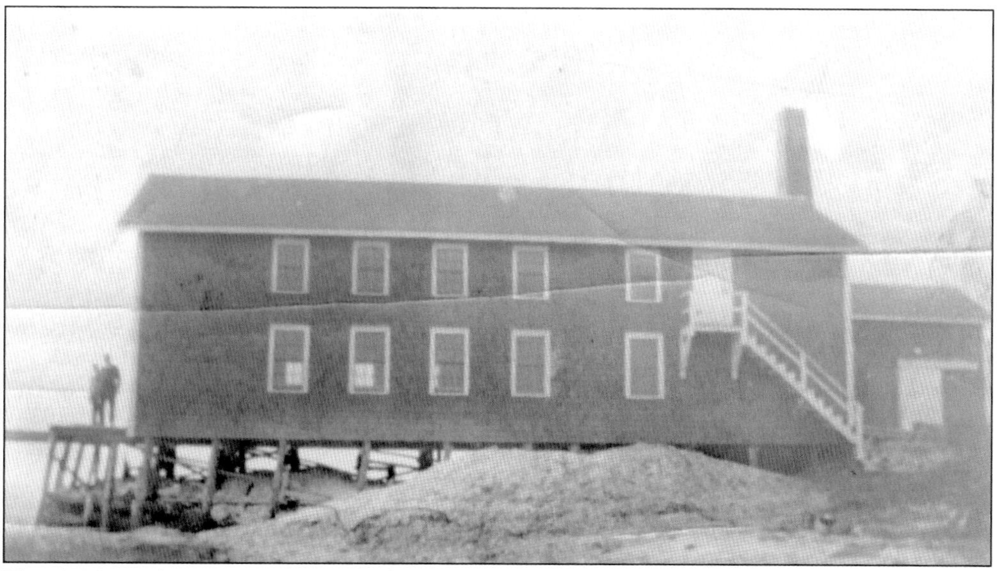

The A.M. Look Canning Company has carried on the tradition of providing gourmet seafood products that are distributed throughout the world. This c. 1940s photograph shows the plant.

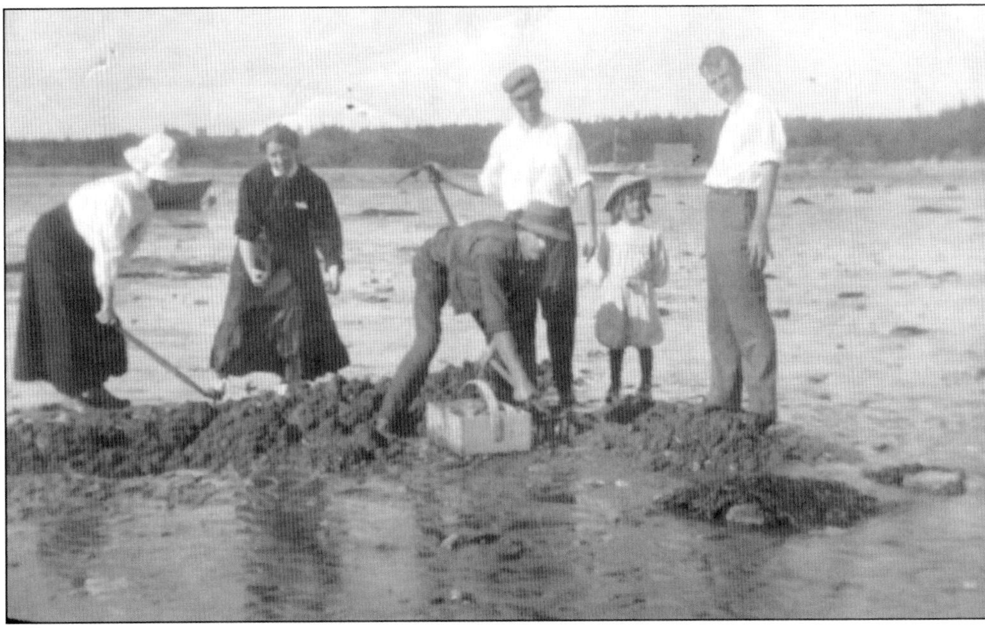

These folks are raking clams during a summer outing at Little Machias in 1908.

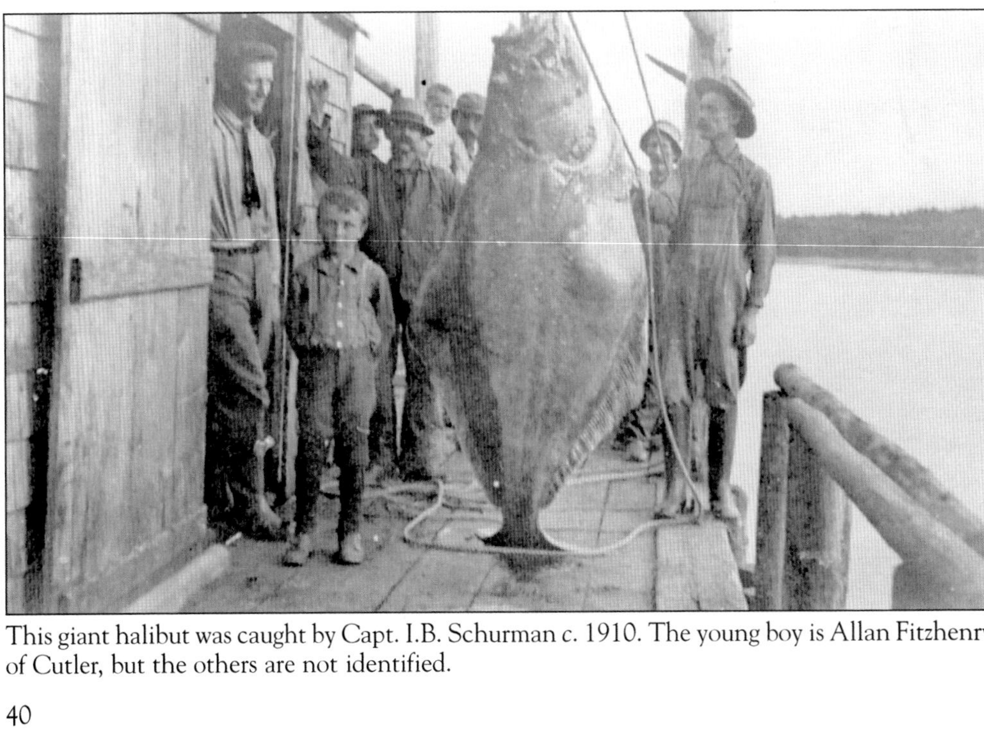

This giant halibut was caught by Capt. I.B. Schurman *c.* 1910. The young boy is Allan Fitzhenry of Cutler, but the others are not identified.

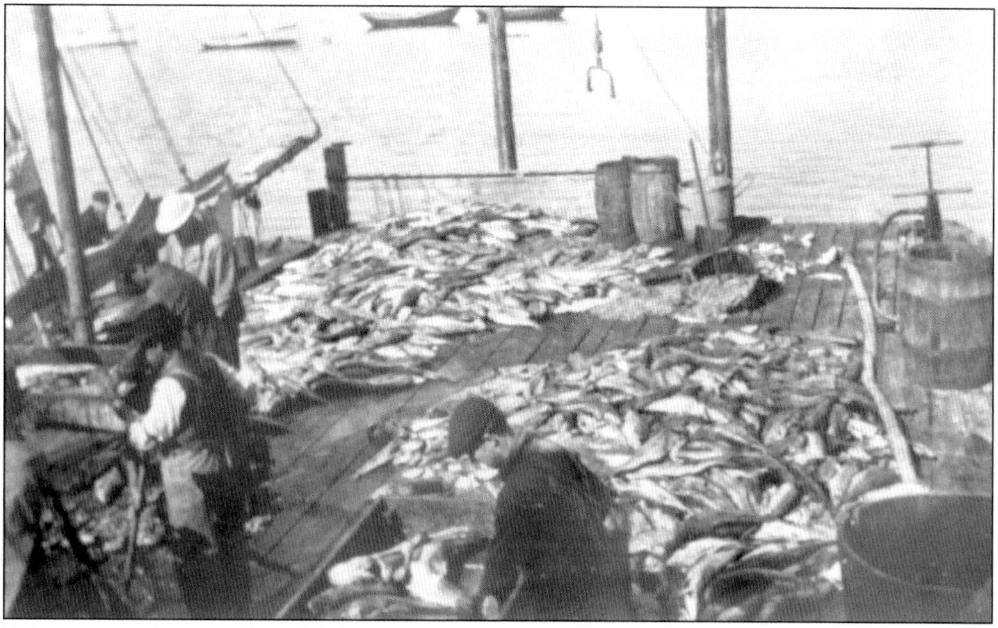

Fish were much more plentiful during the time of this big catch on the Cutler wharf, *c.* 1920s.

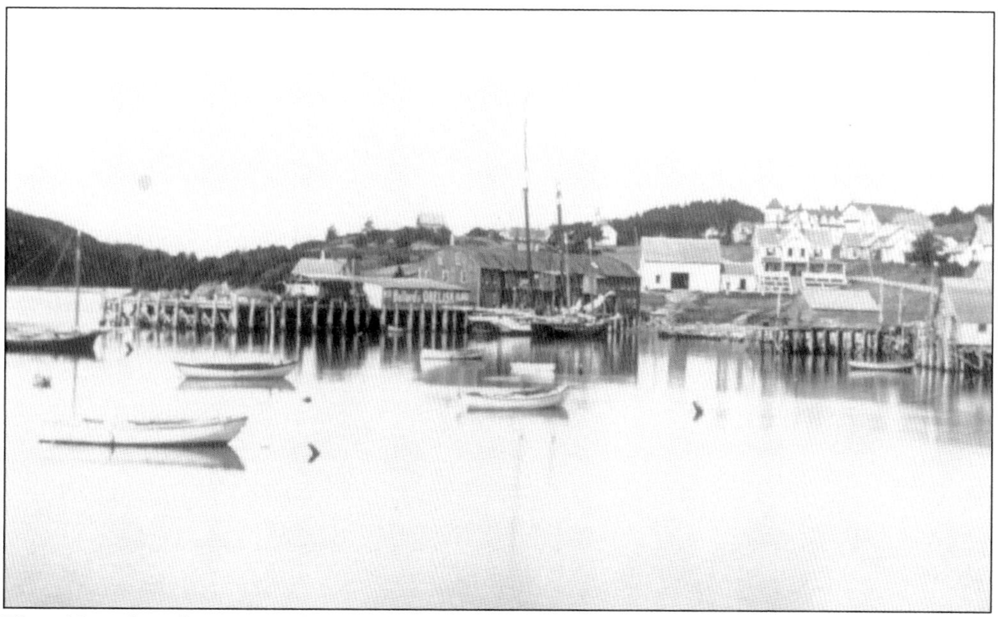

The old sardine factory can be seen here in Cutler Harbor in the late 1890s. Sardines were an economic mainstay of Down East communities.

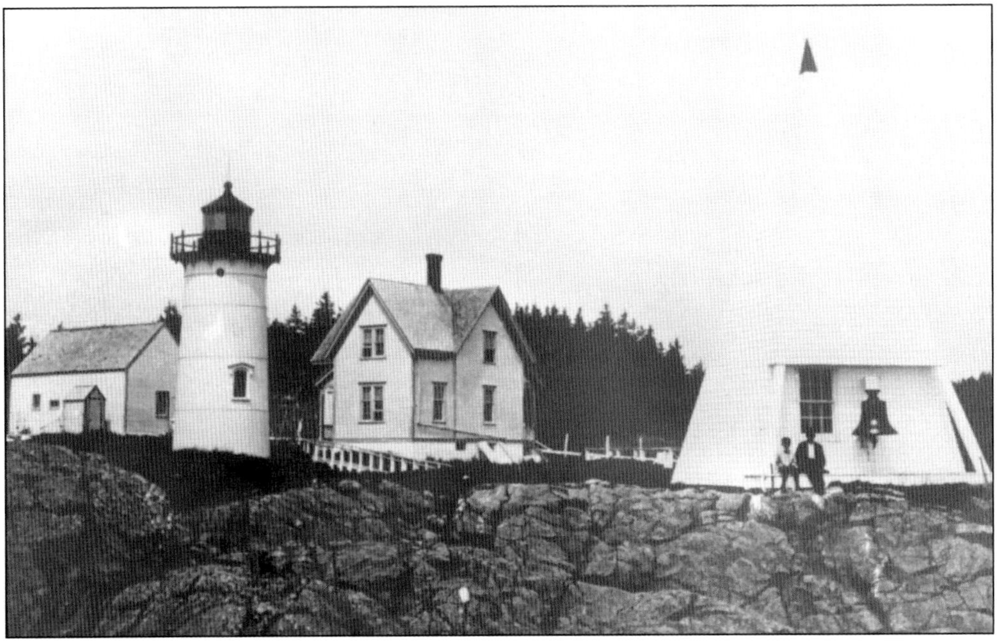

Little River Light is shown *c.* 1920.

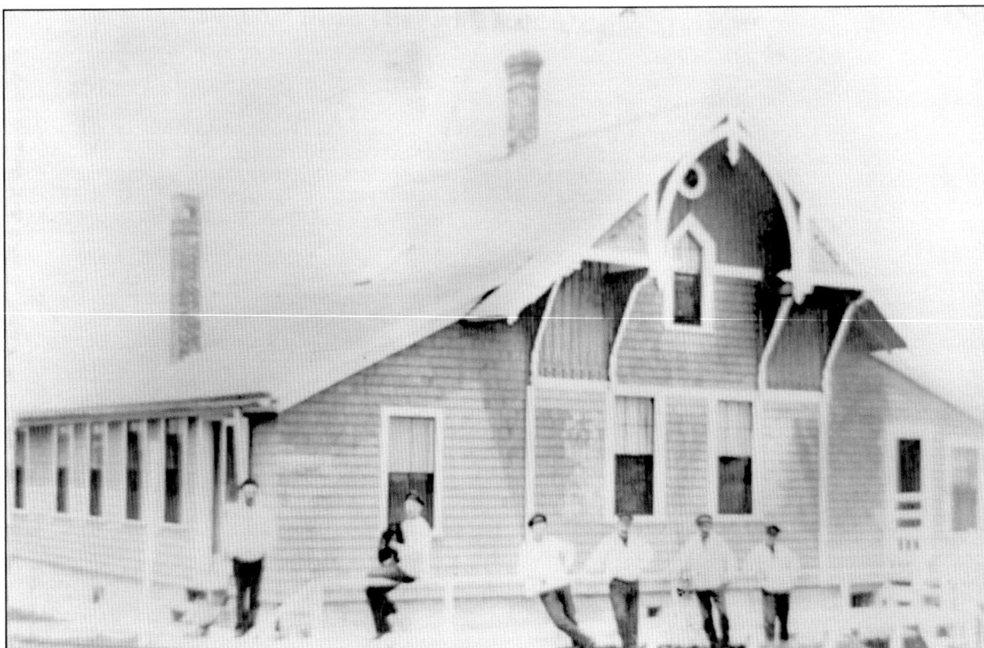

Cross Island Life Saving Station was first manned by the Light House Service and later by the Coast Guard.

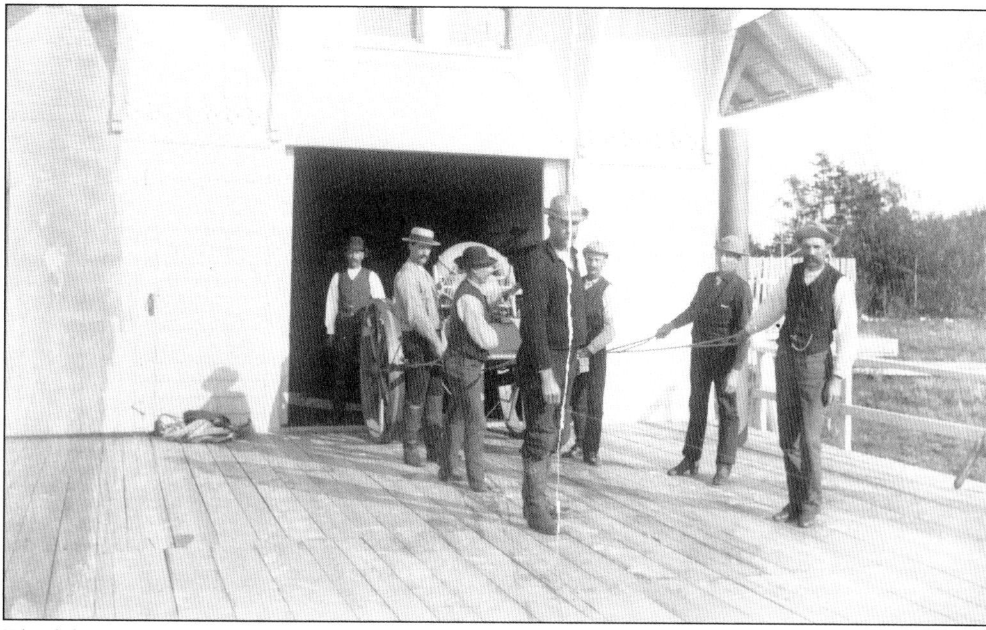

The lifesaving crew at Cross Island is shown *c.* 1890.

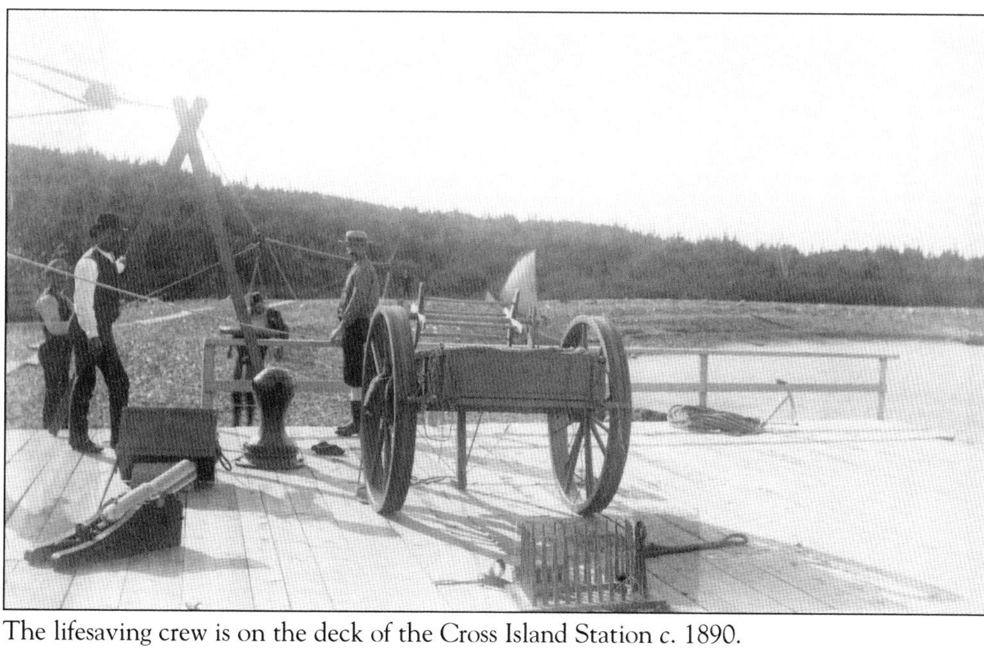

The lifesaving crew is on the deck of the Cross Island Station *c.* 1890.

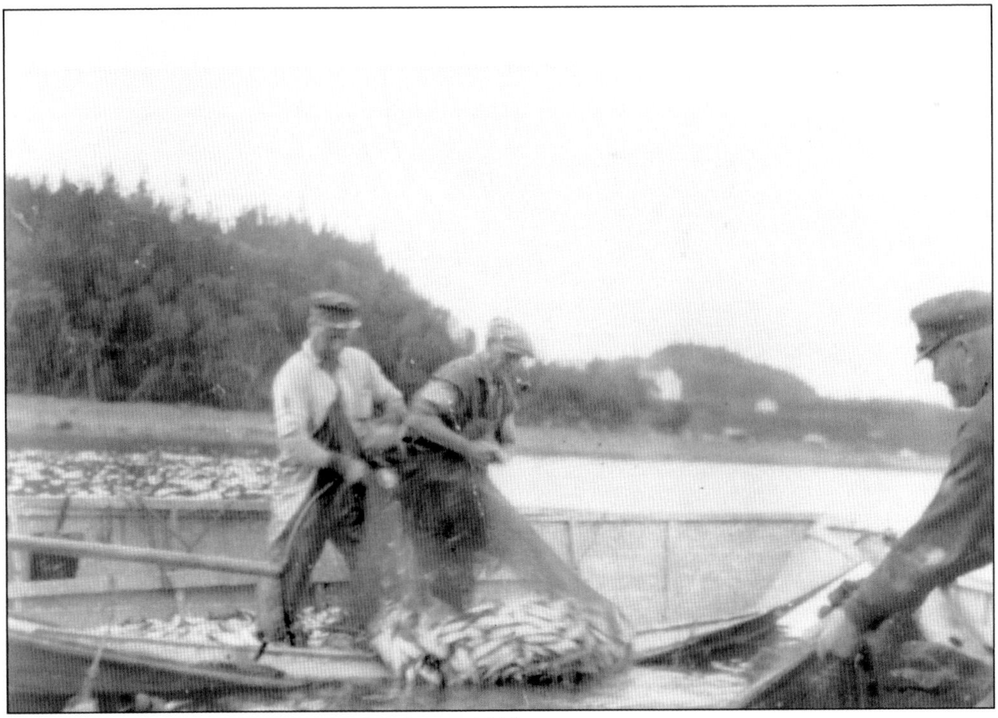

Quite a catch was made at Cutler Harbor *c.* 1915.

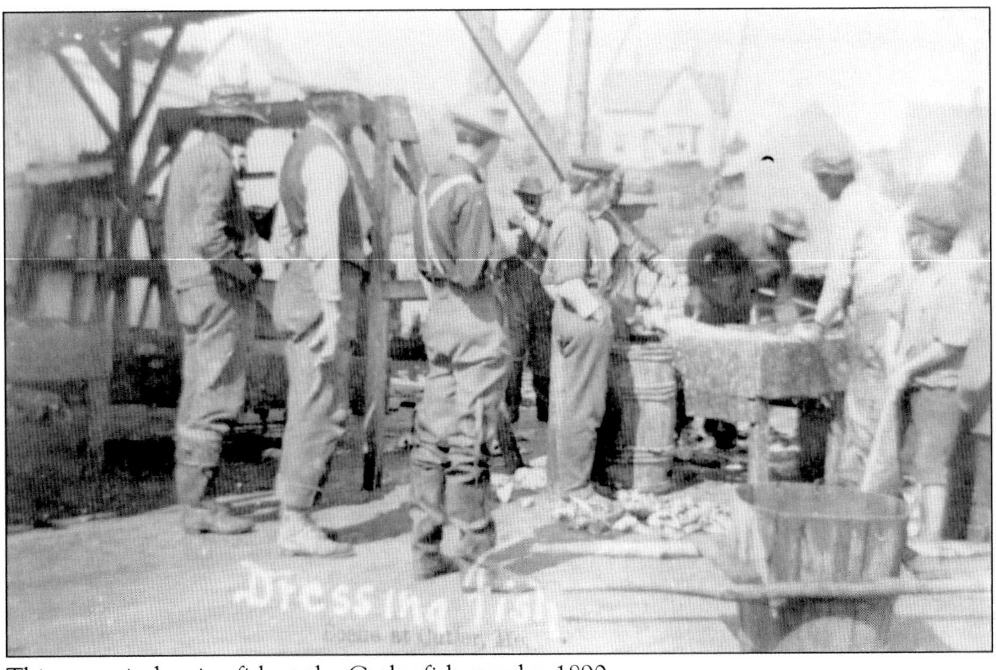

This group is dressing fish at the Cutler fish stand *c.* 1890.

Three

Our Schools

Education has always been important to the people of the Machias Bay Region. Local neighborhood schools under local control were the centerpiece of the educational system. From the colonial era to the early 20th century, education in the schools was quite similar. One of the oldest chartered schools in New England is Washington Academy. It was chartered under the governorship of John Hancock of Massachusetts in 1792.

From 1792 to 1823, Washington Academy classes were held in a public schoolhouse and the Burnham Tavern in Machias as well as in the Masonic Hall in East Machias. In 1823, it was organized as an all-boys school and opened in a new building under the direction of Rev. Soloman Adams, a 26-year-old Harvard and Andover Theological Seminary graduate. Through the years, the academy has added athletic fields and additional educational space.

During the 1950s, the new Machias Memorial High School was completed and, in May 1961, it became fully accredited, offering the usual secondary courses. For over nine decades, the University of Maine at Machias has played a key role in the community. Before it became known as the University of Maine at Machias in 1970, the college had four other names: Washington State Normal School (1909–1952), Washington State Teachers College (1952–1965), Washington State College (1965–1968), and Washington State College of the University of Maine (1968–1970).

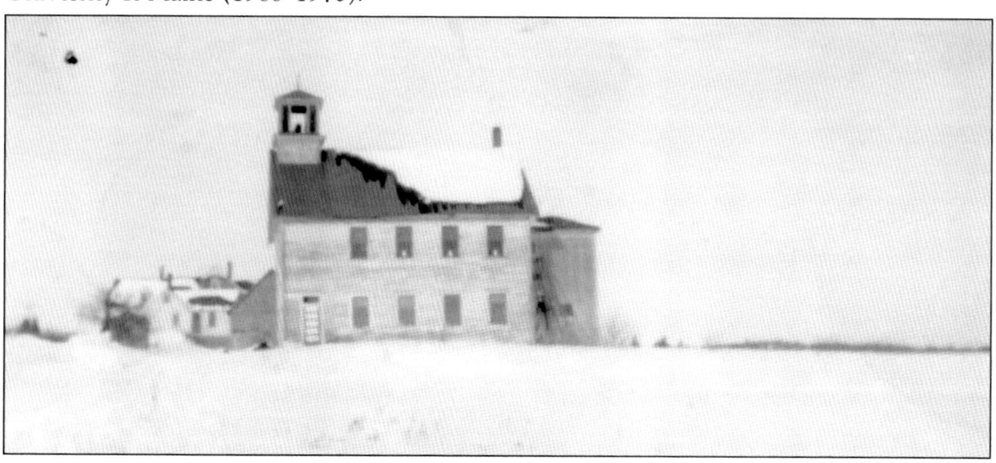

The Bucks Harbor Elementary School was photographed in December 1947.

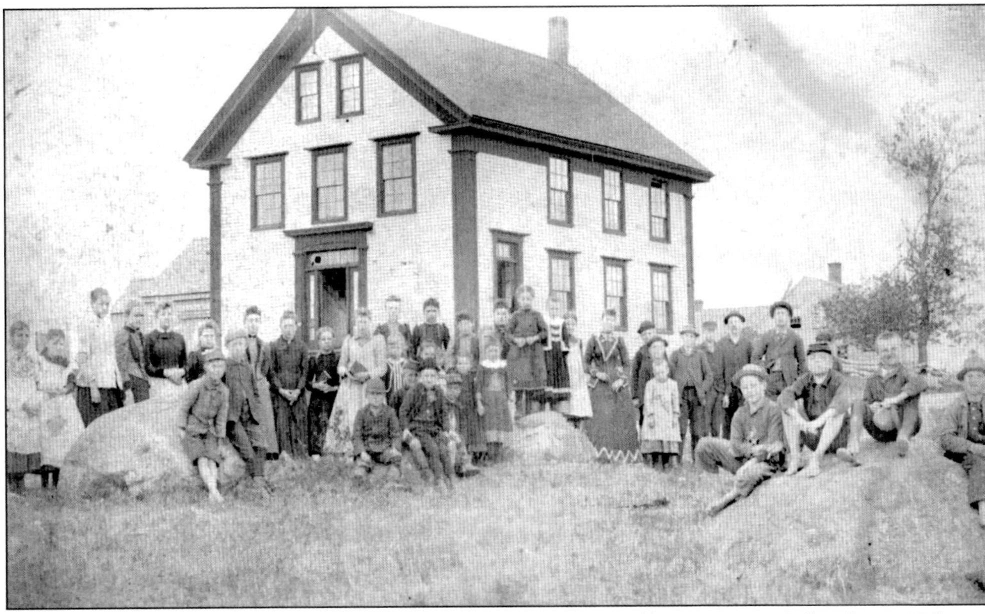

Students and their teacher are seen in front of the Jacksonville Grammar School in 1885.

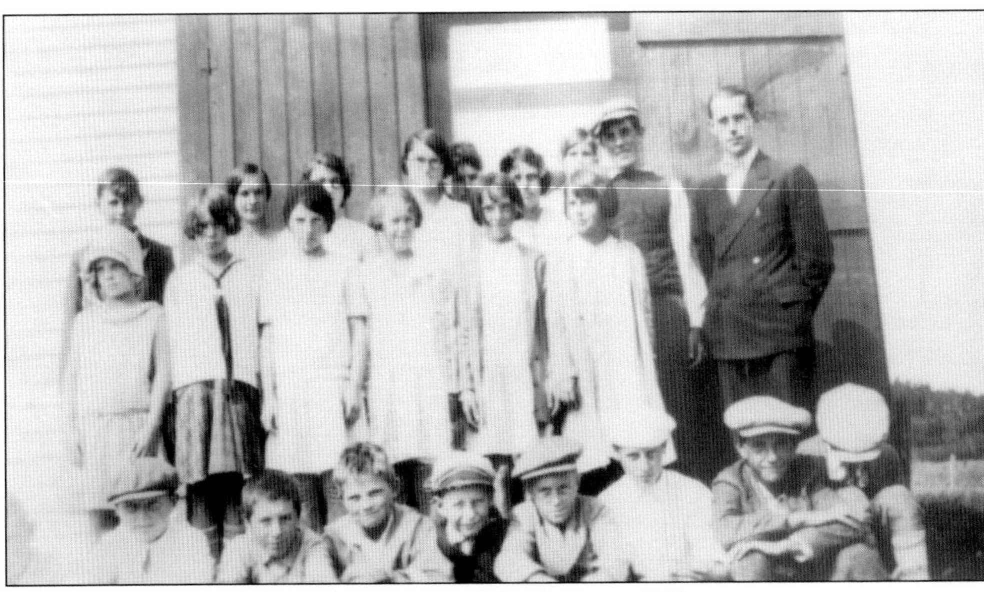

Students and faculty of the Cutler Grammar School pose in 1930.

Cutler Harbor Grammar School served grades one through nine until 1962.

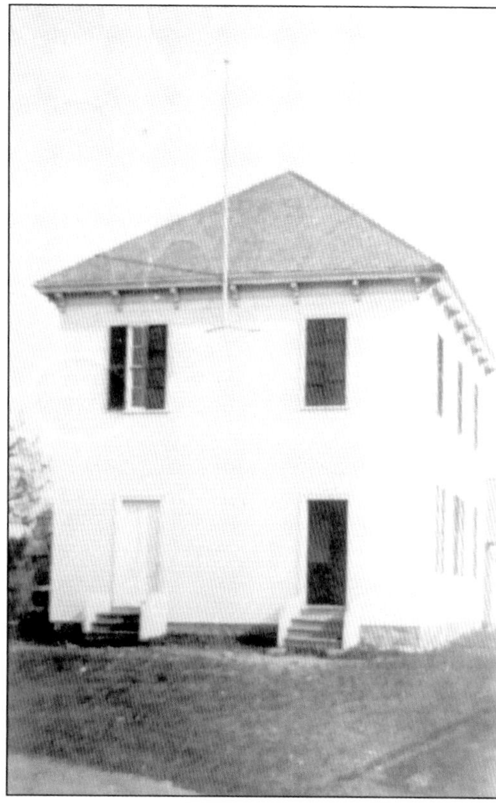

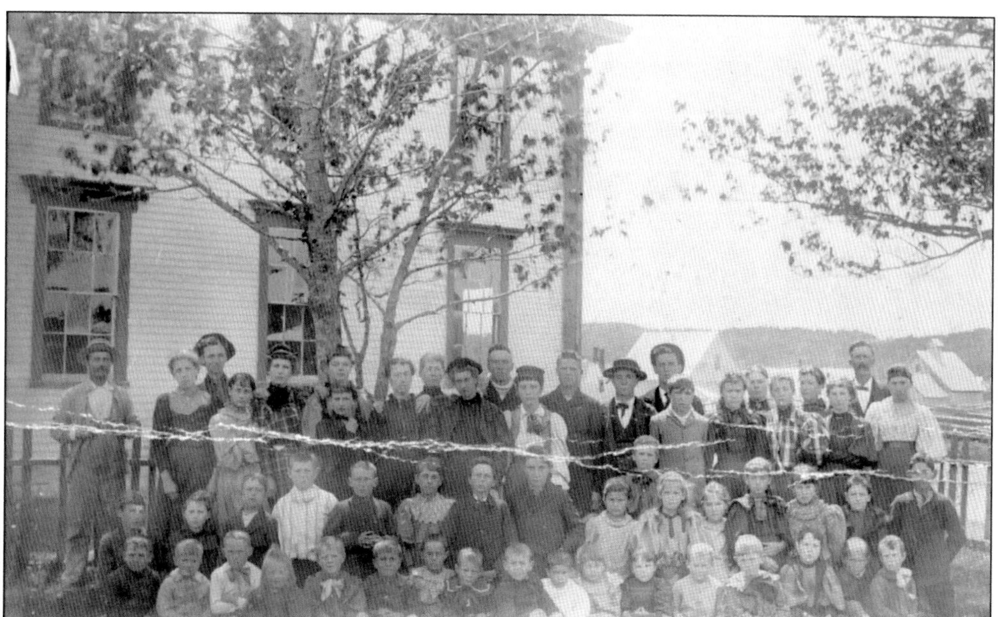

These Cutler Harbor Grammar School students and faculty were photographed in 1885.

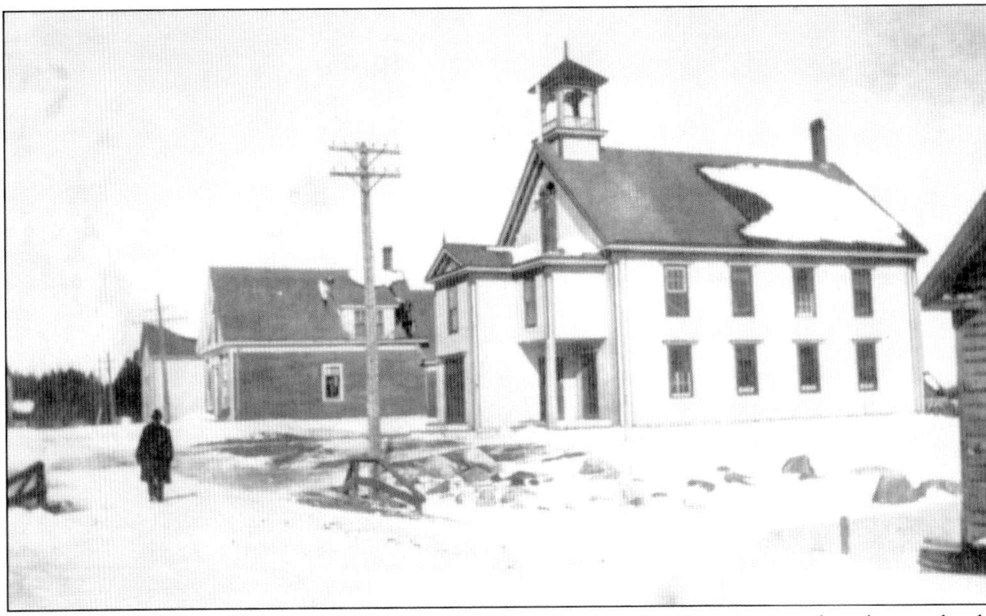

Centrally located in the community, the Jonesboro High School, c. 1920s, played a vital role in the community for many years.

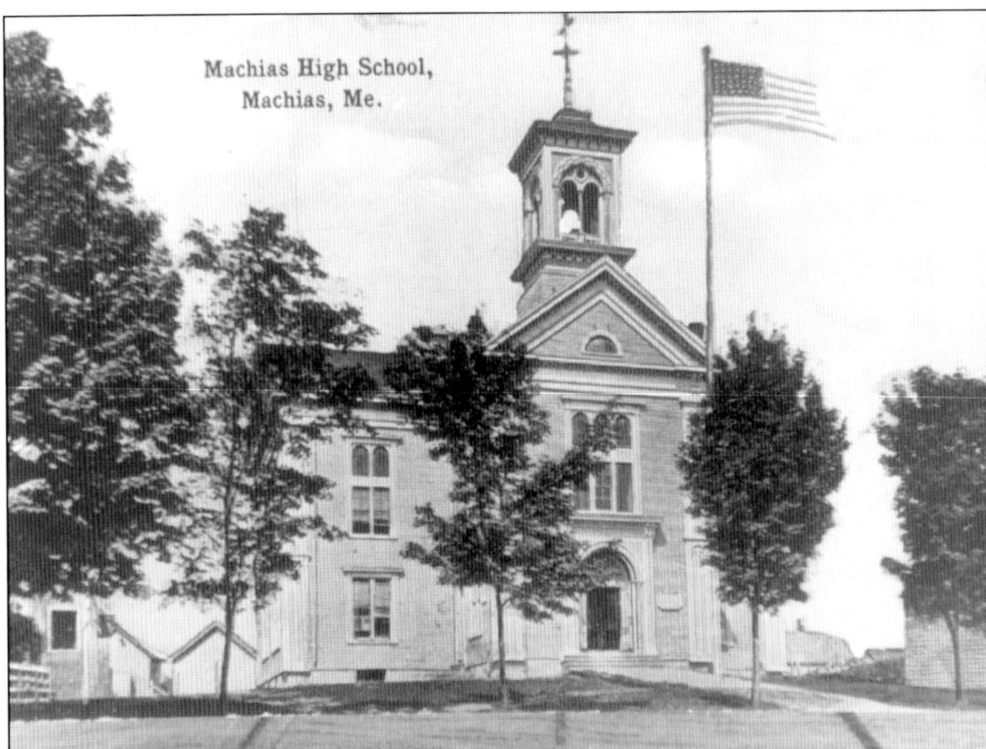

In the 1950s, the new Machias Memorial High School was completed to replace the old Machias High School, photographed c. 1940s.

This is the cover of the 1934 Machias High School yearbook, *The Margaretta*. (See pages 7 and 8 for the story of the ship *Margaretta*.)

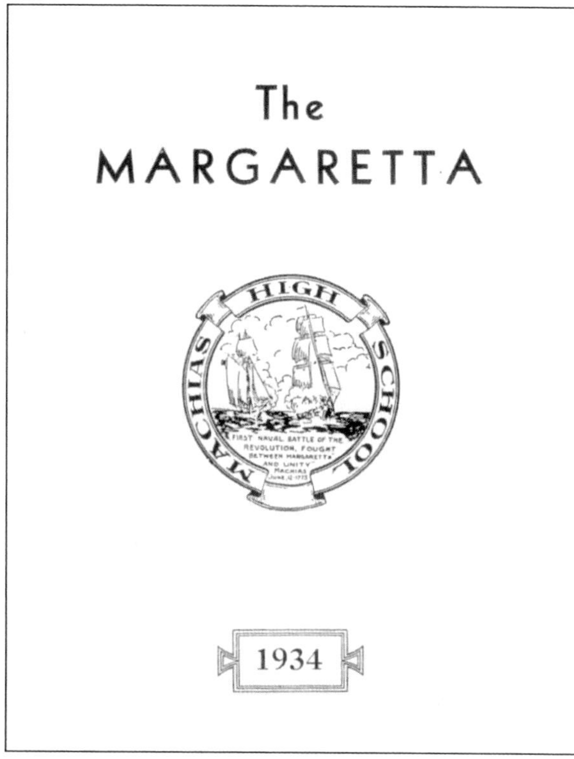

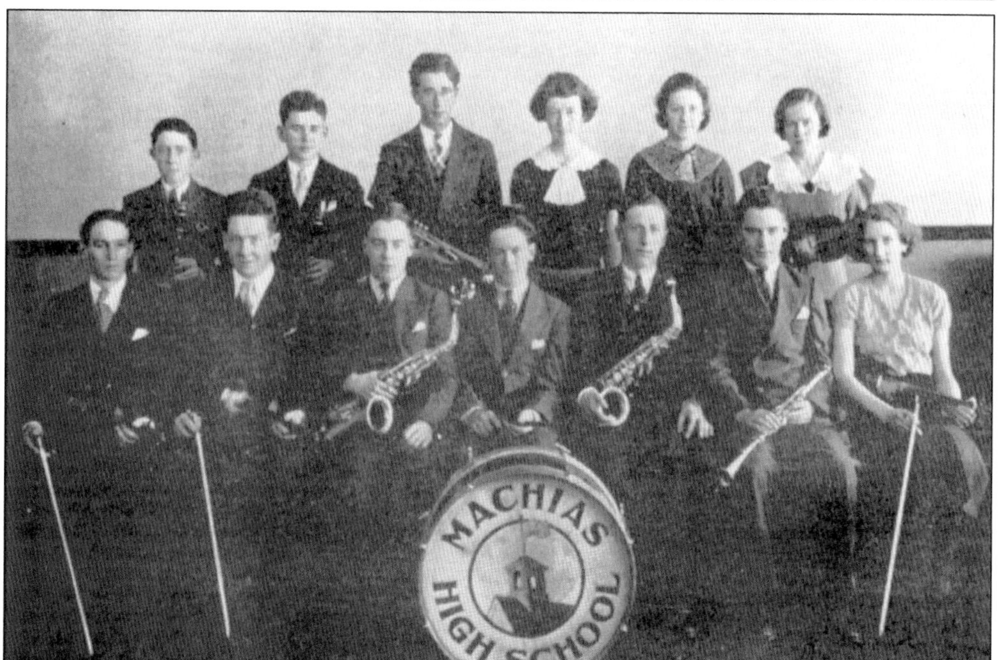

The Machias High School Orchestra was photographed in 1935. Shown from left to right are the following: (front row) V. Rice, E. Watts, R. Saunders, A. Clark, P. Bagley, F. Saunders, and L. Dircksen; (back row) H. DeShon, V. Pettegrew, W. Beverly, I. Vose, J. Rogers, and Miss Tibbetts.

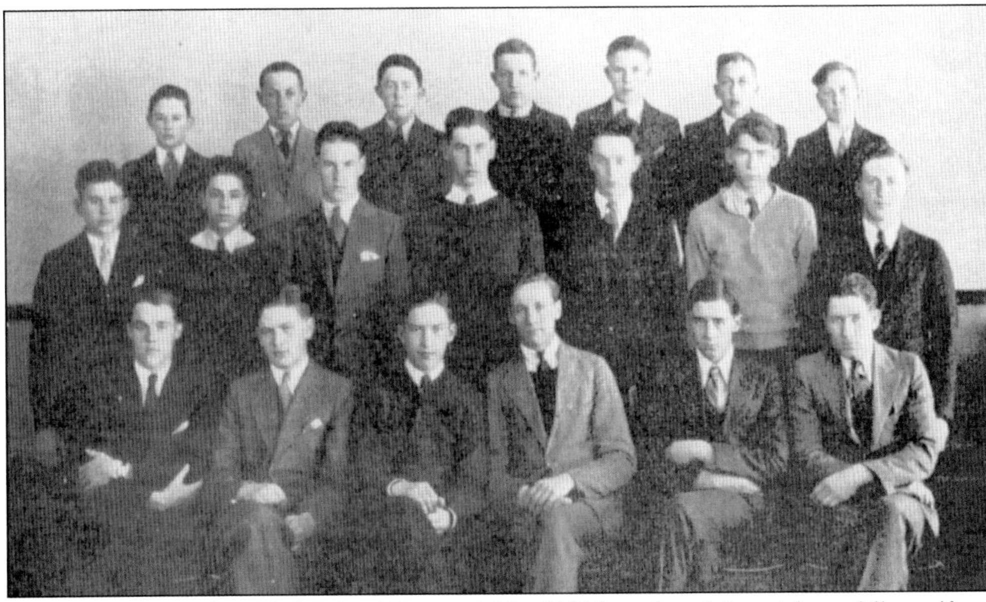

Members of the Machias High School Science Club of 1935 are, from left to right, as follows: (front row) M. Johnson, H. Dolan, B. Woodman, J. Andrews, D. Longfellow, and Mr. Dekin; (middle row) V. Pettegrew, P. Farris, J. Pennell, R. Allen, S. Meserve, N. Mallar, and P. Bagley; (back row) H. Miller, A. Moore, H. DeShon, R. Mealey, R Hatt, M. Farnsworth, and O. Armstrong.

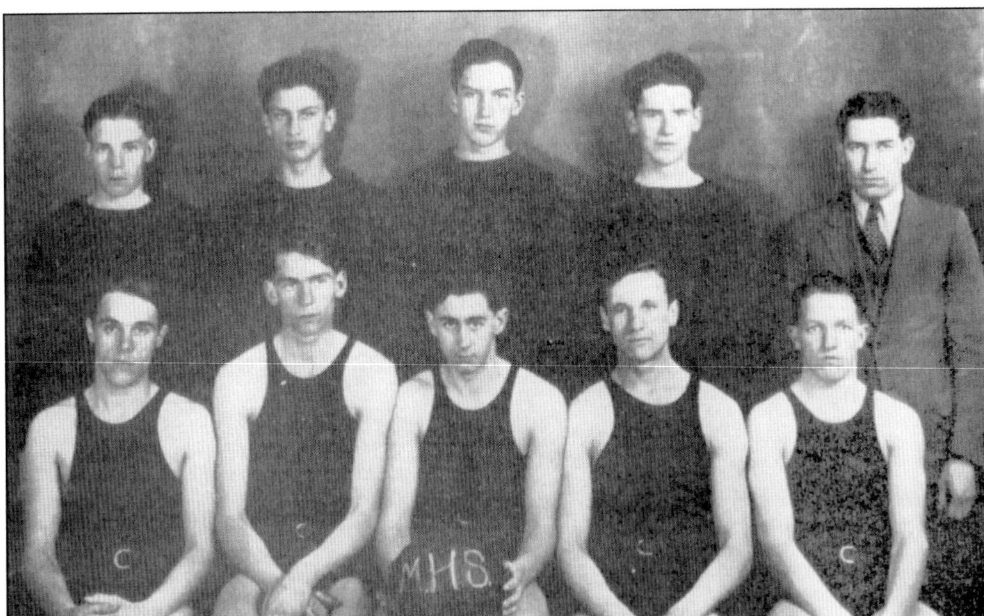

The 1935 Machias High School basketball team had a record of 14 wins and 5 losses. They ended the season on March 1 with a loss to Calais. This gave them a tie for second place in league standings with Calais. Team members included, from left to right, the following: (front row) M. Johnson, N. Mallar, D. Longfellow, J. Andrews, and R. Mealey (back row) R. Hatt, D. Sinclair, B. Woodman, F. Schoppee, and Coach Dekin.

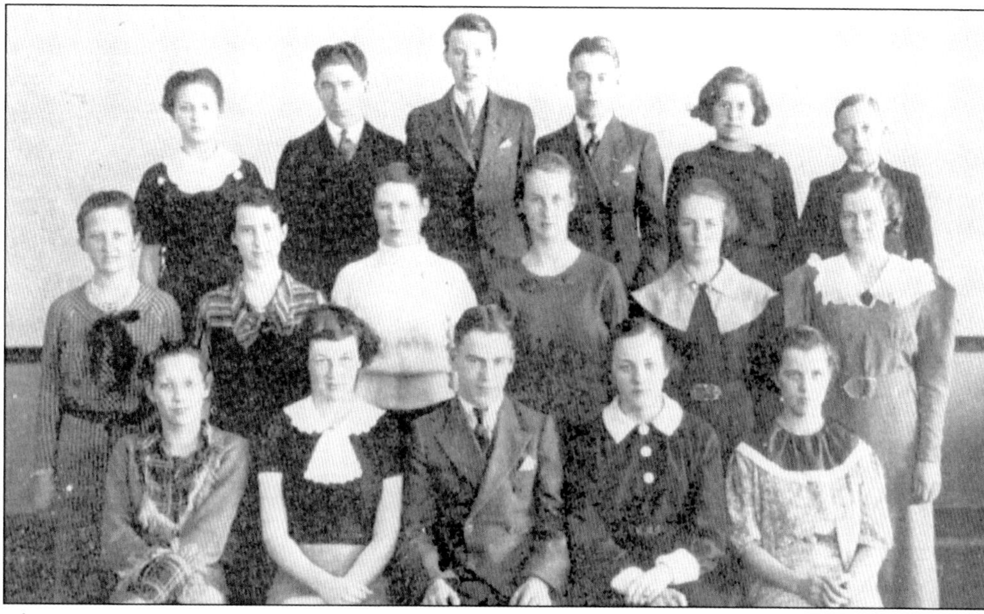

The 1935 Classical Club of Machias High School included, from left to right, the following: (front row) A. Sinford (publicity manager), I. Vose (treasurer), F. Saunders (president), M. Plummer, and L. McLain; (middle row) G. Smith, E. Johnson, M. McGuire, G. Dodge, and Miss Tibbetts (faculty); (back row) B. Sinford, C. Hanscom, R. Saunders, H. Foss, and G. Sprague. Absent from the photograph is C. Hubbard (secretary).

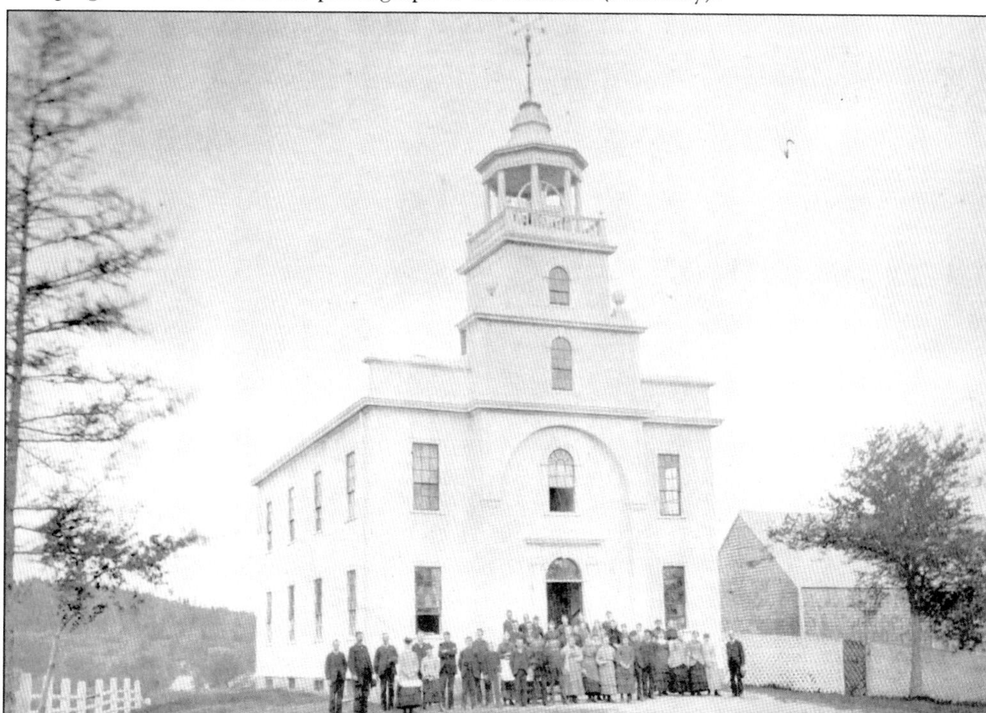

Washington Academy students and faculty, 1883, stand in front of the academy's original permanent facility.

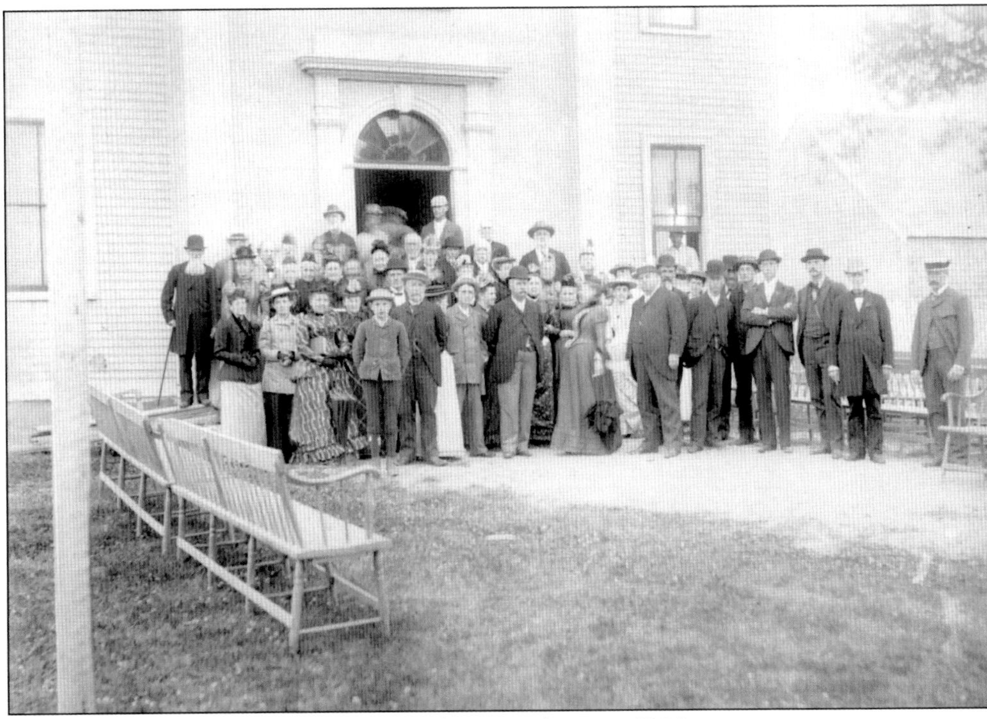

Students and faculty of Washington Academy are shown c. 1900.

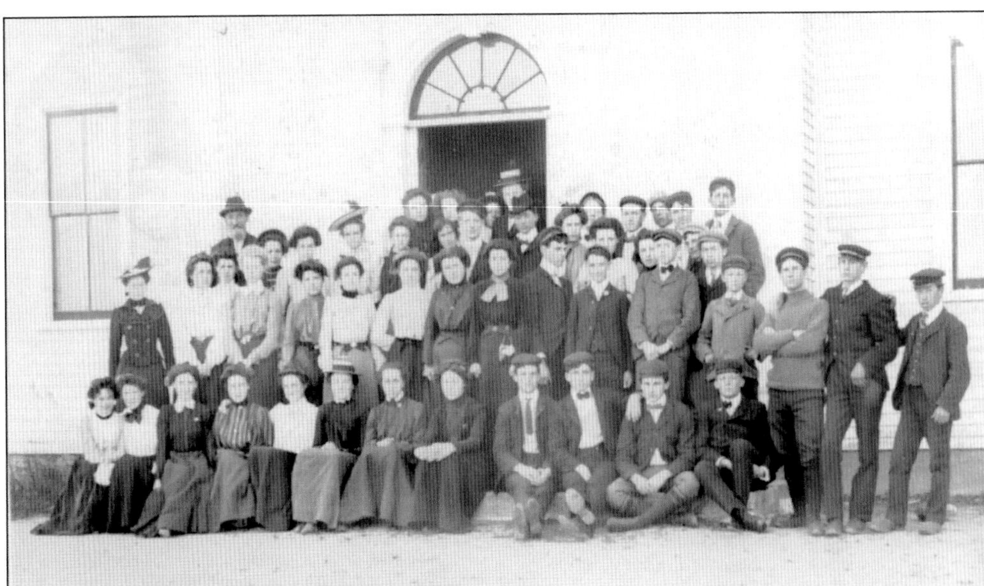

This is an early-1900s photograph of students and faculty in front of Washington Academy.

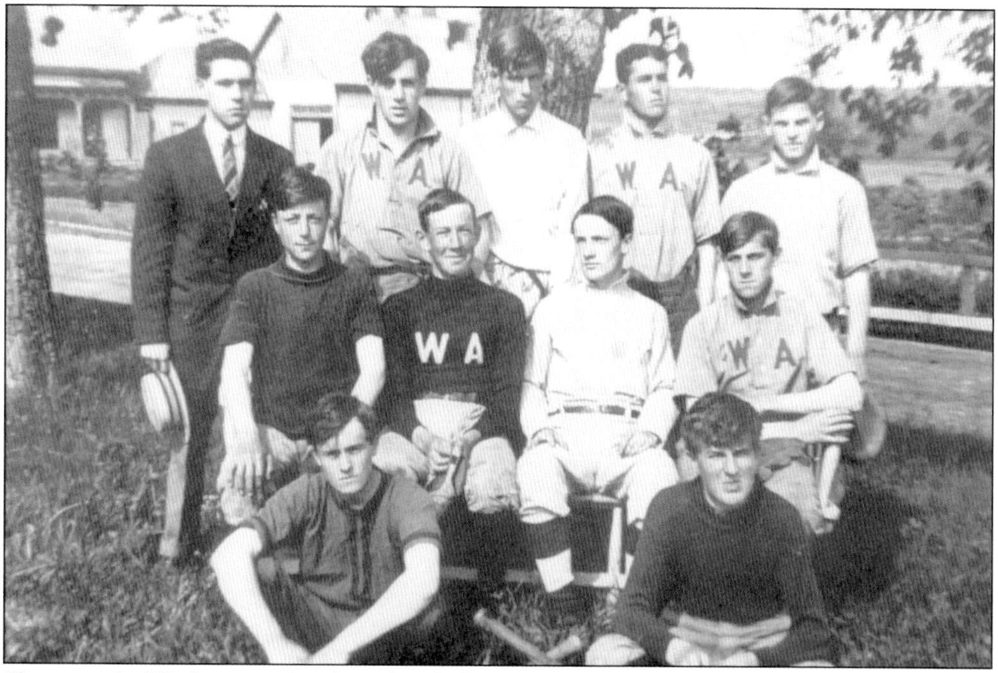

Shown is the Washington Academy baseball team of the early 1920s.

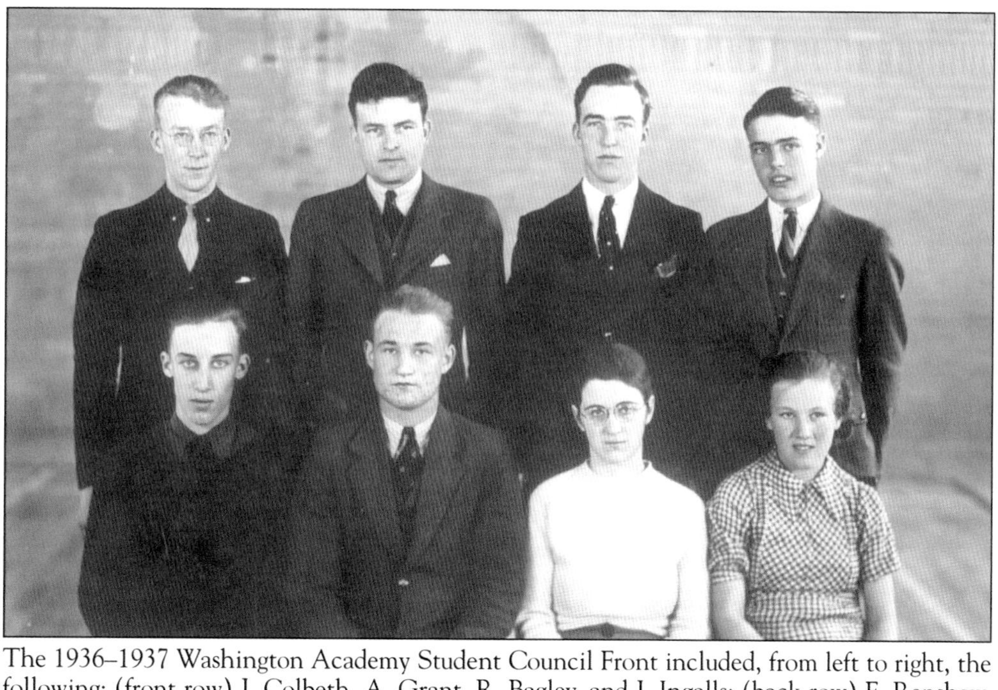

The 1936–1937 Washington Academy Student Council Front included, from left to right, the following: (front row) J. Colbeth, A. Grant, R. Bagley, and J. Ingalls; (back row) E. Renshaw, Ernest Catcomb (principal), W. Talbot, and J. Dow.

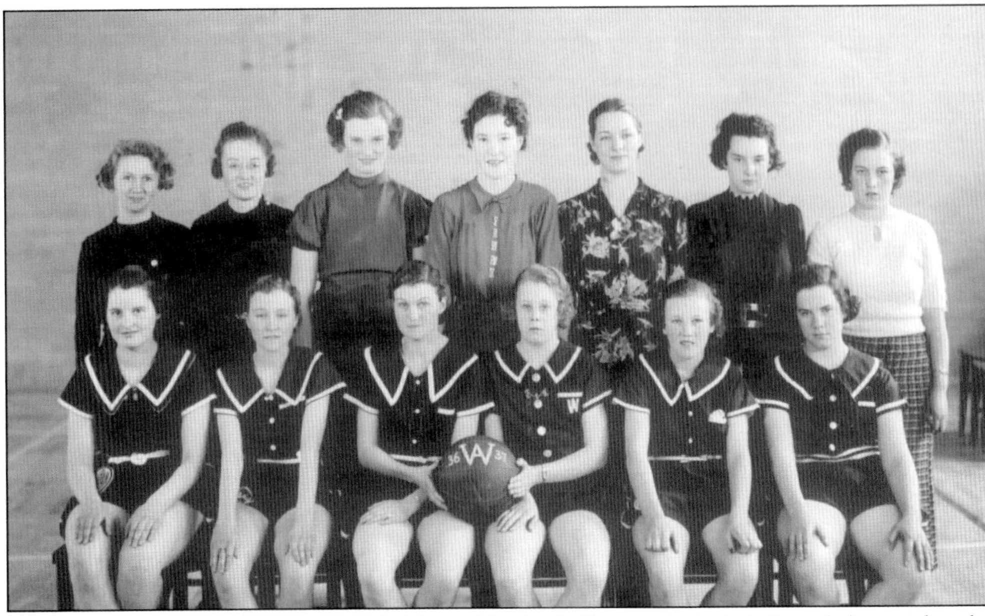

The Washington Academy's 1936–1937 girls' basketball team included, from left to right, the following: (front row) K. Hurley, L. Gilpatrick, A. Durgan (captain), P. Holmes, J. Ingalls, and M. Gardner; (back row) I. Davis. Miss Averill, O. Gatcomb, M. Mcguire, A Hall, G. Holmes, and L. Pettegrow.

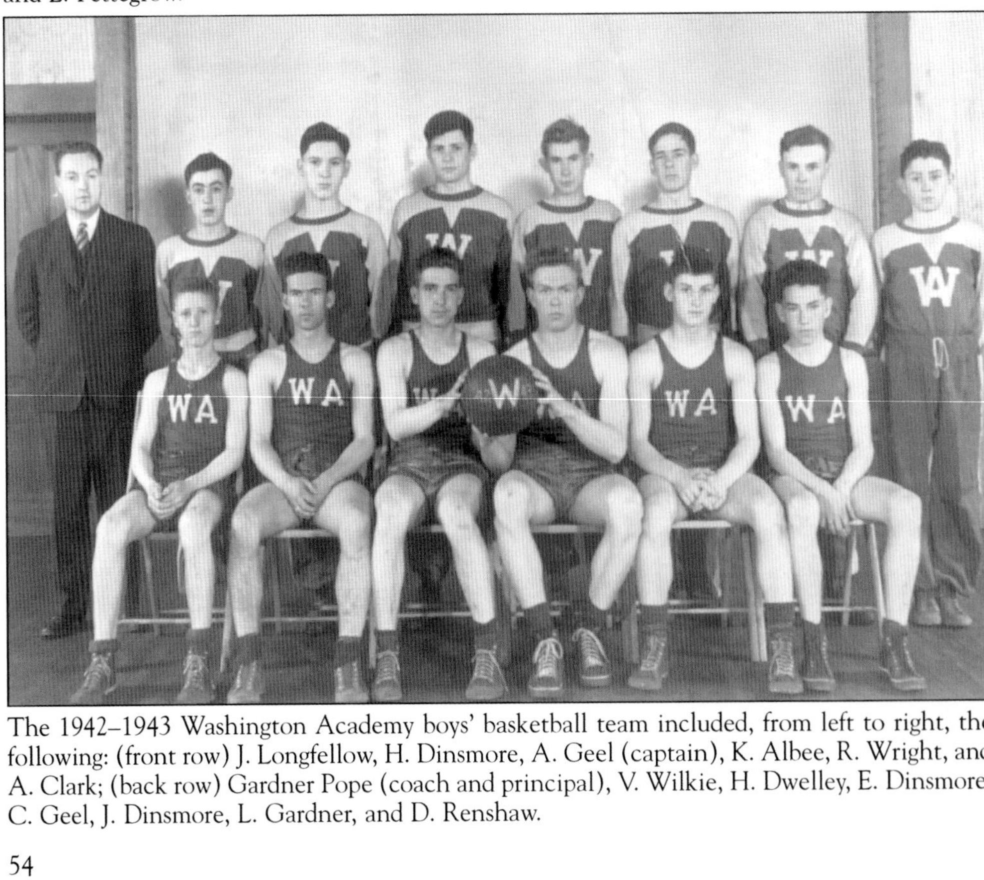

The 1942–1943 Washington Academy boys' basketball team included, from left to right, the following: (front row) J. Longfellow, H. Dinsmore, A. Geel (captain), K. Albee, R. Wright, and A. Clark; (back row) Gardner Pope (coach and principal), V. Wilkie, H. Dwelley, E. Dinsmore, C. Geel, J. Dinsmore, L. Gardner, and D. Renshaw.

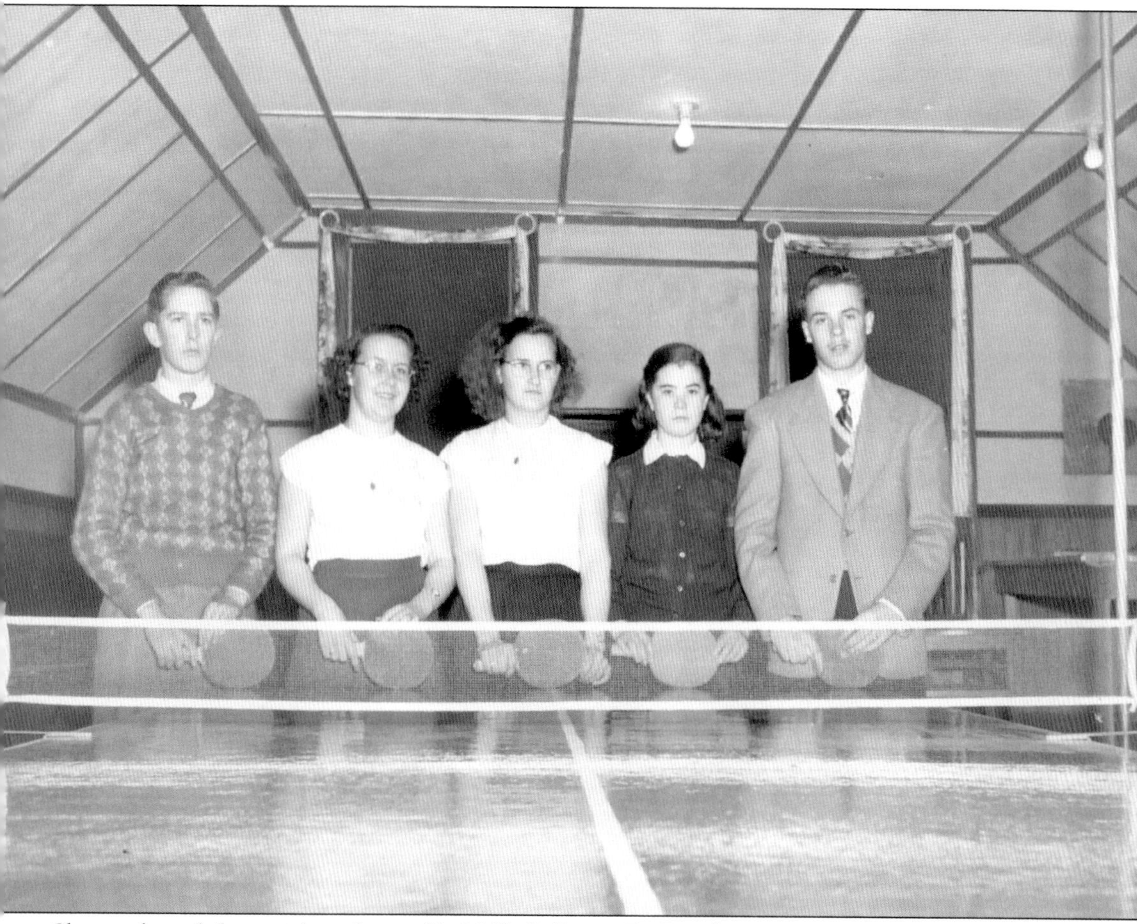

Shown from left to right, players H. Hall, P. Berry, B. Dwelley, E. Gardner, and C. Libby participated in a Ping-Pong match at Washington Academy, c. 1950.

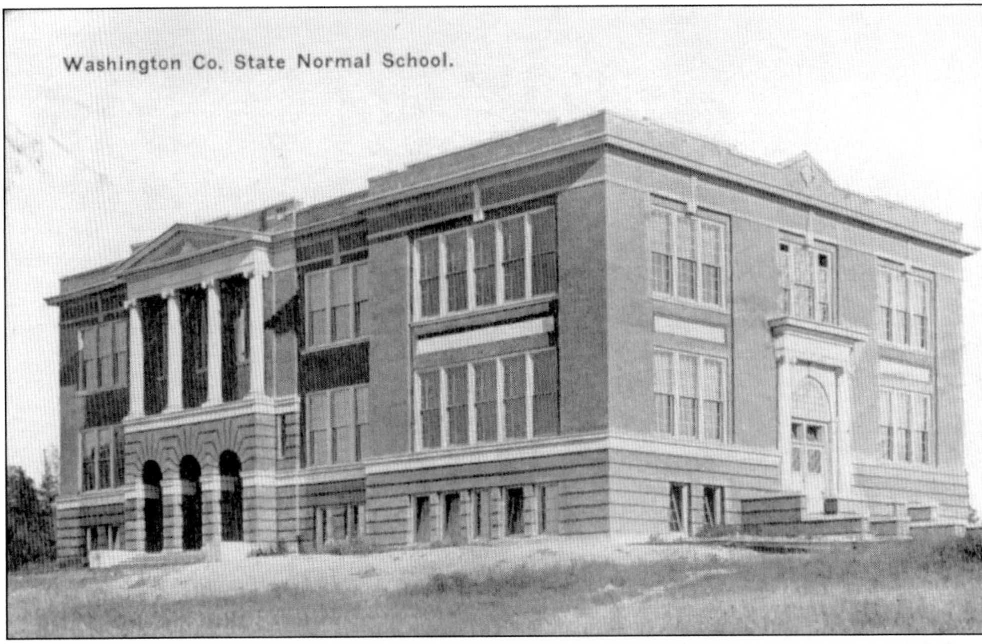

The University of Maine at Machias (UMM) was known as Washington State Normal School from 1909 to 1952. The original Powers Hall, shown here c. 1920s, was destroyed by fire in 1936 but was rebuilt, opening again in March 1937.

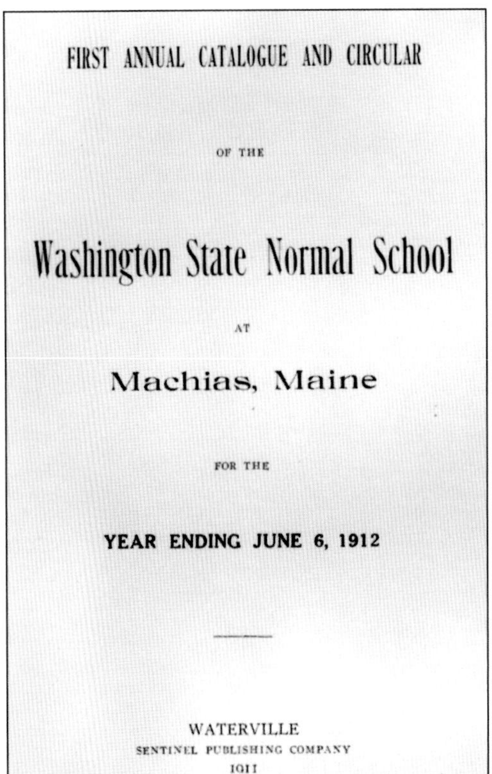

FIRST ANNUAL CATALOGUE AND CIRCULAR

OF THE

Washington State Normal School

AT

Machias, Maine

FOR THE

YEAR ENDING JUNE 6, 1912

WATERVILLE
SENTINEL PUBLISHING COMPANY
1911

In June 1912, the Normal School issued its first annual catalogue and circular.

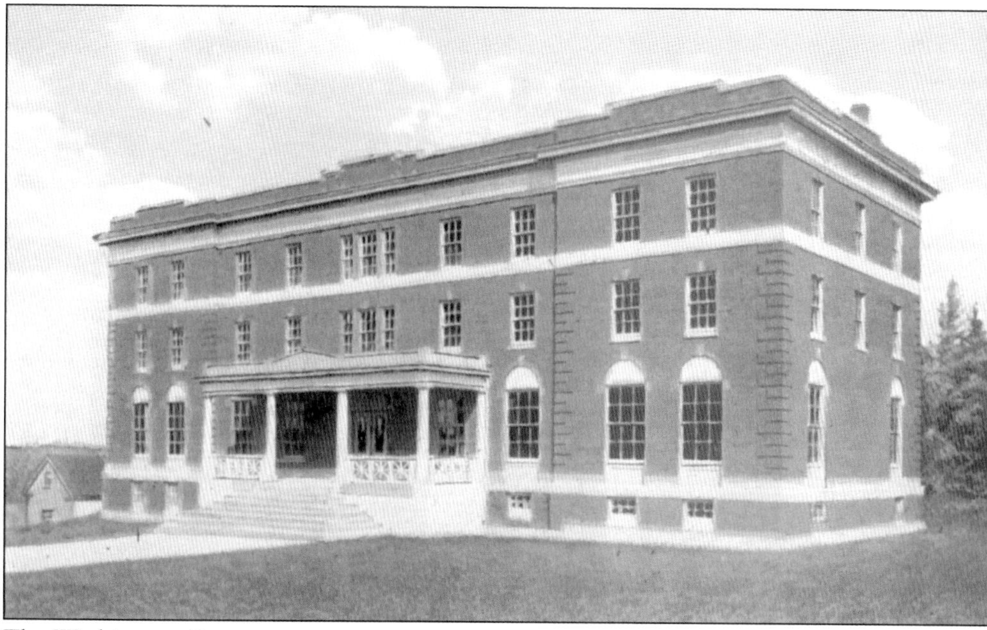

The Washington State Normal School's growth demanded expansion of facilities. This photograph of the new dormitory was taken in the 1920s.

STATE NORMAL SCHOOL

MACHIAS, MAINE

GENERAL RULES

Students are Required:

1. To be in their rooms for the night each day except Saturday and Sunday from 7:30 to 9:30 P.M. for study, and on every night to refrain from all activities after 7:30 which would disturb the quiet of the house for purposes of study or rest. Students are required to be in their rooms at 9 on Sunday evening.
2. To retire for the night not later than 10 P.M. on every night except Saturday when the time is extended to 10:30.
3. To scrupulously observe the usages which prevail among ladies and gentlemen in good society, to refrain from making calls upon all persons of the opposite sex, and to refrain from walking or riding with all such persons, other than immediate family connections, except on the main streets within this village, but calls from gentlemen may be received in the Reception Room at such hours as do not interfere with other regulations. Entertainment of gentlemen friends from out-of-town must be arranged for in advance of the visit.
4. To refrain from attending dances and similar functions except those provided by the school.
5. To appropriately observe the entire Sabbath and to attend public morning worship each Sabbath at the church which they or their parents may select. To observe as quiet hours each Sabbath from 4 to 6 P.M.
6. To leave town only by permission of the Principal if such absence would result in any infraction of school regulations.
7. In all cases of illness severe enough to prevent attendance at school, the boys shall report to the principal and the girls shall report to the teacher of physical education. No person shall enter a sick room in the dormitory without permission from the Dean.
8. Dancing will be allowed in the dormitory two evenings a week, Tuesday and Friday, until 7:30 o'clock. The normal school boys are allowed in the dormitory after supper until 7:30 on Tuesday, Friday, Saturday and Sunday evenings. On all other occasions they shall leave as soon as meals are over.
9. The girls may leave the dormitory after supper only when absolutely necessary and by permission of the Dean, except on Saturday. On Sunday evening the girls may be excused to go to church or any other special occasion.
10. Meals will be served in the dormitory at 7:30 in the morning, 12:15 at noon, and 6 at night; on Sundays at 8:30, 1:15 and 6:00. Boys who board in the dormitory are not to appear there more than 10 minutes before the meal is served.

DORMITORY RULES

1. The house must be quiet from 7:30 to 9:30 and no unnecessary noise between 9:30 and 10. No baths can be taken during study hours or before 7 A.M.
2. A high standard of conduct shall be maintained in the dining room.
3. In all cases of illness severe enough to prevent attendance at school the sick person must report to the teacher of physical education. No person will be allowed to enter a sick room without permission from the Dean.
4. Dormitory rooms must be in a condition to be inspected at any time. Formal inspection will occur once in two weeks.
5. There shall be no noise or talking before 7 A.M. Persons rising before that time shall wear bedroom slippers and shall maintain quiet.
6. The walls of the rooms must not be defaced in any way. Pictures must be hung from mouldings.

SCHOOL BUILDING RULES

1. Communication of students with each other during the hours school is in session must be limited to brief questions or consultations on matters pertaining strictly to school work, but in the recitations the teacher in charge will control this matter.
2. To report to the Principal absence and tardiness with reasons, in writing, during the first session of subsequent attendance. Every unexcused absence takes 5 off the pupil's rank.
3. To be careful of textbooks loaned by the school.
4. To remain at the school building throughout a session unless excused.

NOTE.—All infractions of the rules which may occur from emergency or otherwise must be reported as soon as possible to the Principal. Permission may be obtained in advance on all reasonable requests.

These are some school rules of an earlier era.

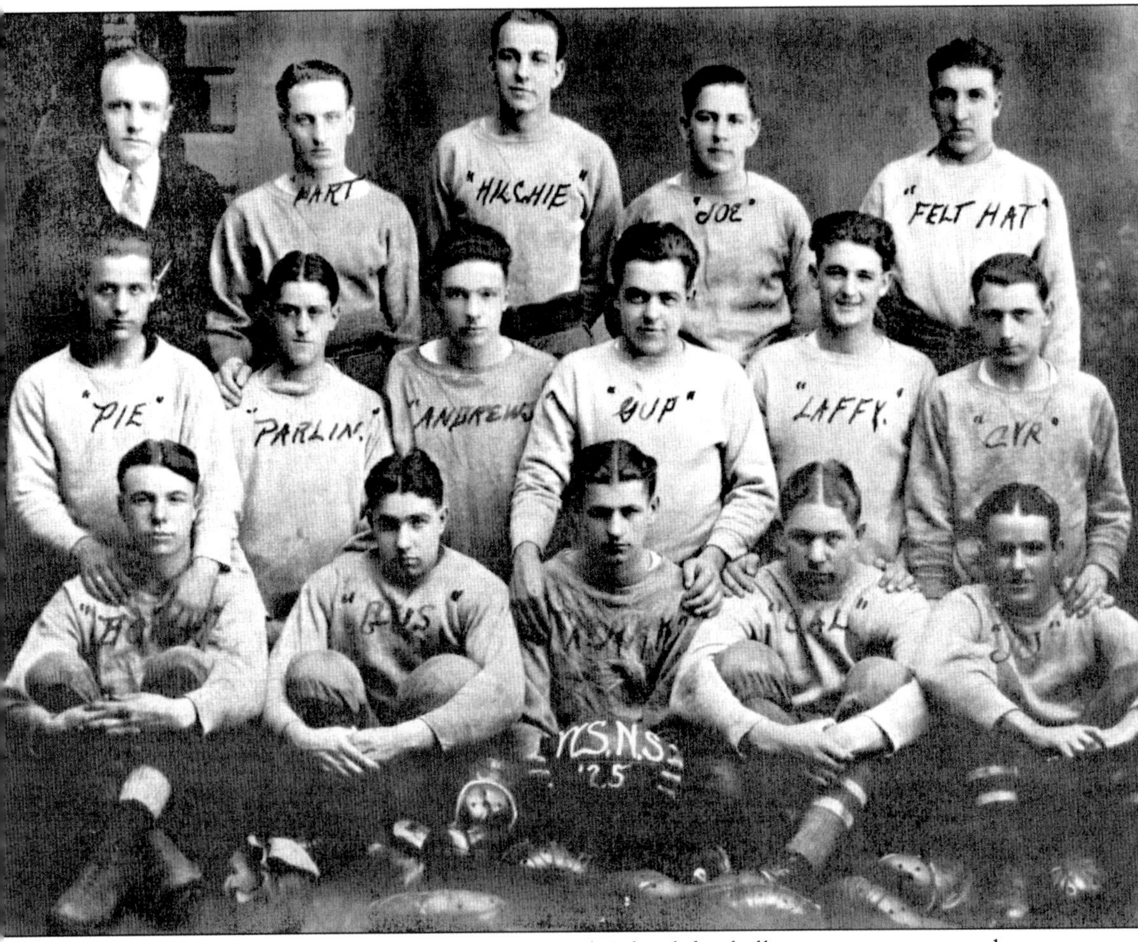

The Class of 1925 Washington State Normal School football team was not scored on once during the season. Sports have always played an important role in the development of well-rounded students.

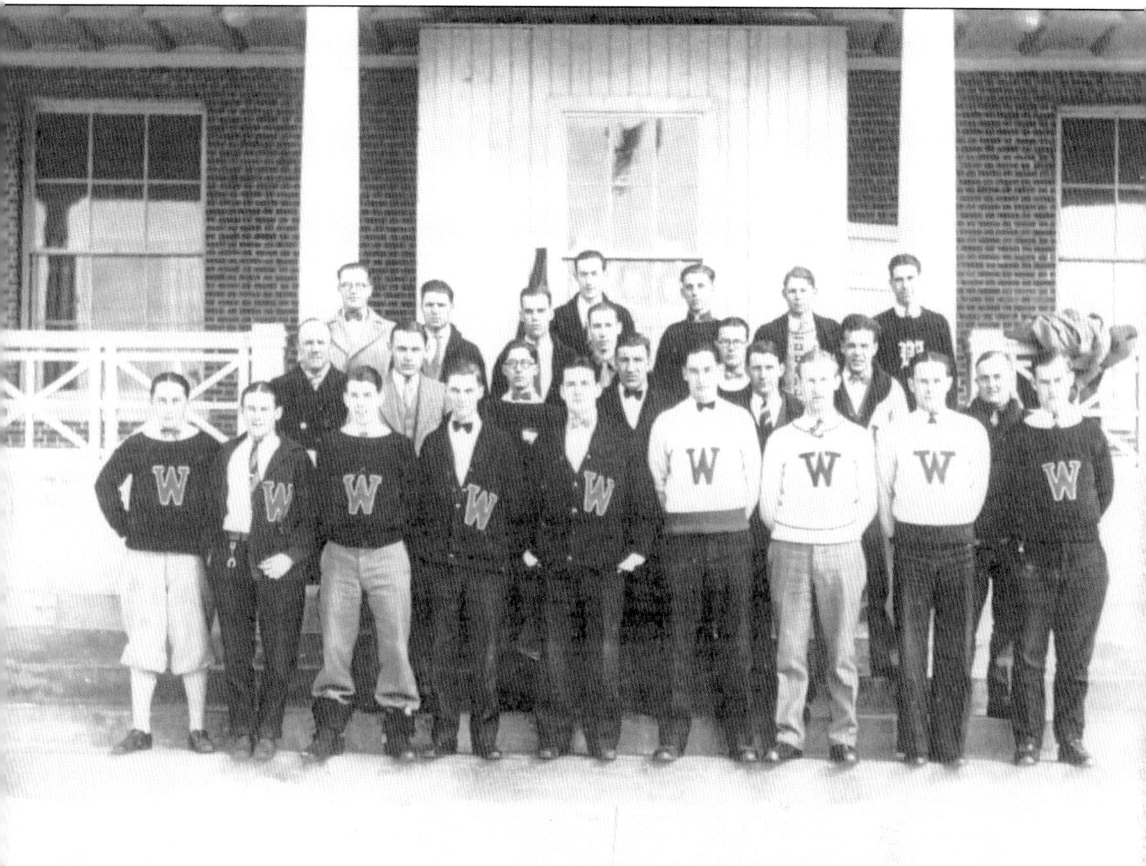

Proud lettermen of the Washington State Normal School stand in front of Powers Hall.

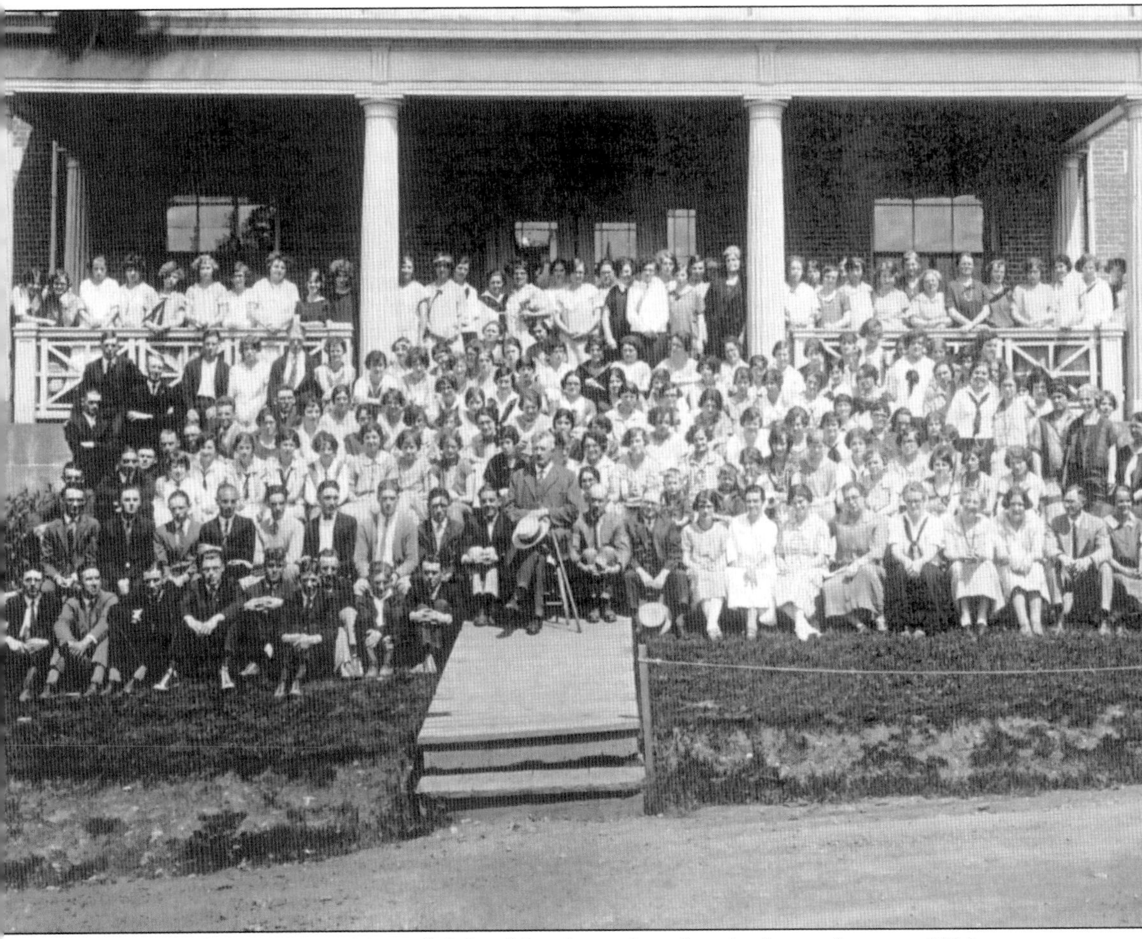

The Washington State Normal School faculty and student body are shown c. 1930.

Four

THE BERRIES

Glacial deposits provided Maine with a perfect terrain for growing wild, lowbush blueberries. Because much of southern and central Maine's acreage turned from farming to other industries (such as shopping malls and other real estate development), the growing and harvesting of blueberries significantly decreased. In Washington County, however, blueberry growing, harvesting, and processing continues to be a major industry.

The tradition of commercial harvesting and processing of blueberries can be traced to just after the Civil War, when the first blueberry canning plant in America was started in Millbridge in 1868. During the mid-1970s, the Machias Centre Street Congregational Church initiated, as a community project, the Annual Machias Wild Blueberry Festival.

In mid-August each year, the celebration gives the community an opportunity to gather and enjoy the blessing of a successful harvest.

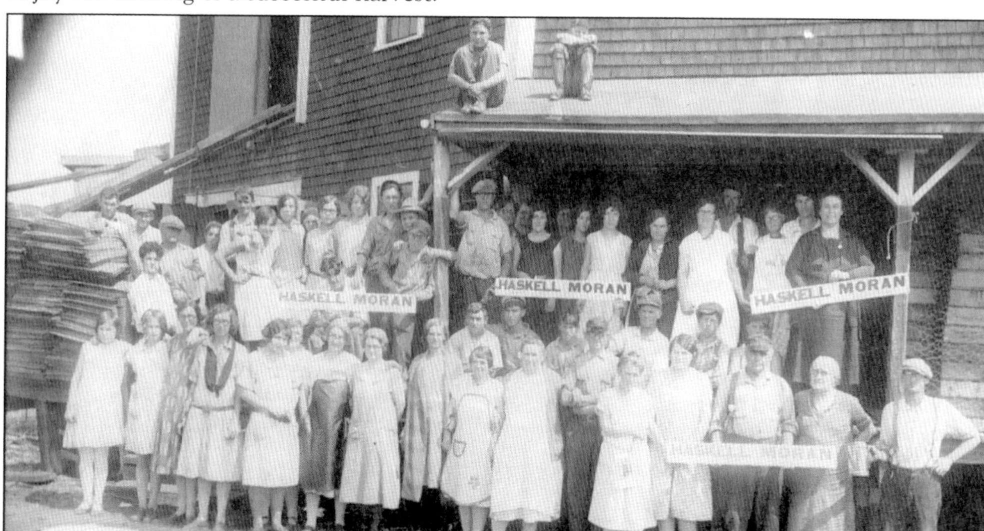

Gaddis Brothers Mill and Blueberry Factory was located in East Machias. The first plant was built in 1912 and burned to the ground on January 20, 1913. The second plant was built in the spring of 1913. This photograph shows the factory during the 1920s. It too burned down with a total loss on May 15, 1936.

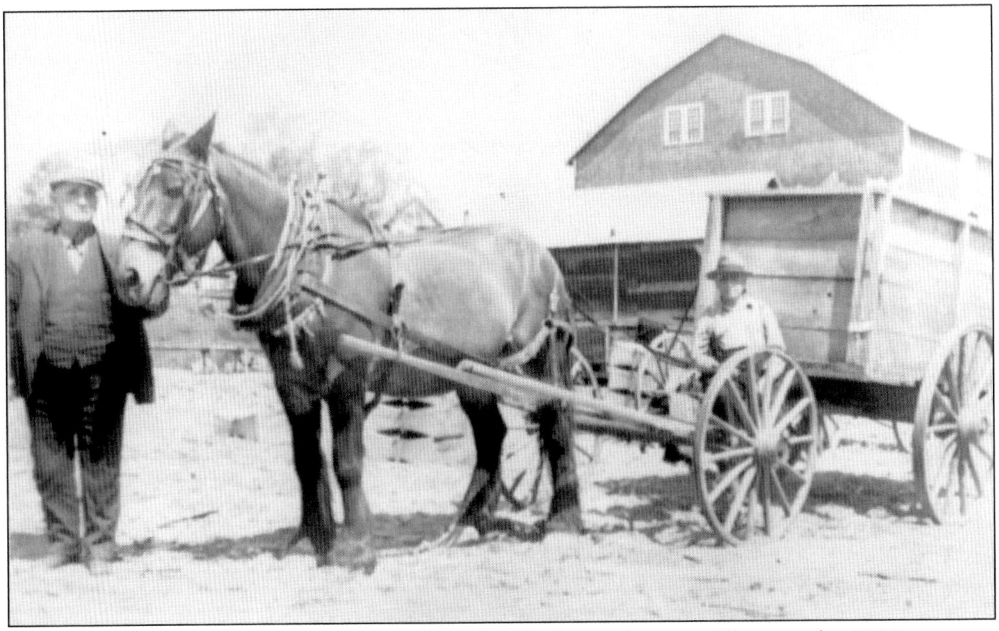

A horse-drawn cart is shown in front of Gaddis Blueberry Canning Plant in the 1920s.

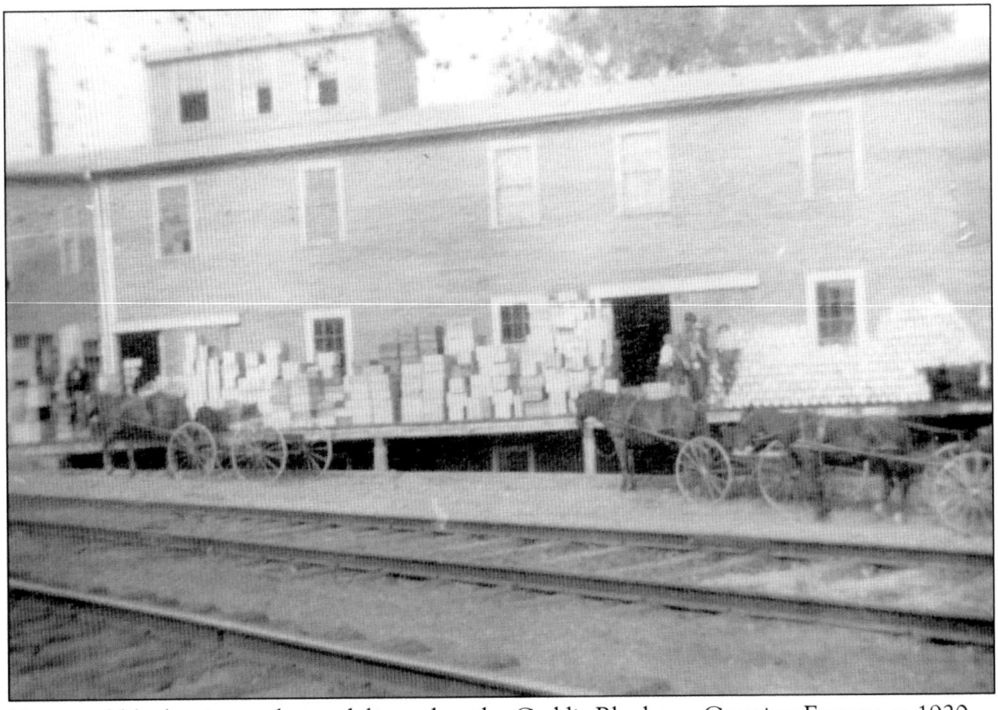

Harvested blueberries are being delivered to the Gaddis Blueberry Canning Factory, c. 1920.

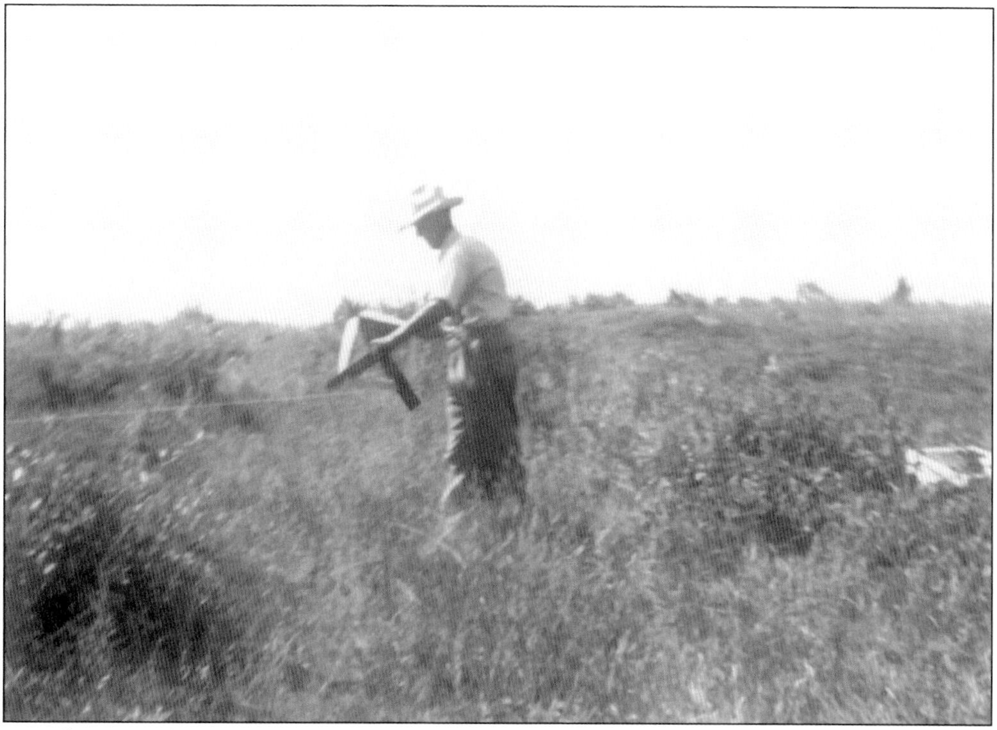

Lowell Hayward is "stripping out" a nine-foot-wide section for rakers, August 1947.

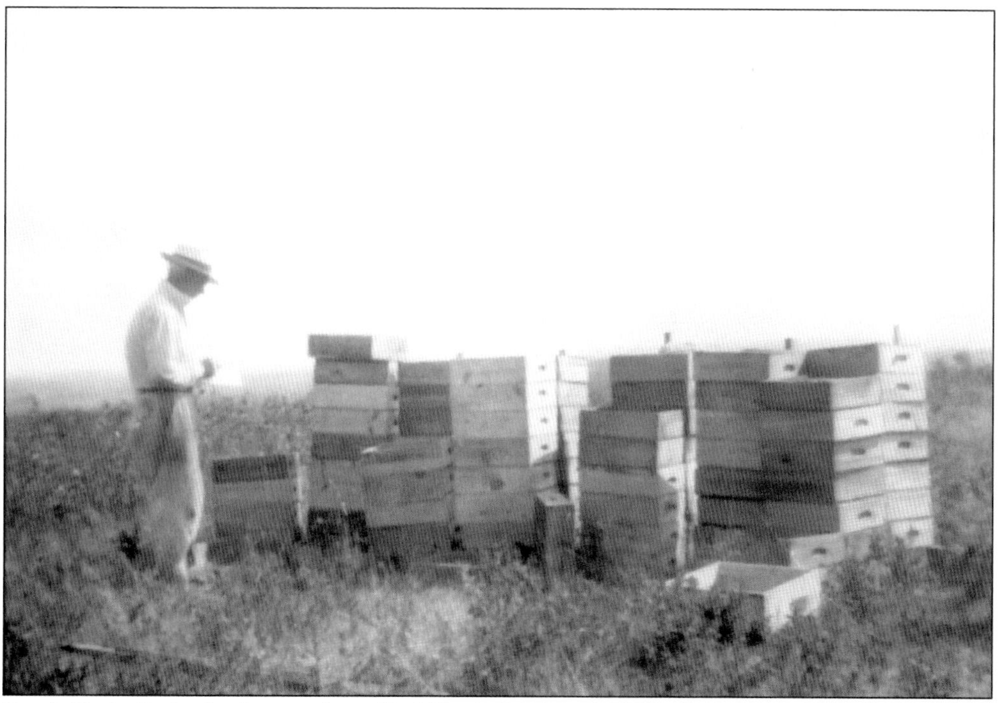

Frank Haskell checks the number of half-bushels of stacked blueberries.

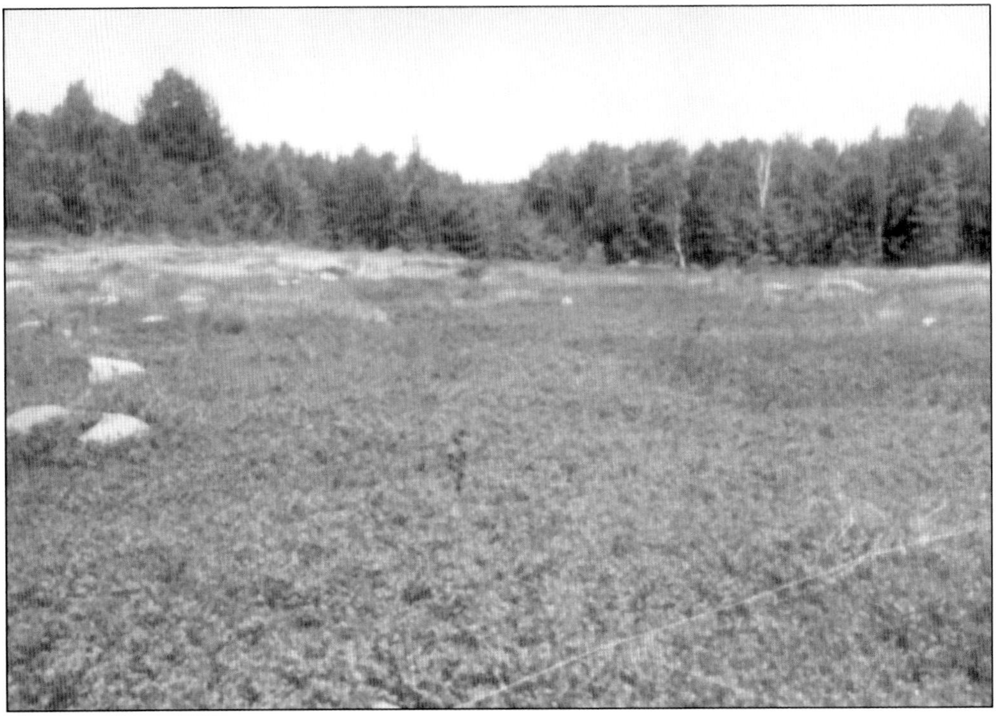

A rolling carpet of blueberry plants promises a fine harvest each August.

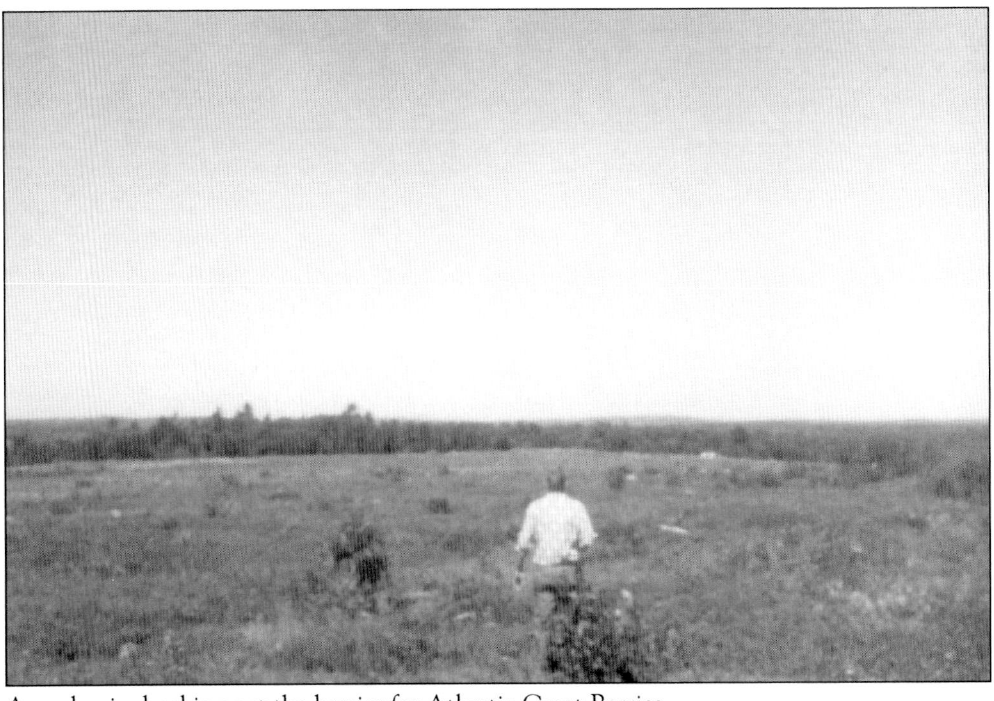

A worker is checking out the berries for Atlantic Coast Berries.

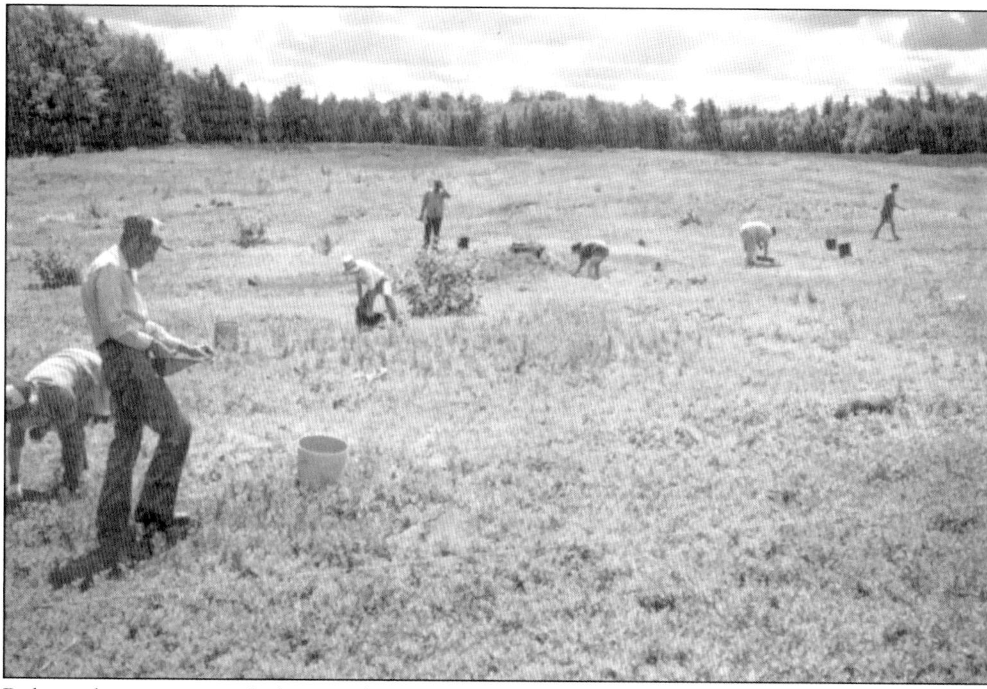

Raking the crop is a task that employs immigrant workers as well as locals.

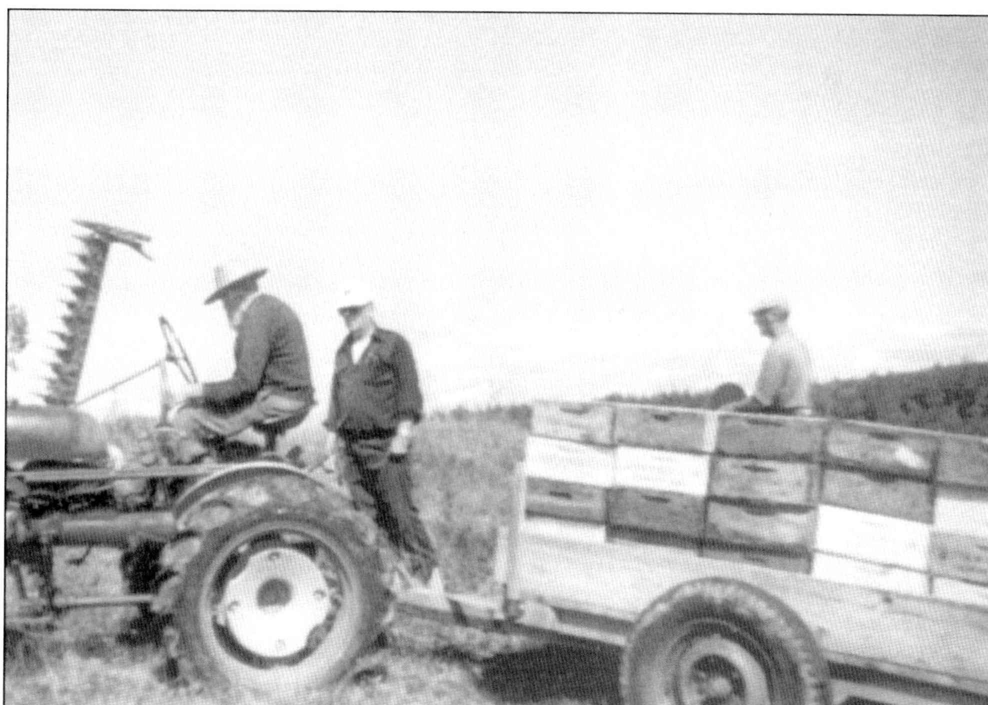

Sam Watts (on the tractor), with his son Phil Watts, and Richard Hayward are bringing in the berries.

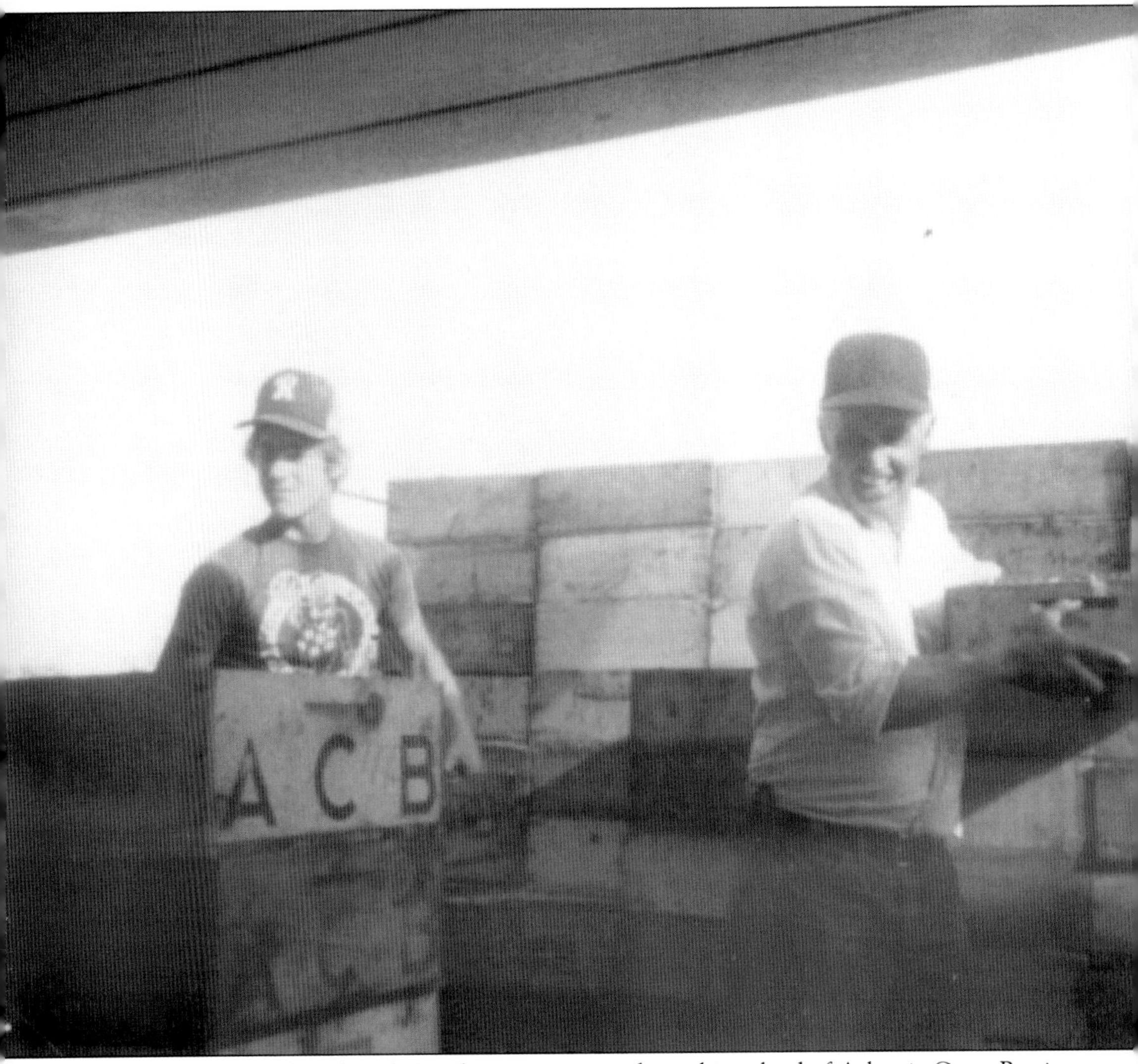

Bob Orlletta (left) and Herb Smith are getting ready to ship a load of Atlantic Coast Berries.

Five

Celebrating Our Heritage

From our nation's founding days, the Machias Bay Region has been blessed with men and women of vision and integrity. Upon hearing of the battles at Concord and Lexington, the local citizenry erected a liberty pole, which symbolically committed the region to the cause of freedom.

On June 12, 1775, patriots from the region engaged the British schooner *Margaretta* in Machias Bay and were victorious. In this skirmish, British Captain Moore of the *Margaretta* was wounded and died the next day. The Burnham Tavern, where the patriots had met to plan their course of action, served as a hospital for many of the wounded.

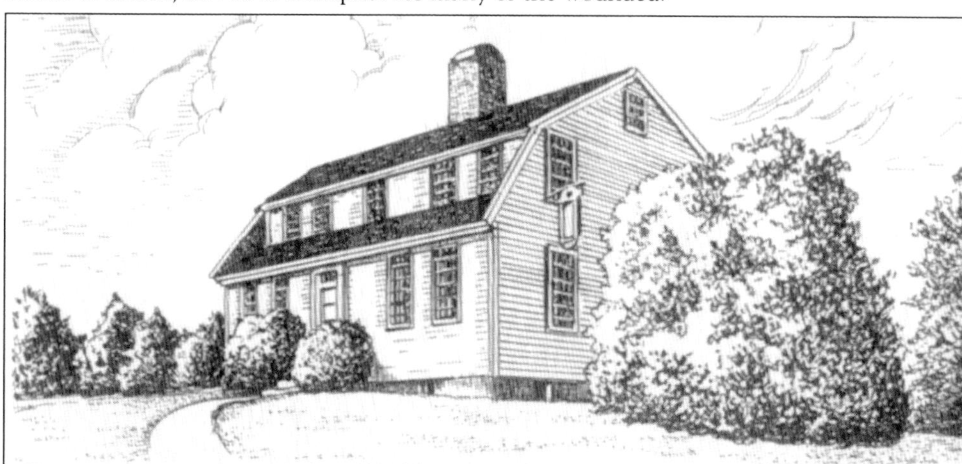

This line drawing of the Burnham Tavern represents the official portrayal of this historic home that was authorized by the Hannah Weston Chapter of the Daughters of the American Revolution. Since 1910, the Burnham Tavern has been maintained as a museum by this group. In 1973, the Burnham Tavern was designated a National Historic Site by the U.S. Department of the Interior.

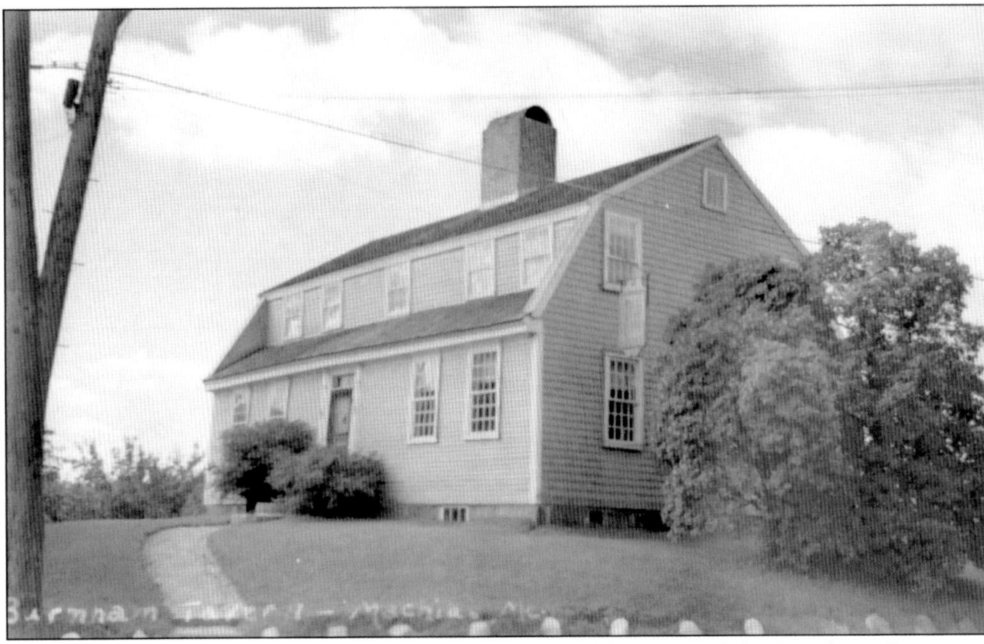

The historic Burnham Tavern, c. 1920, is the oldest building east of the Penobscot River and the only building in eastern Maine that has a direct link to the Revolutionary War.

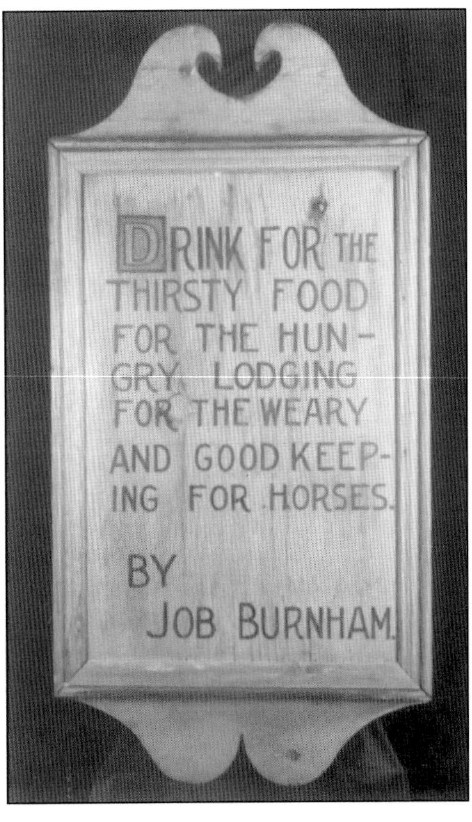

This is Job Burnham's hostelry sign.

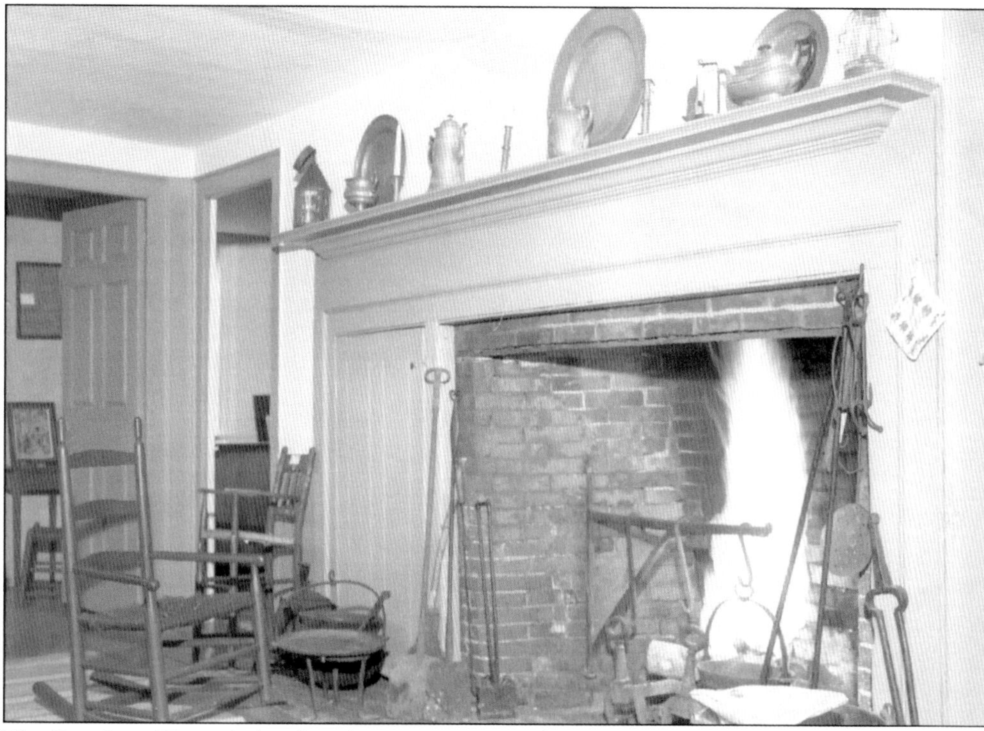

The Burnham Tavern's fireplace kept guests warm during cold winter days.

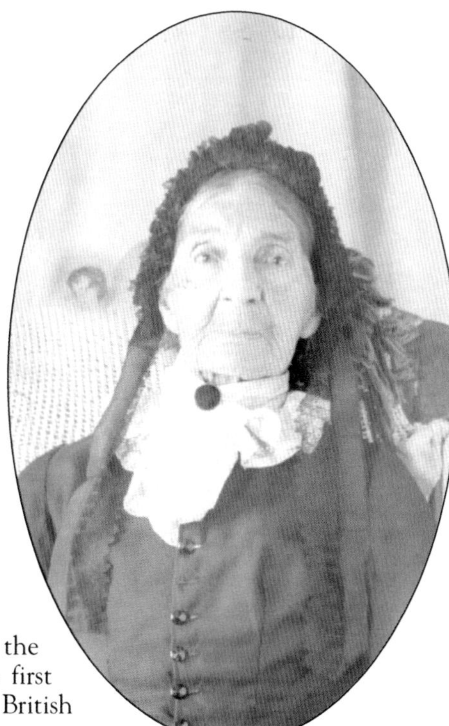

Sabrina Watts Hall was a true daughter of the revolution. Her father, Samuel Watts, fired the first shot in the patriots' engagement and capture of the British schooner *Margaretta* on June 12, 1775.

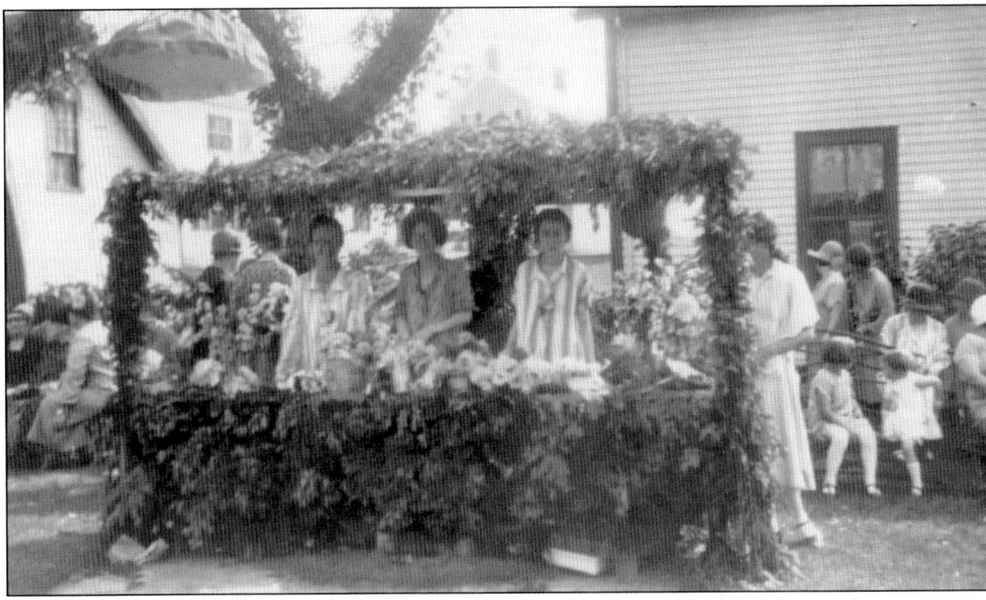

These women tend a flower booth at a fair put on by the Hannah Weston Chapter of the Daughters of the Revolution (DAR) on July 15, 1926.

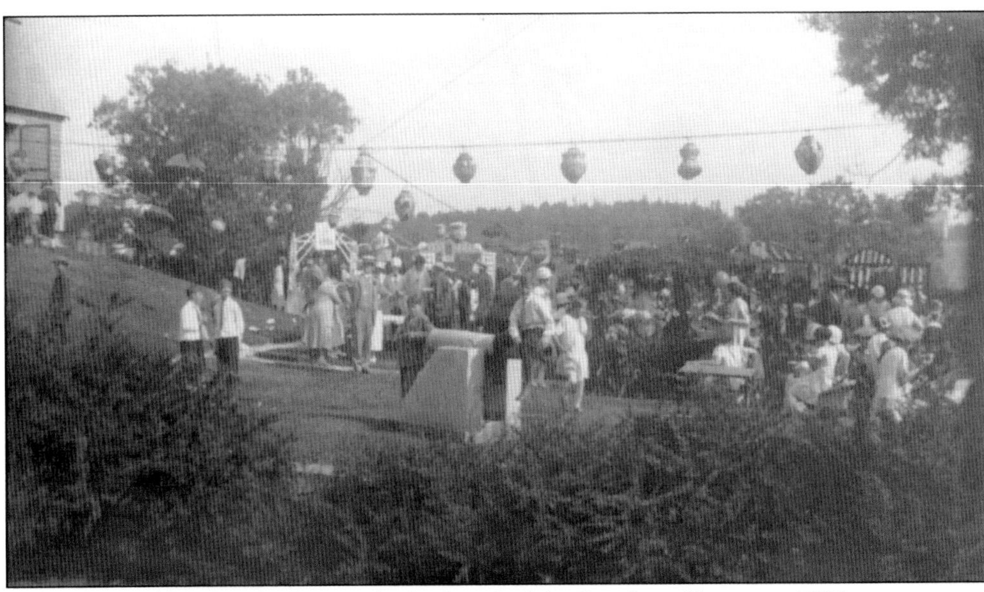

Annual lawn parties took place in the backyard of the Burnham Tavern, *c.* 1920s.

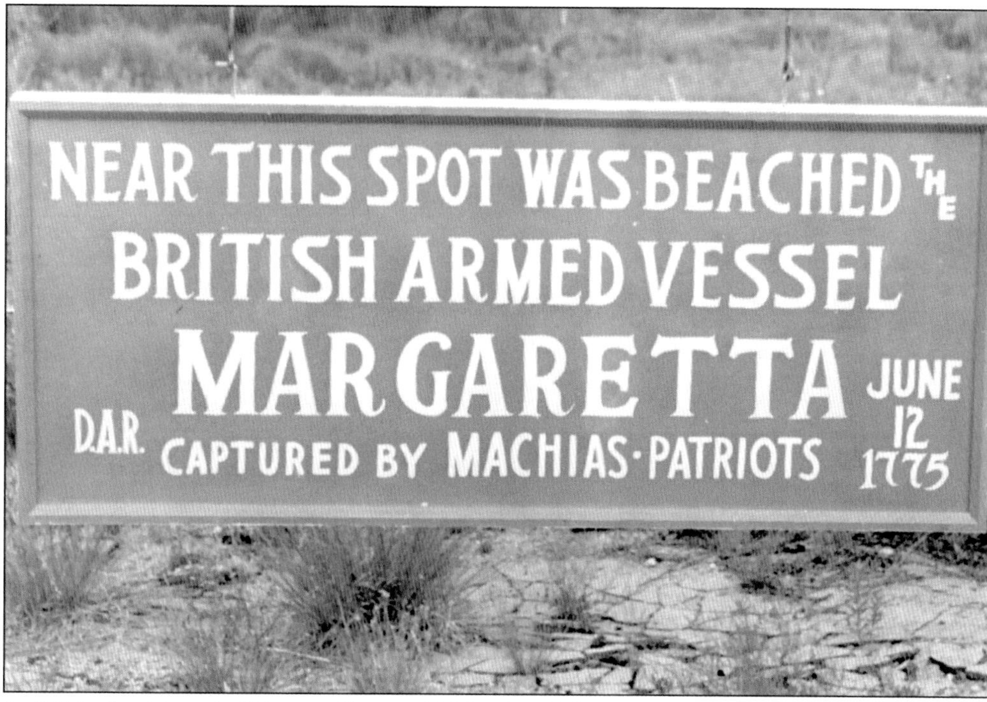

In 1913, the Hannah Weston Chapter DAR placed this marker at the bridge in Marshfield, where the *Margaretta* was beached to hide it from the British.

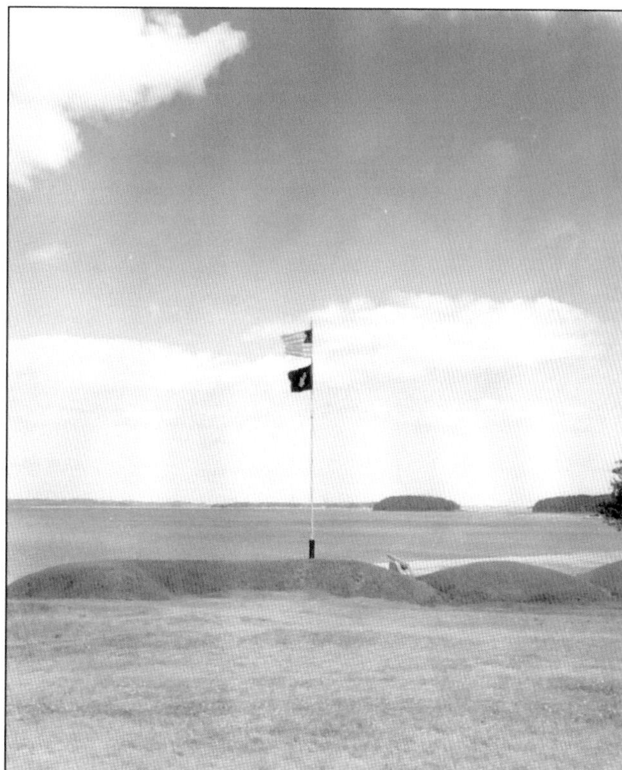

Fort O'Brien State Memorial marks the site of the first fort, which was constructed in 1775. (It was off Round Island, shown to the right of the flagpole, that the Battle of the *Margaretta* took place.) During the War of 1812, the fort was captured and held by the British until 1814. When it was rebuilt in 1863, it was renamed Fort O'Brien in honor of the Revolutionary War hero Jeremiah O'Brien. In 1923, the state of Maine purchased the site.

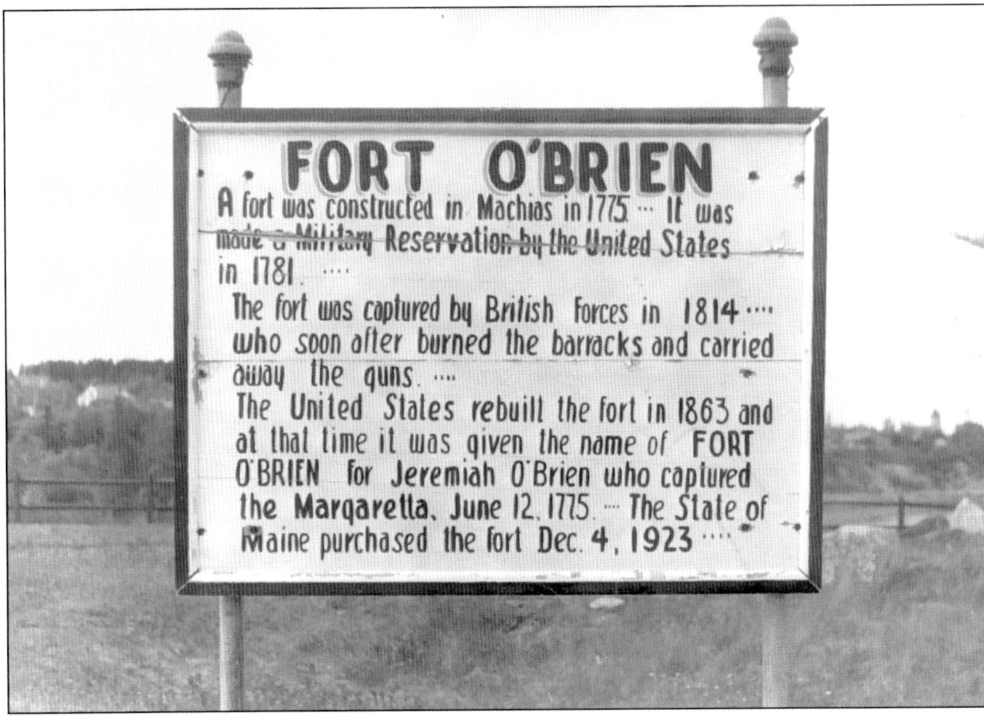

This sign was erected to mark the location of Fort O'Brien.

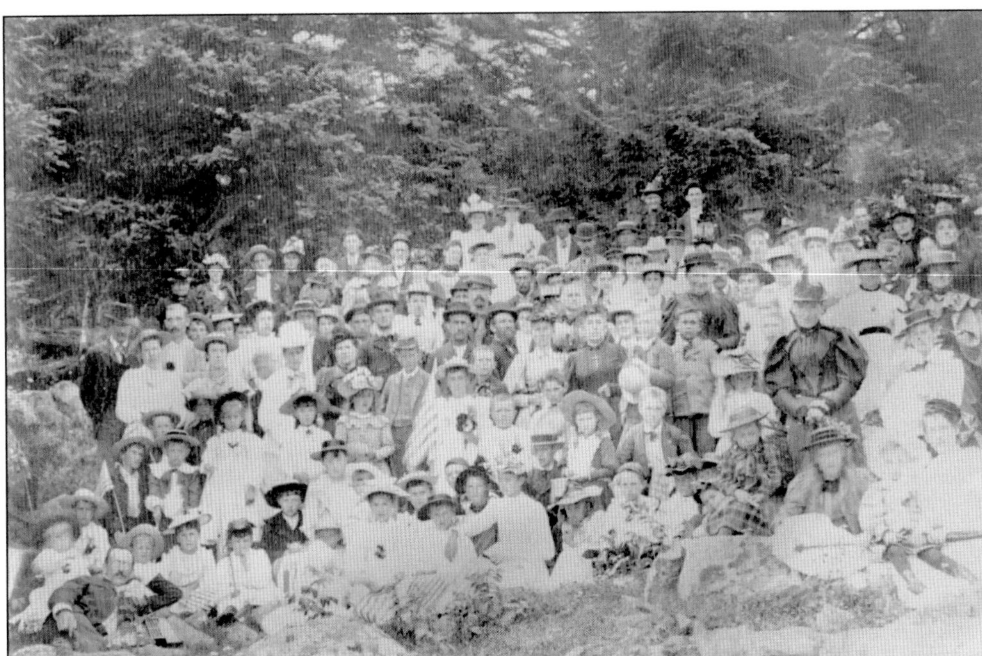

These folks were part of the Cutler celebration of Independence Day 1890.

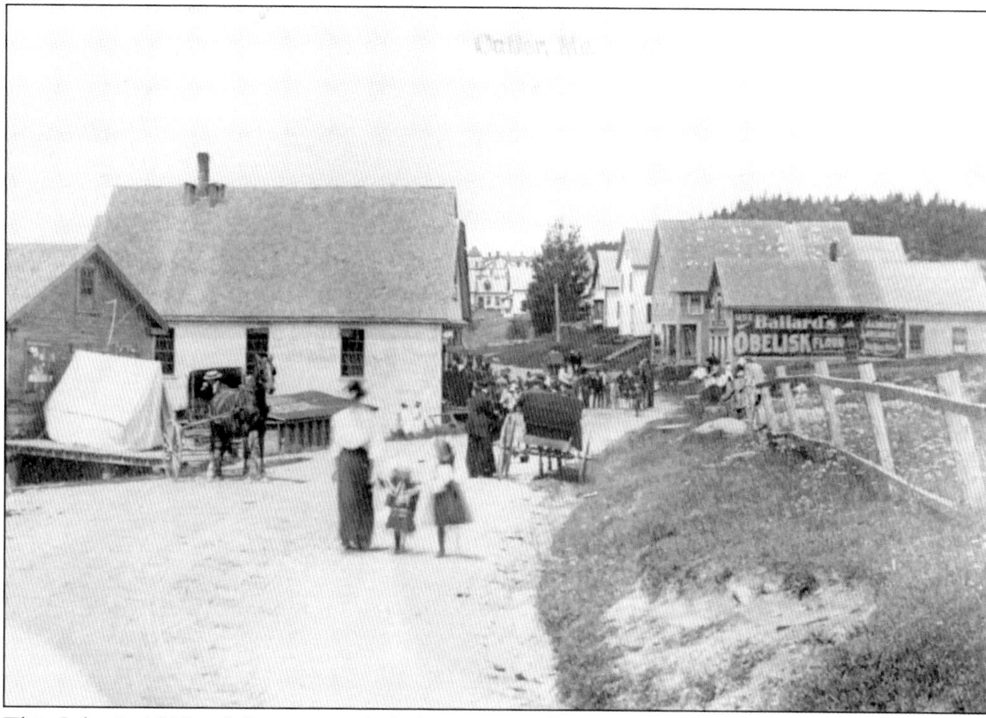

This July 4, 1902 celebration included many people in Cutler. The tent shown to the left with a horse and carriage in front of it was a soda concession stand operated by a gentleman from East Machias.

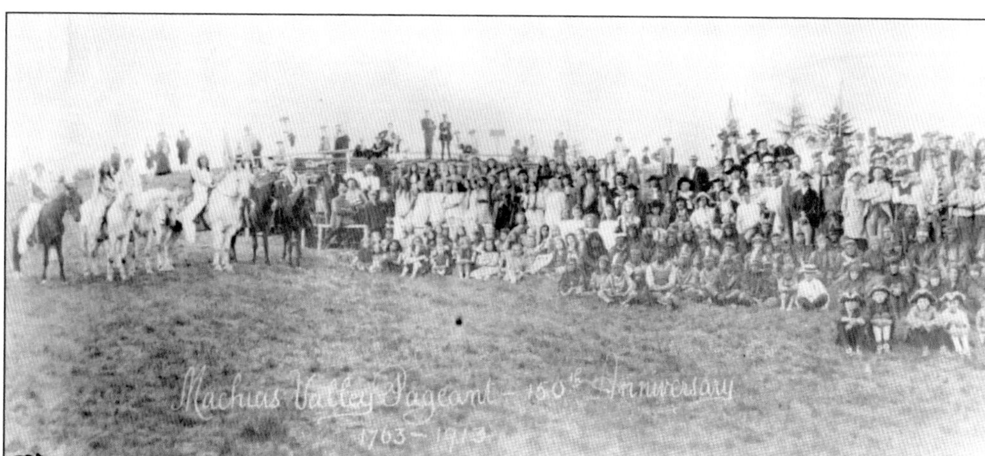

On the banks of the Machias River, citizens celebrated the 150th anniversary of the settlement of the region with a pageant.

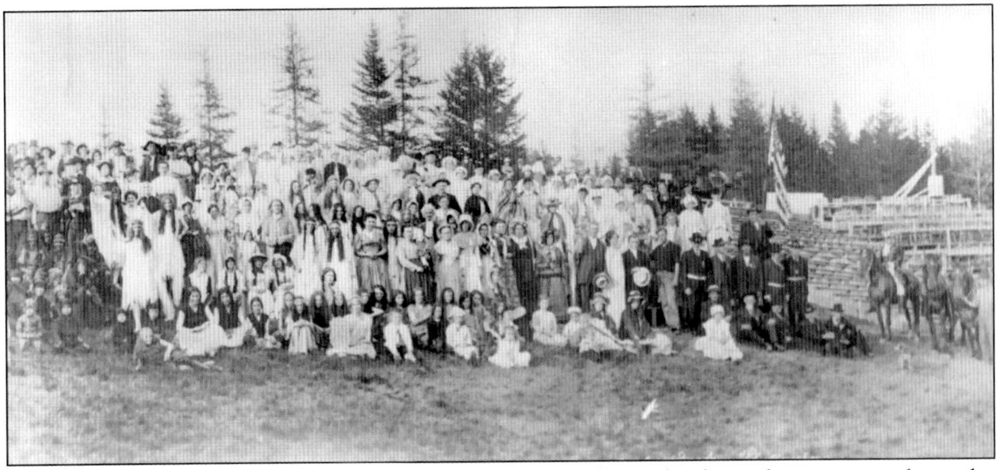

The 150th anniversary pageant lasted several days and involved nearly everyone from the community in some way.

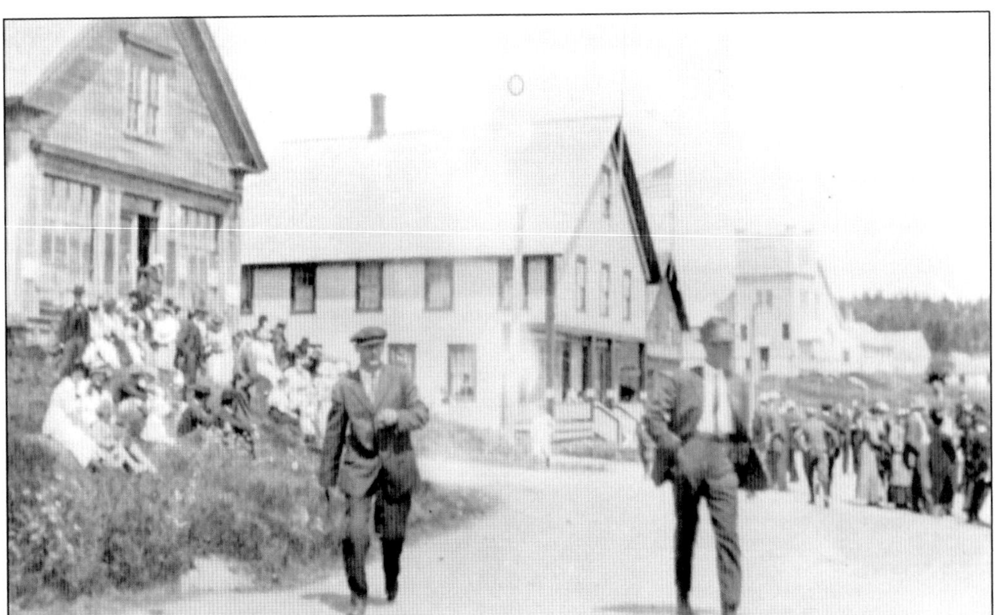

Cutler folks enjoy July 4, 1920 celebrations.

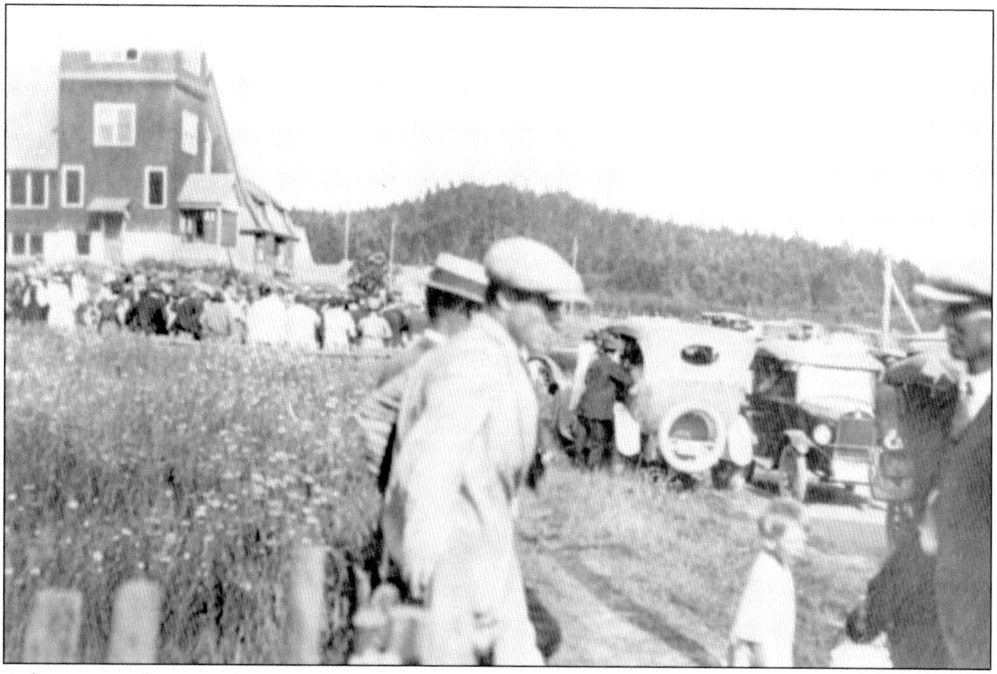

A large crowd enjoyed Independence Day in Cutler, 1925.

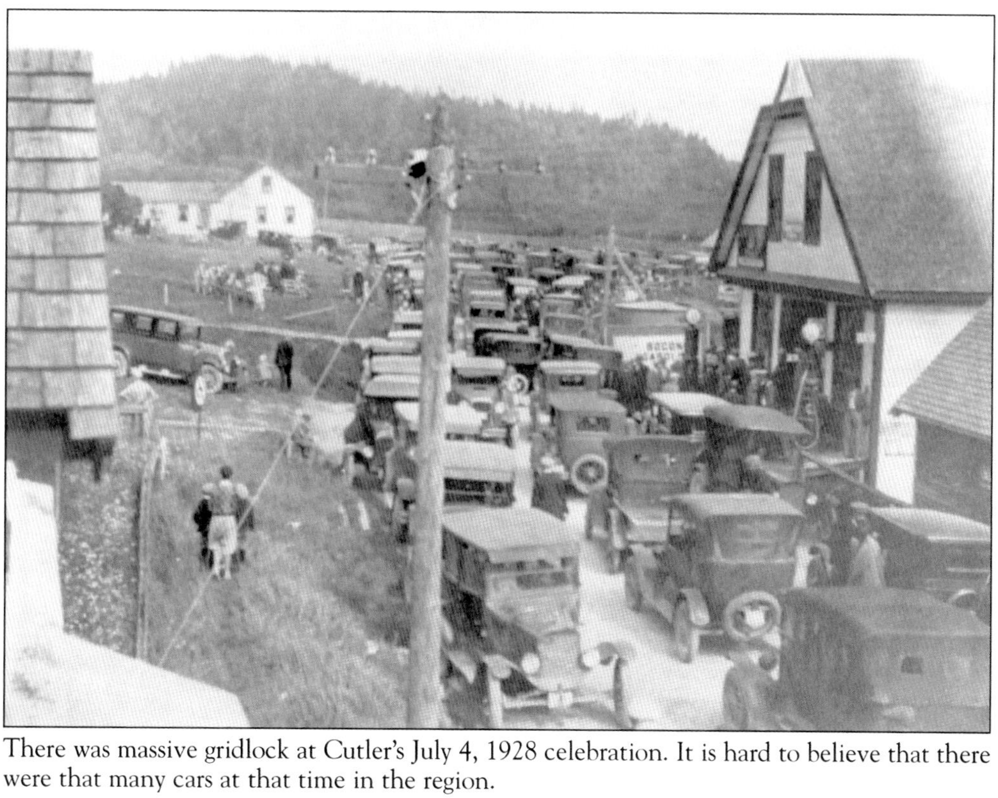

There was massive gridlock at Cutler's July 4, 1928 celebration. It is hard to believe that there were that many cars at that time in the region.

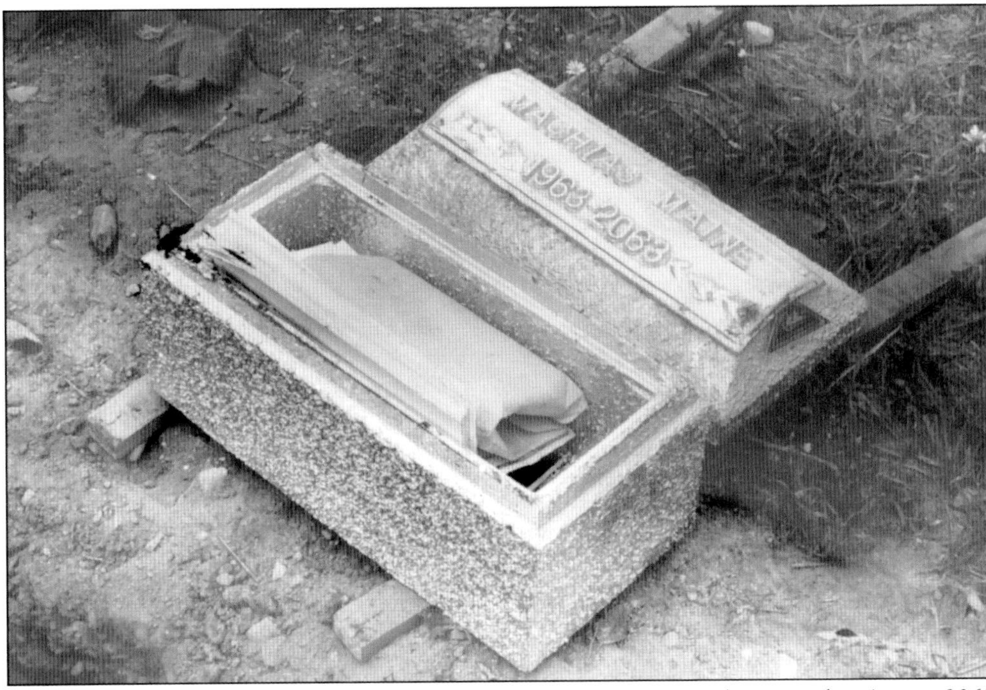

A time capsule was sealed at the bicentennial in August 1963. It is to be opened in August 2063 on the 300th anniversary of the settlement of the region.

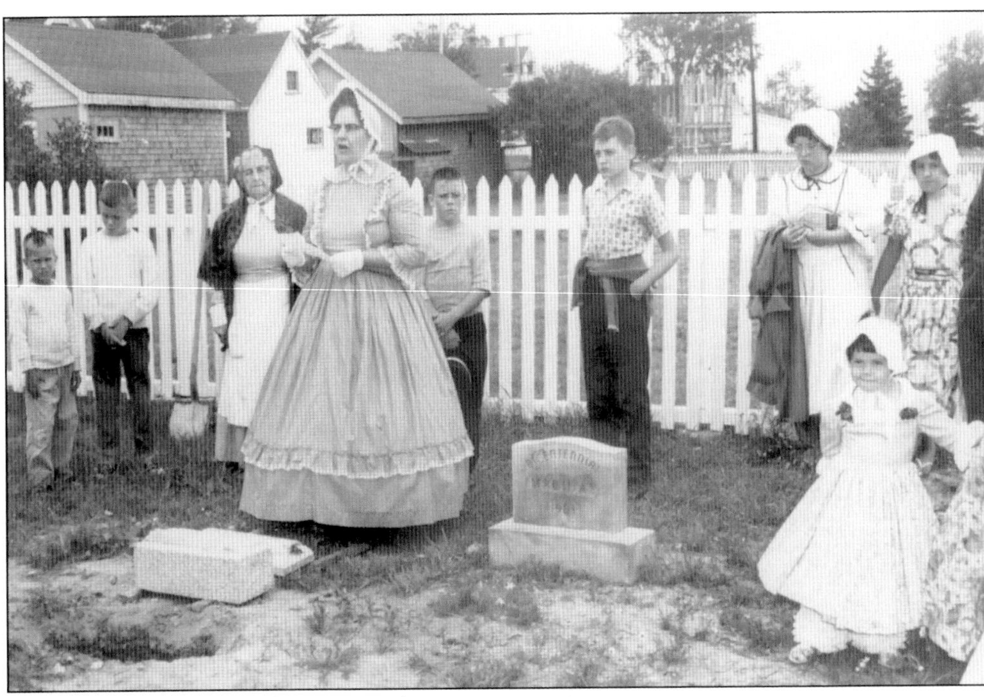

Shown is the August 1963 time capsule commemoration.

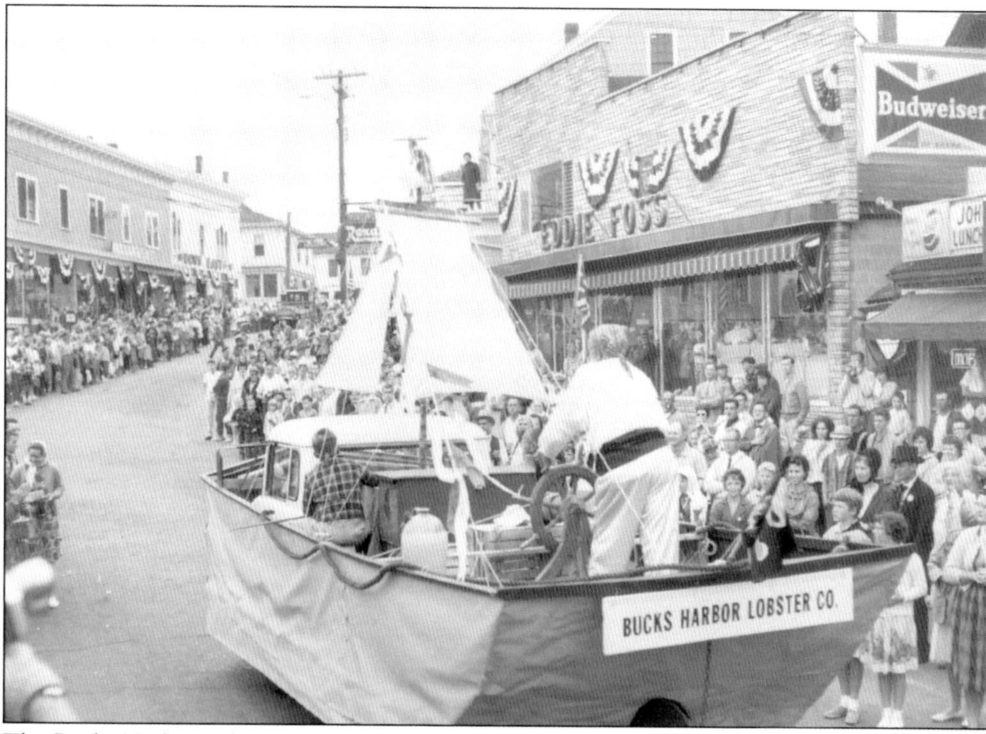

The Bucks Harbor Lobster Company's float was one of the many floats that participated in the August 1963 bicentennial parade.

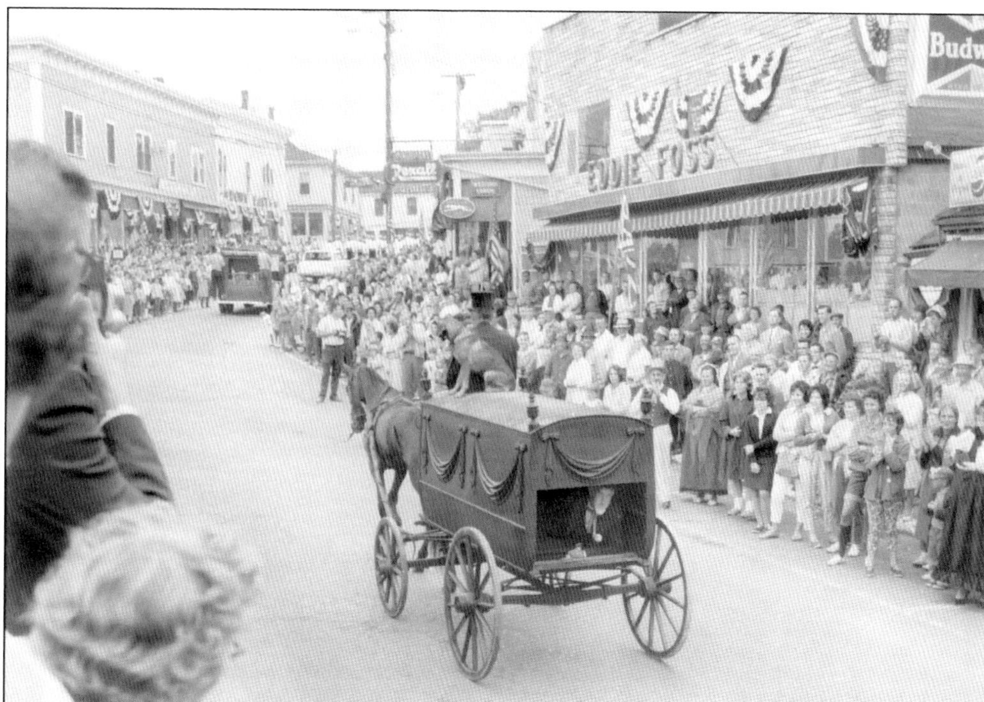

A great parade was a highlight of the bicentennial celebrations in August 1963.

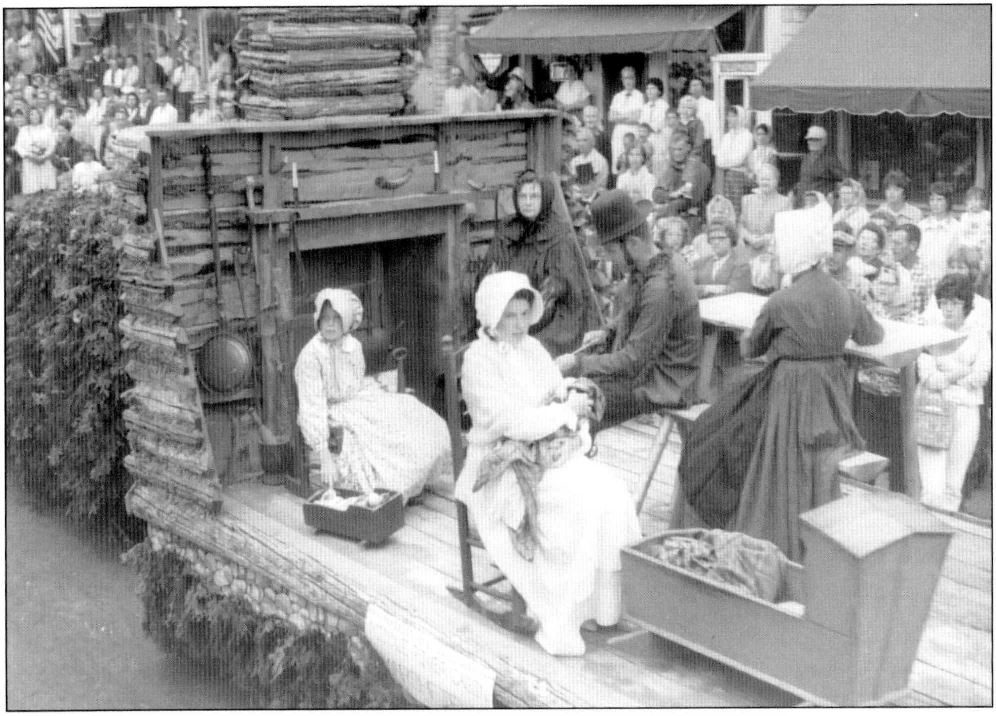

Our heritage was portrayed by many floats in the bicentennial parade.

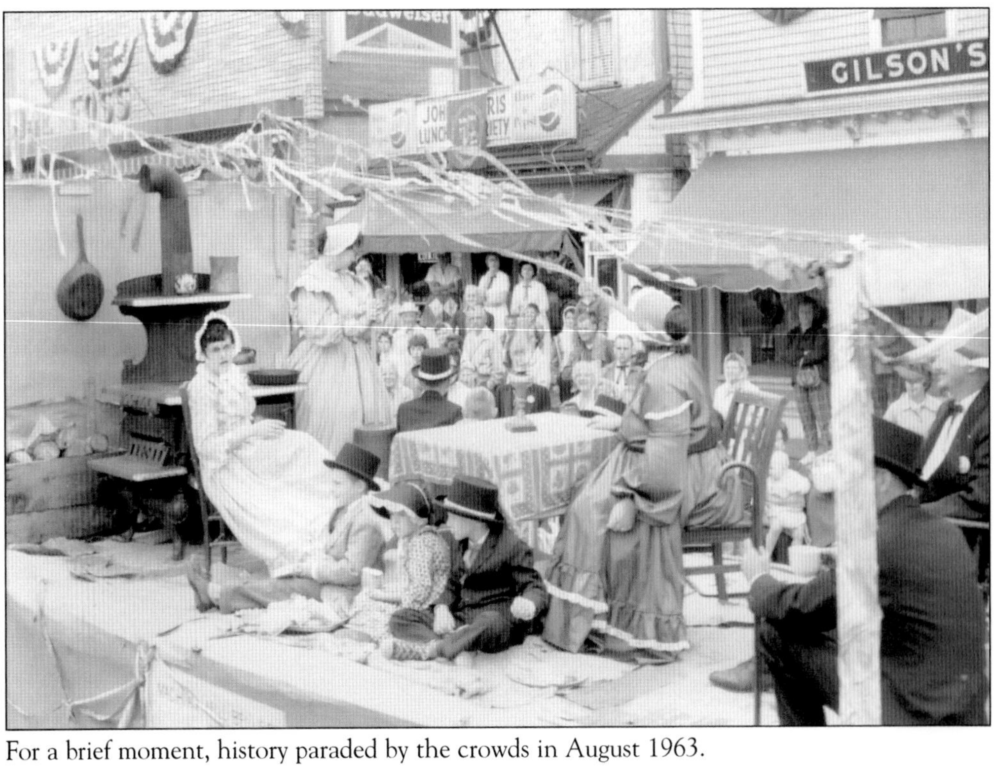

For a brief moment, history paraded by the crowds in August 1963.

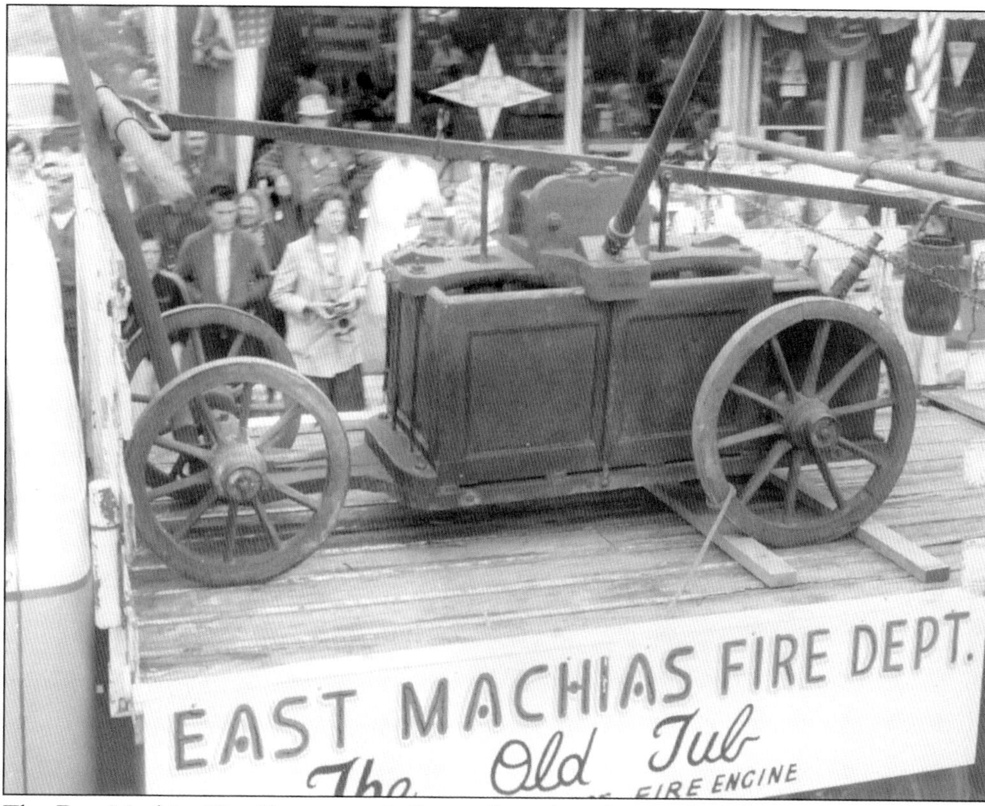

The East Machias Fire Department's float reflected on how a firefighter worked in da The Bicentennial Historical Spectacular was a high point of the celebration.

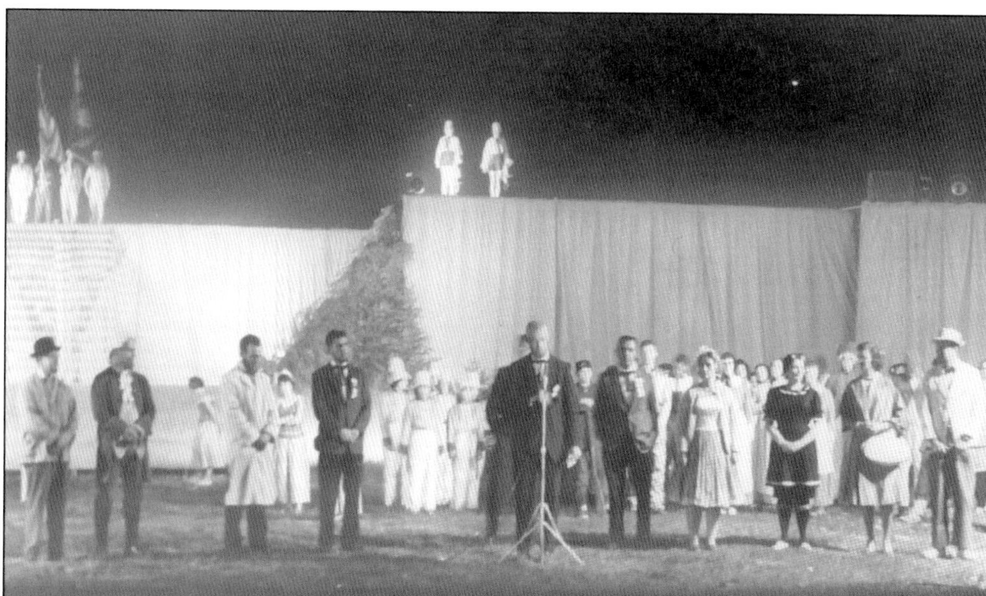

The Bicentennial Publicity Committee included Mrs. Pennell Worcester, Douglas Smith,

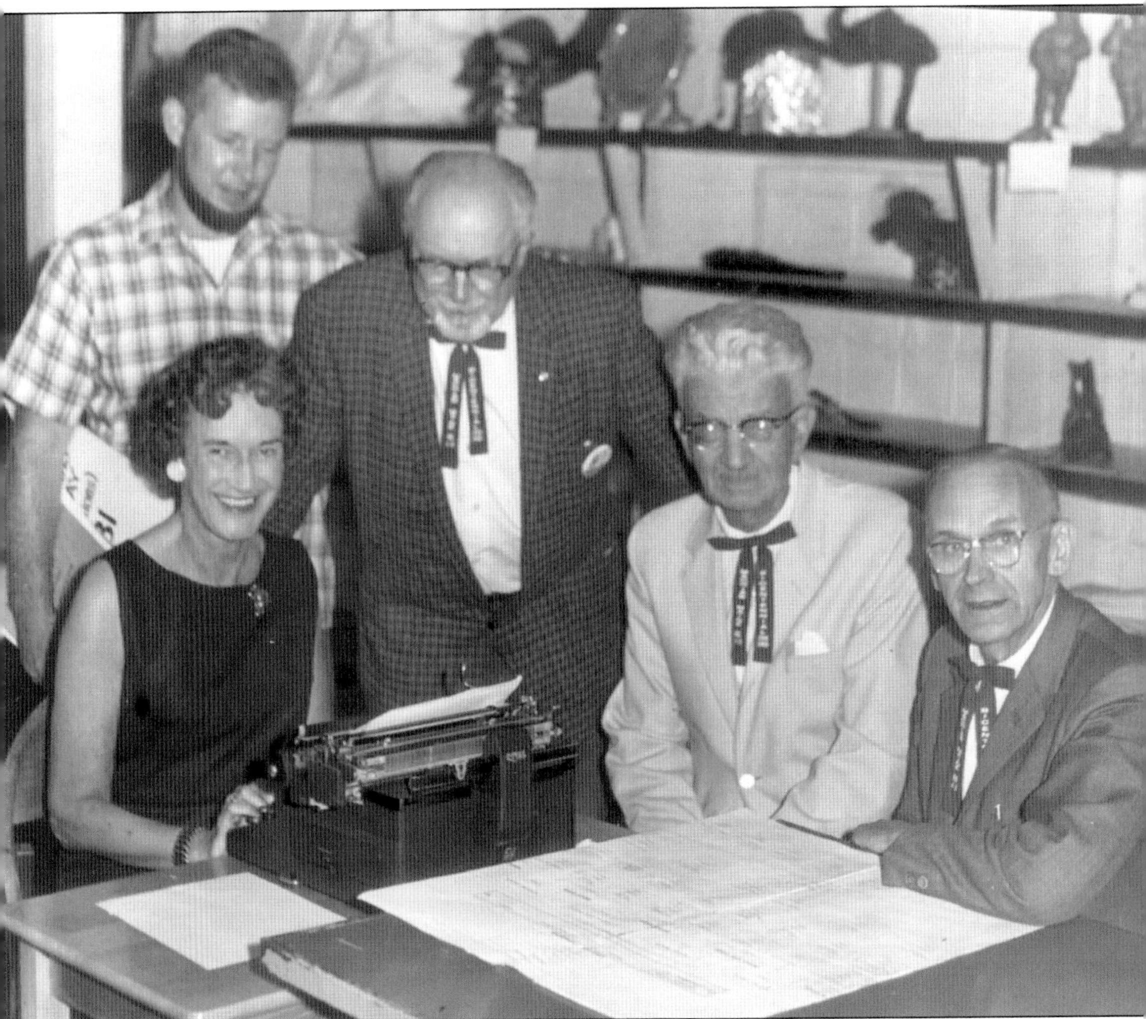

Charles Messer, Abe Farris, and Rev. William Riddiough. These dedicated people helped to make the celebration a most memorable event for the region.

Six

Our Forest Treasures

In the fall of 1762, Isiah Foster, Isaac Larabee, and others from the settlement in Scarborough sailed eastward aboard a large whale boat. They were in search of a hay supply and wanted to explore the possibility of establishing a lumbering operation, as the forests of western Maine had been destroyed by forest fires of the preceding two summers. In the Machias region, they found extensive pine forests that met their plans to build a sawmill. In 1763, a settlement was made in Machias and, by 1765, they had built a double sawmill on the southerly side of the Machias River.

Lumbering remained the major industry of the region until the 1890s. Although its heyday was gone, lumbering was still an important industry with annual long log runs into the 1960s. Today our forest treasures remain one of our most valued resources.

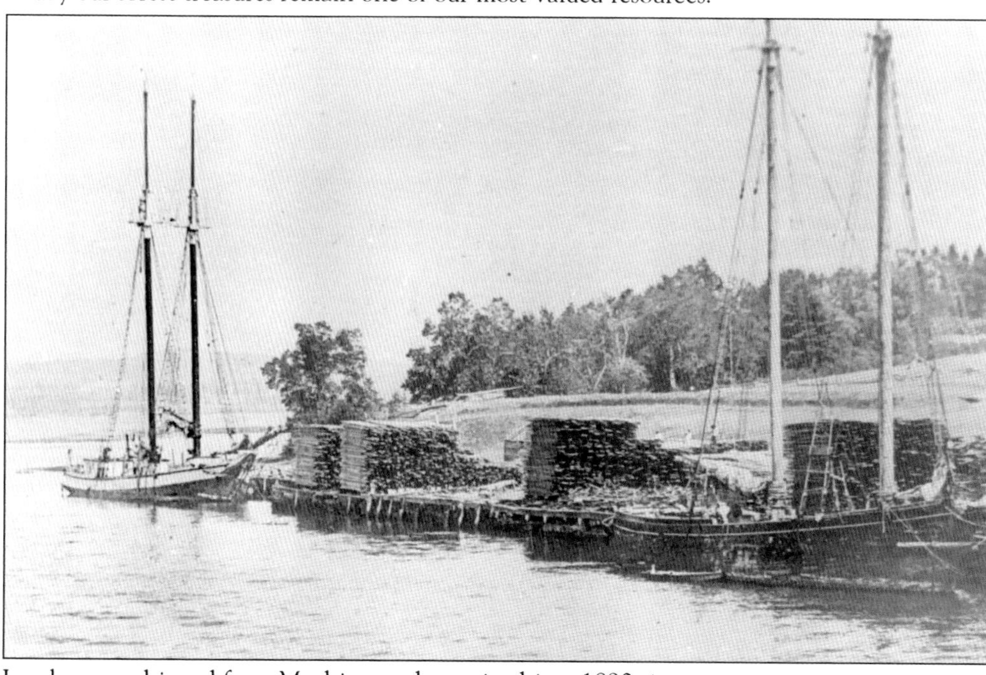

Lumber was shipped from Machias, as shown in this c. 1890s image.

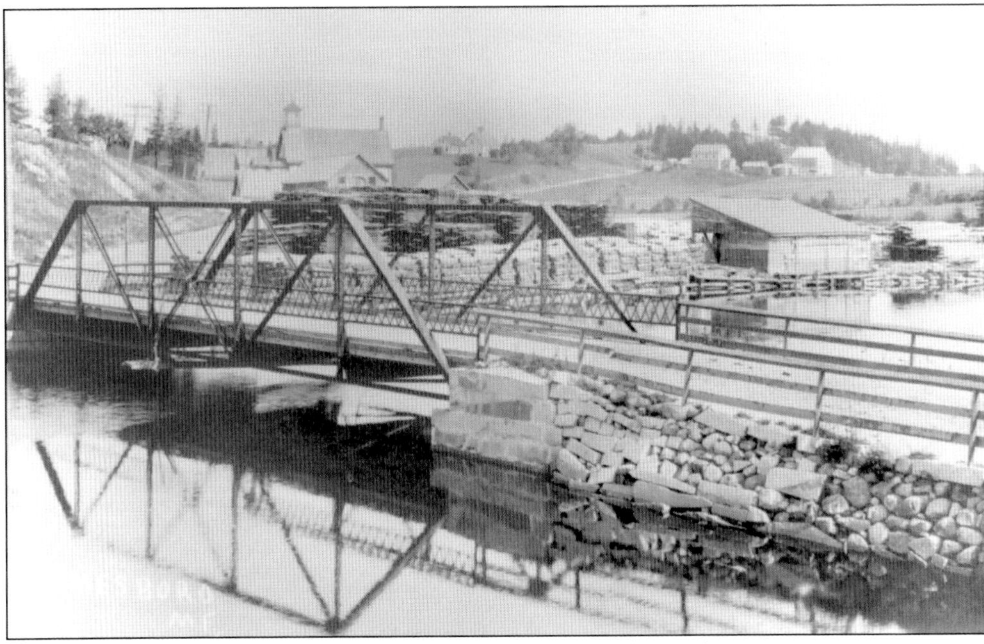

This lumberyard was by the Chandler River Bridge in Jonesboro, shown *c.* 1900.

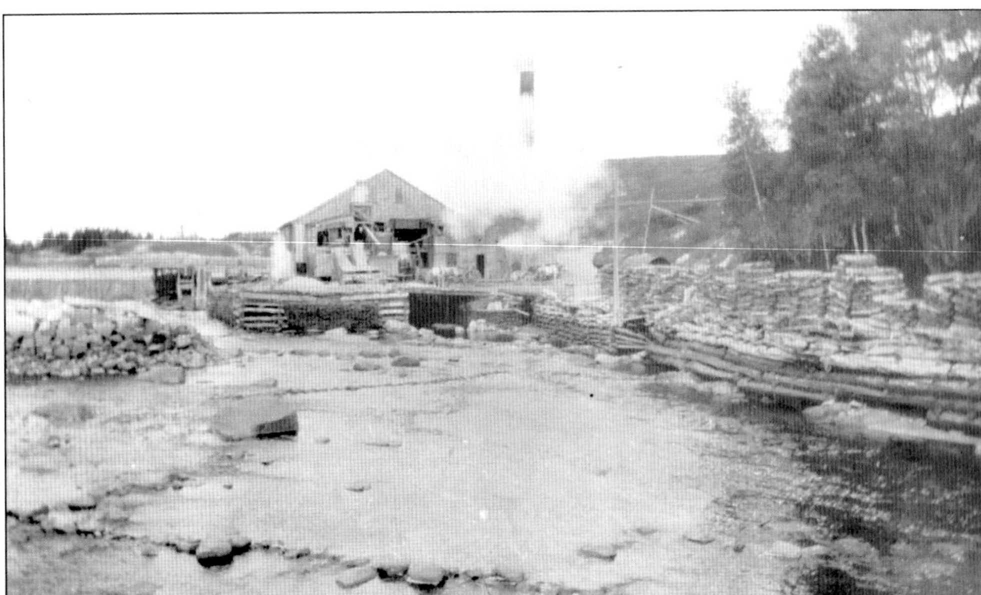

Although the heyday of lumbering had passed, the industry was still quite important. This photograph of a sawmill on the Chandler River, Jonesboro, dates to *c.* 1900.

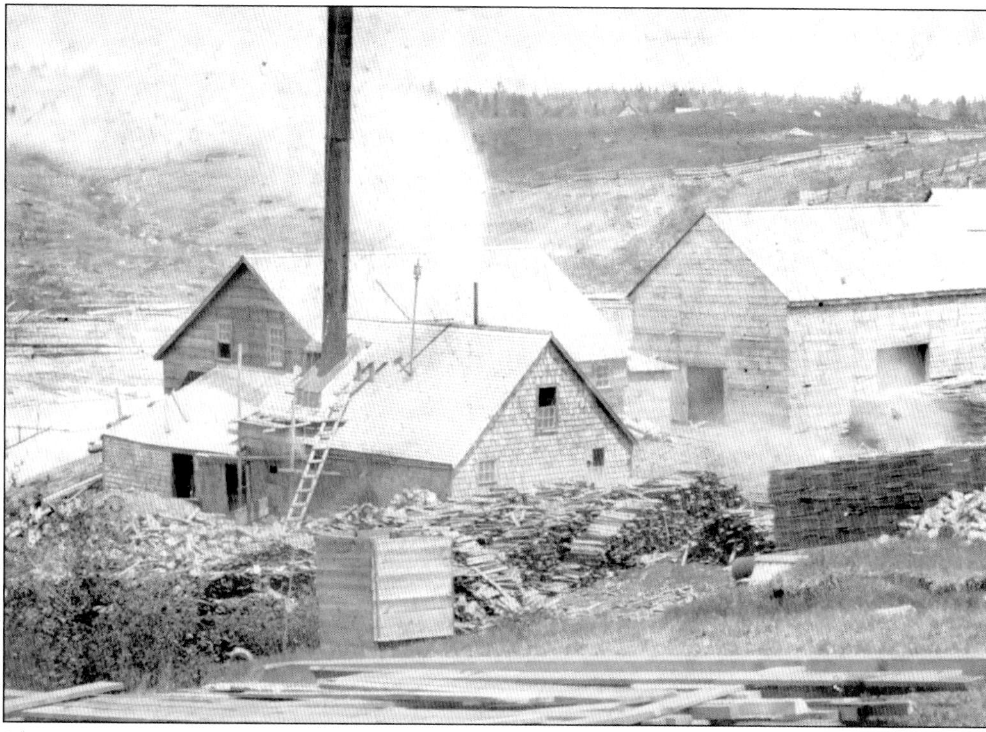

This sawmill was on the west side of the Chandler River, Jonesboro, and was photographed *c.* 1900.

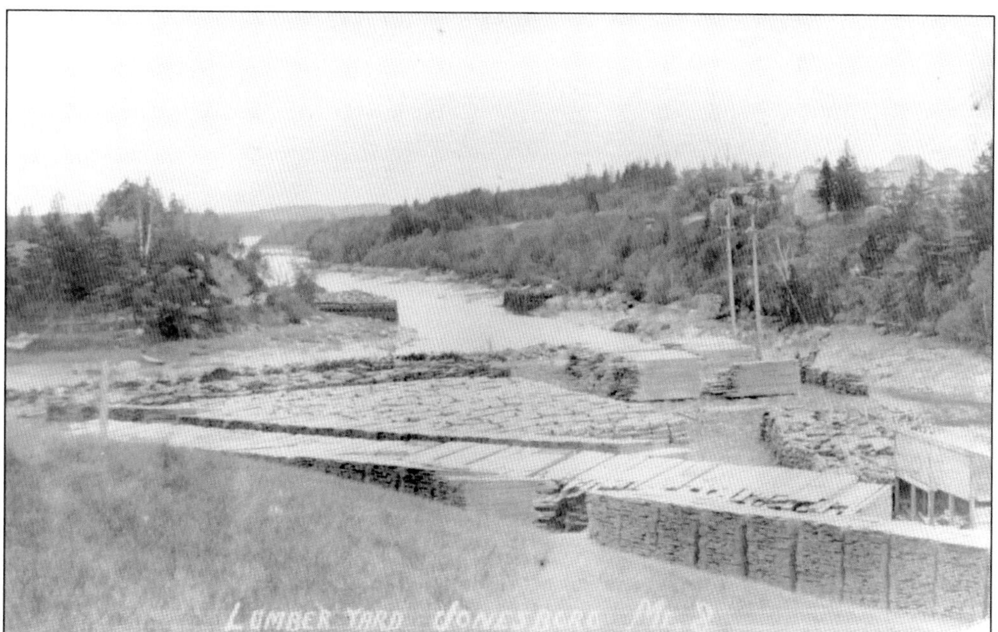

This *c.* 1910 view of a lumberyard looks down the Chandler River in Jonesboro. Lumber is ready and waiting to be shipped from the yard.

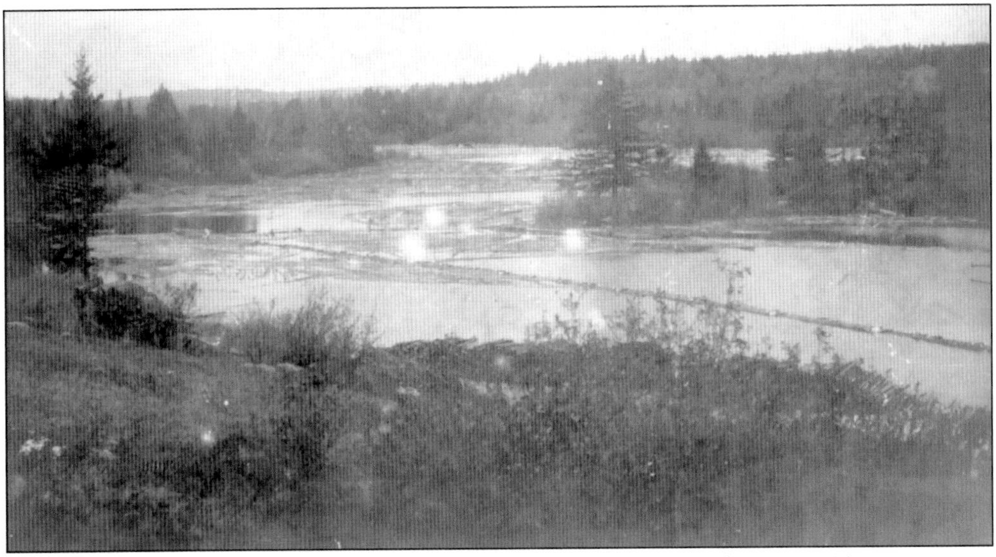

These logs above the dam on Mill Pond were photographed in Jonesboro c. 1900.

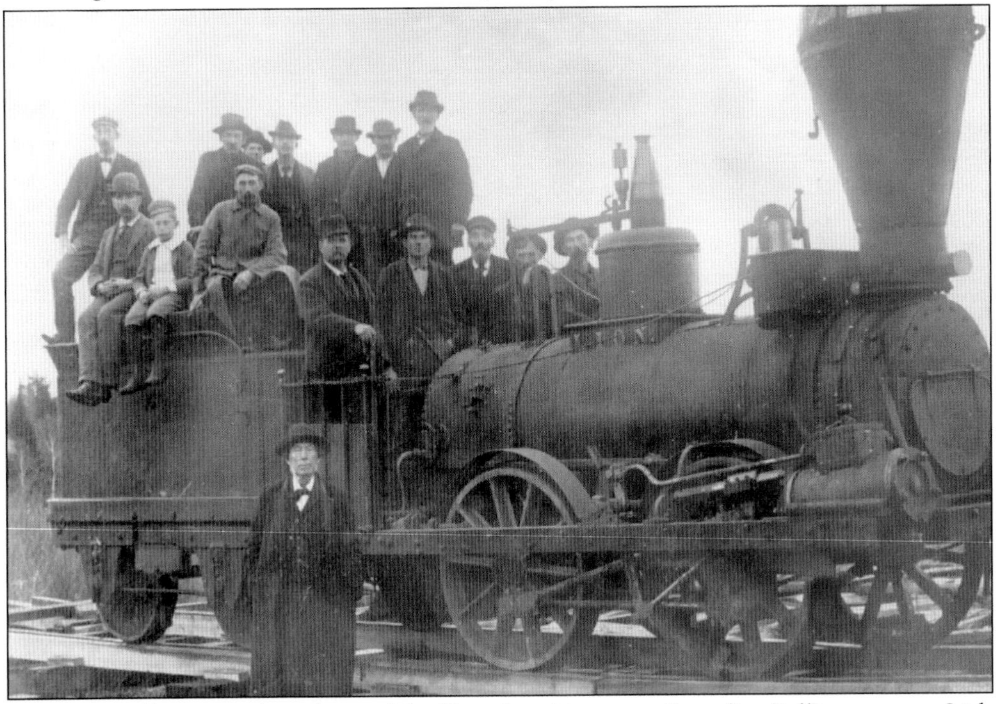

Cornelius Sullivan stands in front of the "Lion" and its crew. Cornelius Sullivan was an Irish immigrant who arrived in New Brunswick, Canada, in 1839. At age 18 , he walked to Machias and obtained a job building the new railroad from Whitneyville to Machiasport. By 1869, he had accumulated enough money to buy the railroad. In 1870, he renamed the burgeoning railroad the Whitneyville and Machiasport Railroad. During the 1870s and 1880s, the railroad carried large amounts of lumber from Whitneyville to Machiasport for shipment to Boston, New York, and other ports. By the early 1890s, the heyday of lumbering had ceased and, by 1892, the trains had stopped. The "Lion" can now be seen at the Natural History Museum at the capital building in Augusta.

Lumber awaits shipment from Machias. The old gristmill can be seen in the left foreground area of this *c.* 1900 photograph.

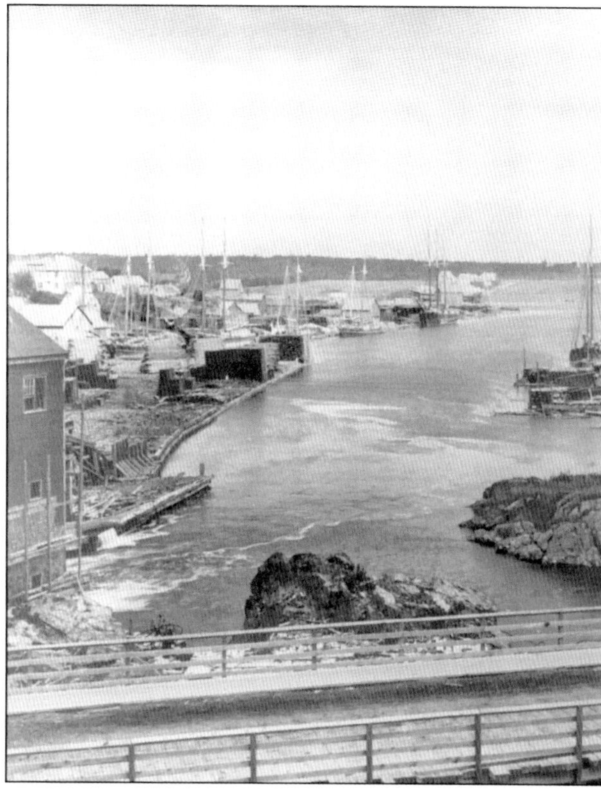

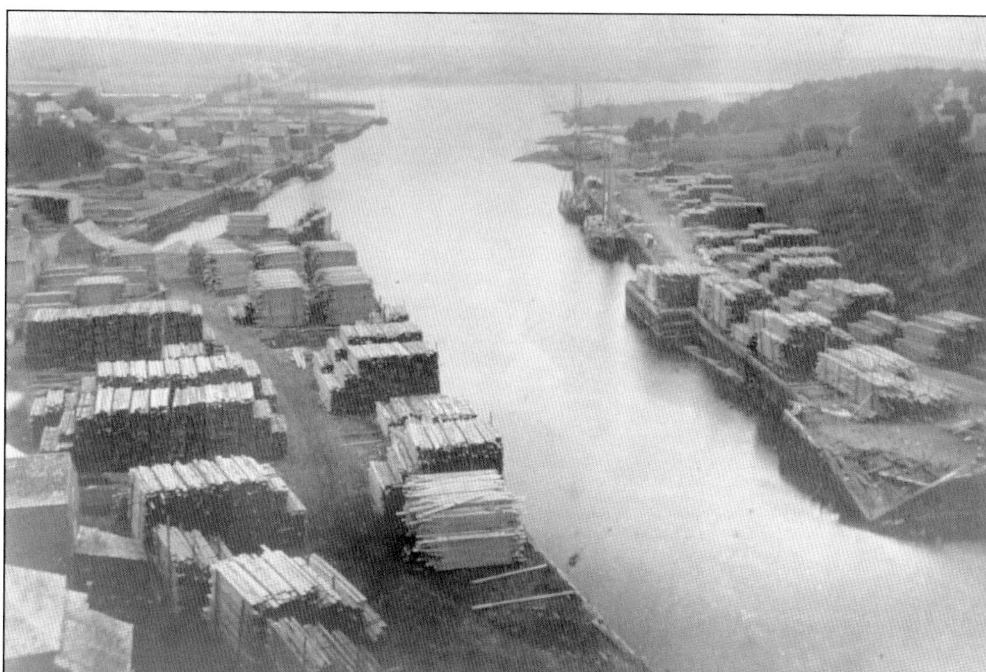

A large inventory of lumber on both sides of the river is stacked in Machias for shipping in the early 1920s.

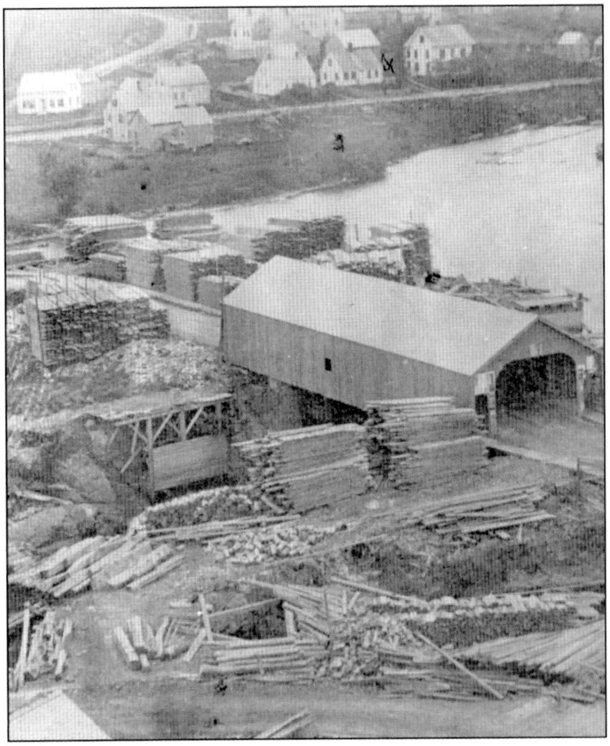

Lumber is stacked for shipment by the covered bridge in Machias, c. 1920s.

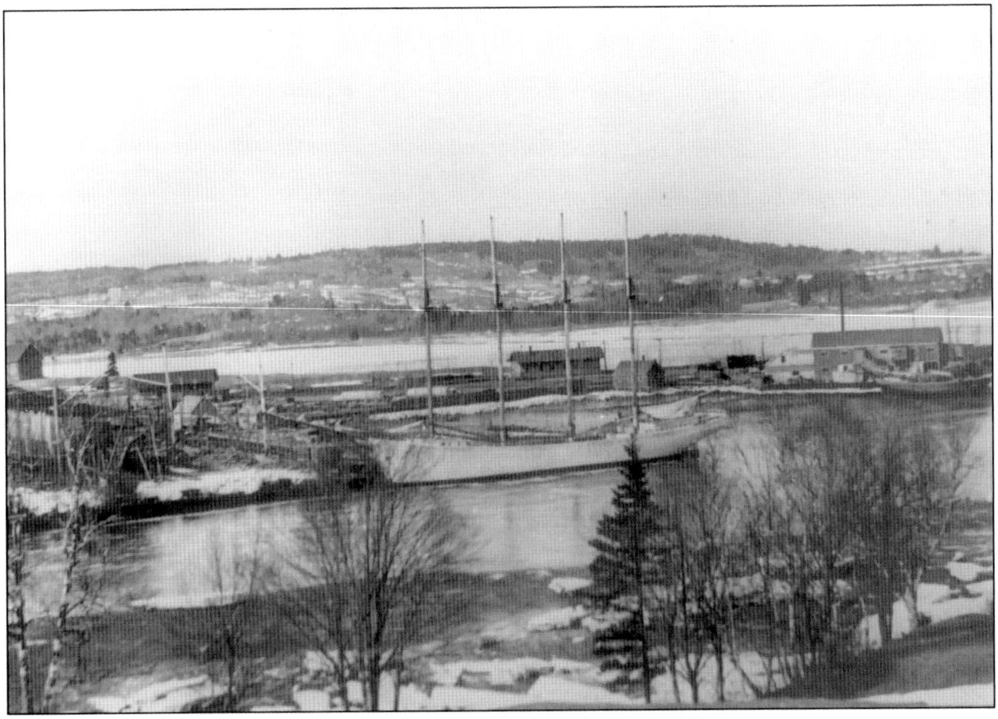

A four-masted schooner is docked awaiting to ship lumber, c. 1930s.

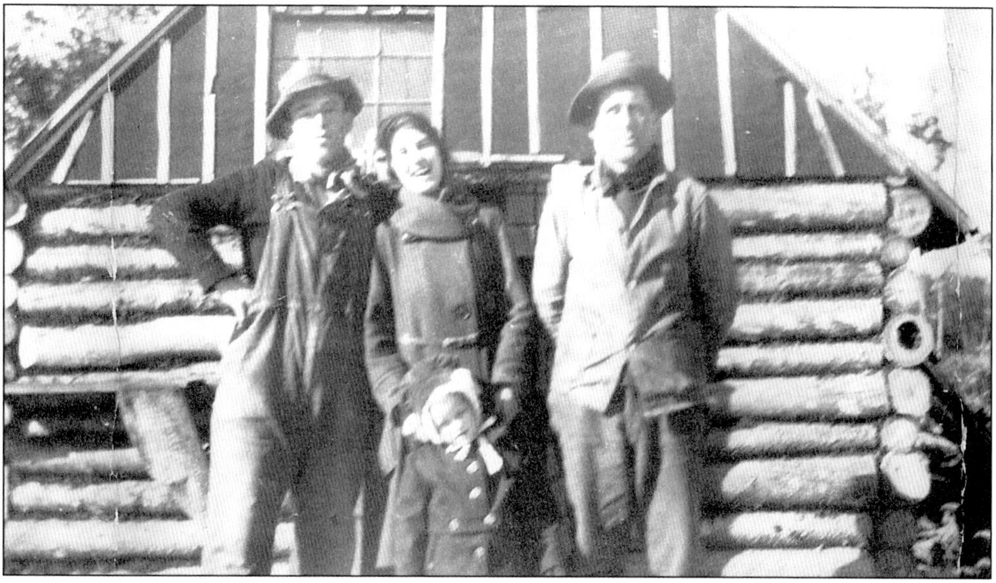

Gilbert L. Berry, Addie Scott Giel, Alec Kennedy, and Madeline Scott pose in front of a logging camp in 1920.

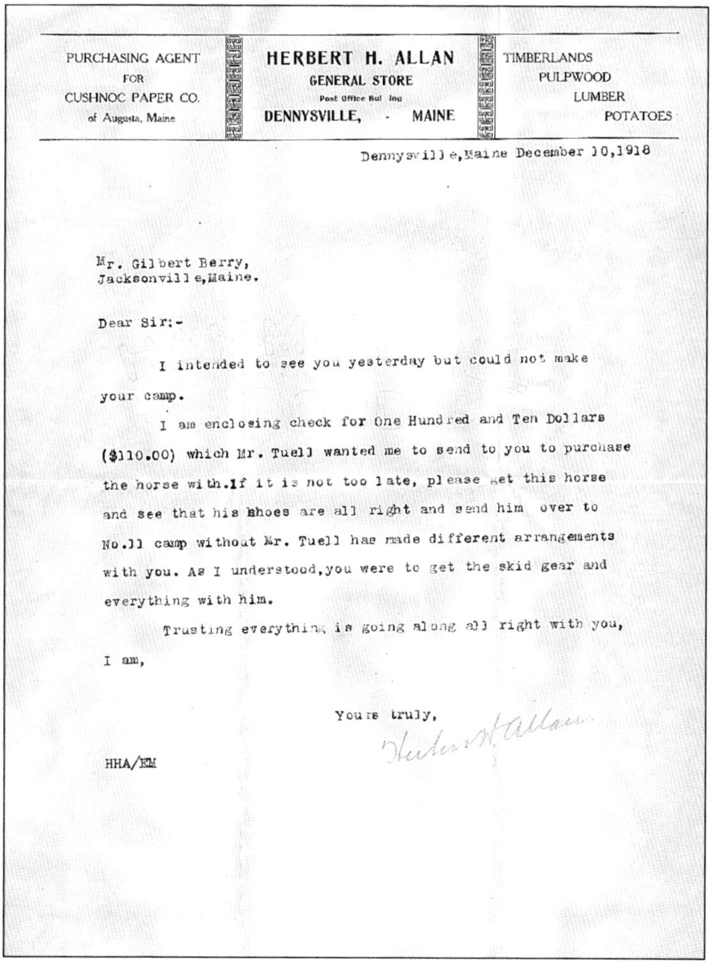

PURCHASING AGENT
FOR
CUSHNOC PAPER CO.
of Augusta, Maine

HERBERT H. ALLAN
GENERAL STORE
Post Office Bui ing
DENNYSVILLE, MAINE

TIMBERLANDS
PULPWOOD
LUMBER
POTATOES

Dennysvill e,Maine December 10,1918

Mr. Gilbert Berry,
Jacksonvill e,Maine.

Dear Sir:-

I intended to see you yesterday but could not make your camp.

I am enclosing check for One Hundred and Ten Dollars ($110.00) which Mr. Tuell wanted me to send to you to purchase the horse with. If it is not too late, please get this horse and see that his shoes are all right and send him over to No.11 camp without Mr. Tuell has made different arrangements with you. As I understood, you were to get the skid gear and everything with him.

Trusting everything is going along all right with you,

I am,

Yours truly,

HHA/EM

This business letter was written to Gilbert Berry at his logging camp.

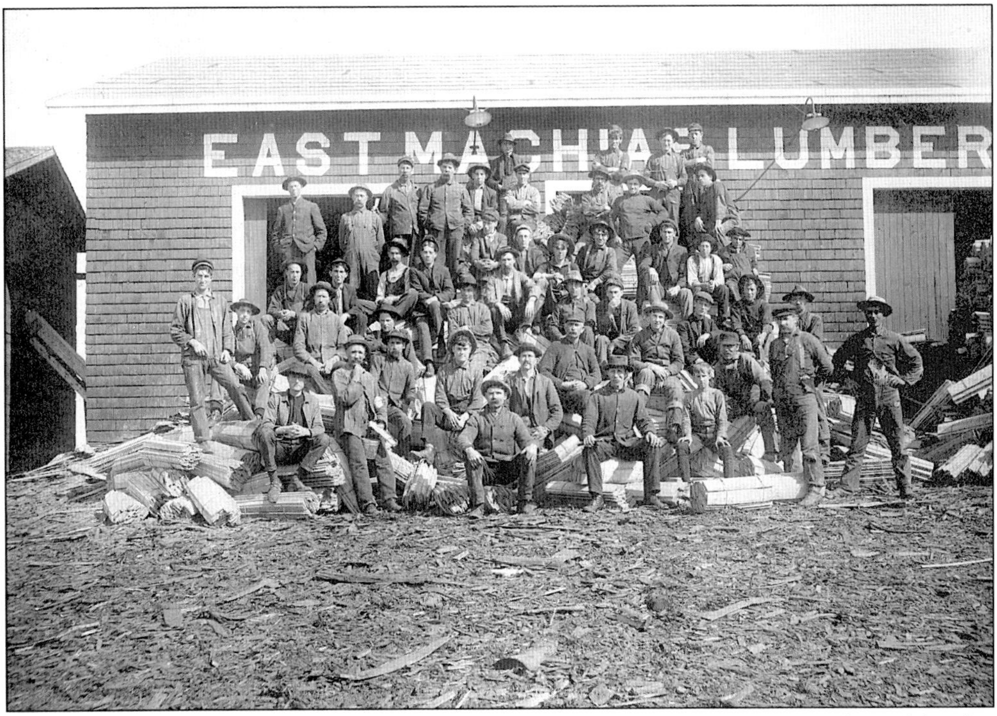

The lumber industry was a major employer in the region for many years, evidenced by this *c.* 1900 photograph of the East Machias Lumber Company crew.

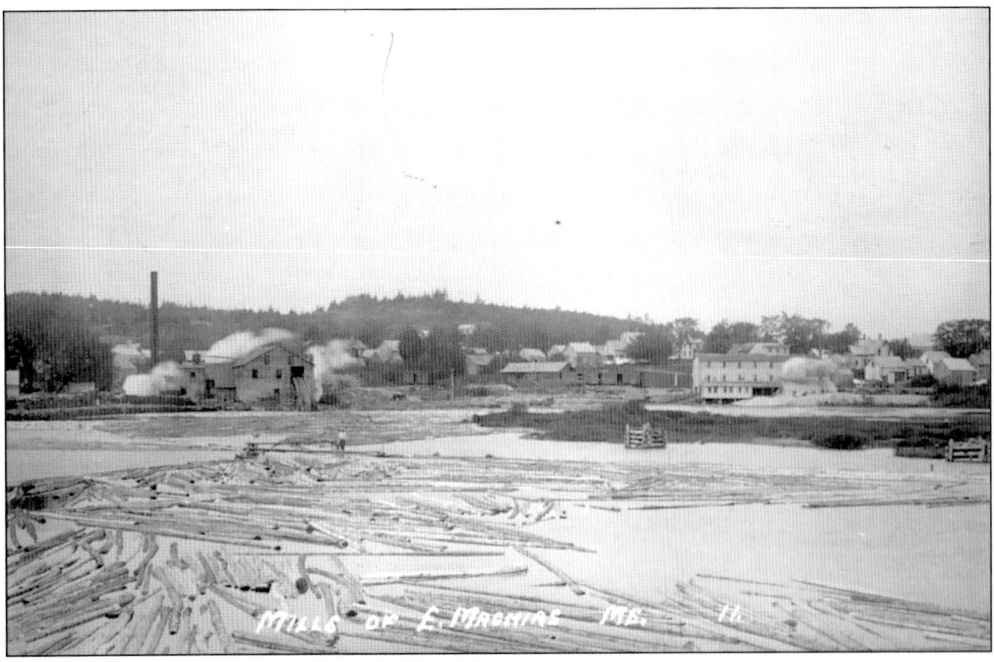

This is Mill Pond at East Machias Mills, *c.* 1900.

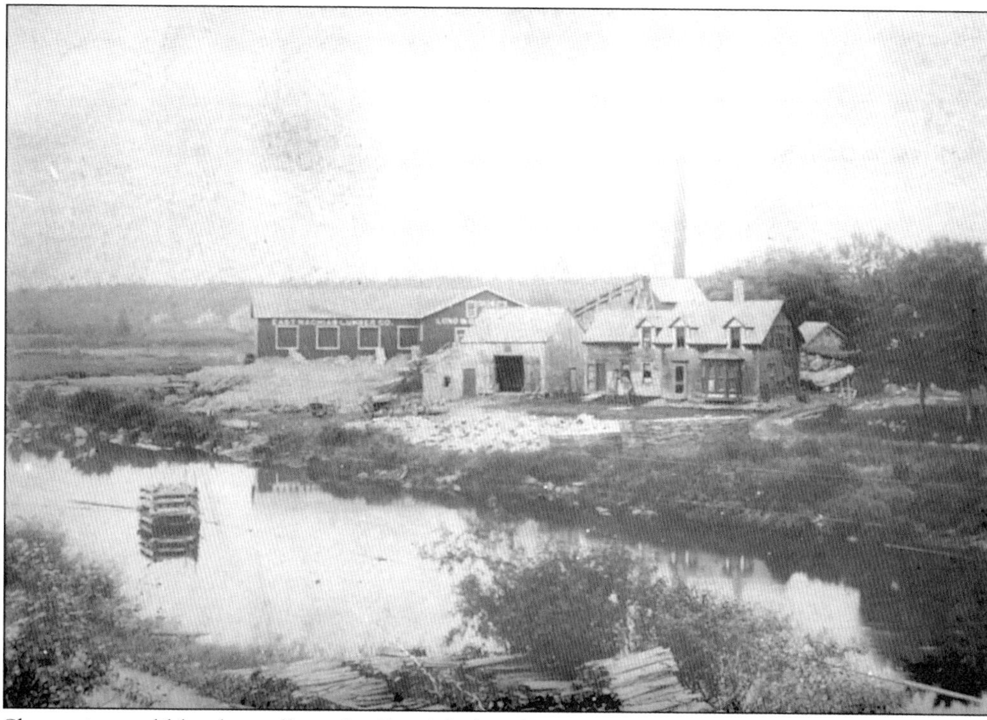

Shown is an old lumbermill on the East Machias River, *c.* 1900.

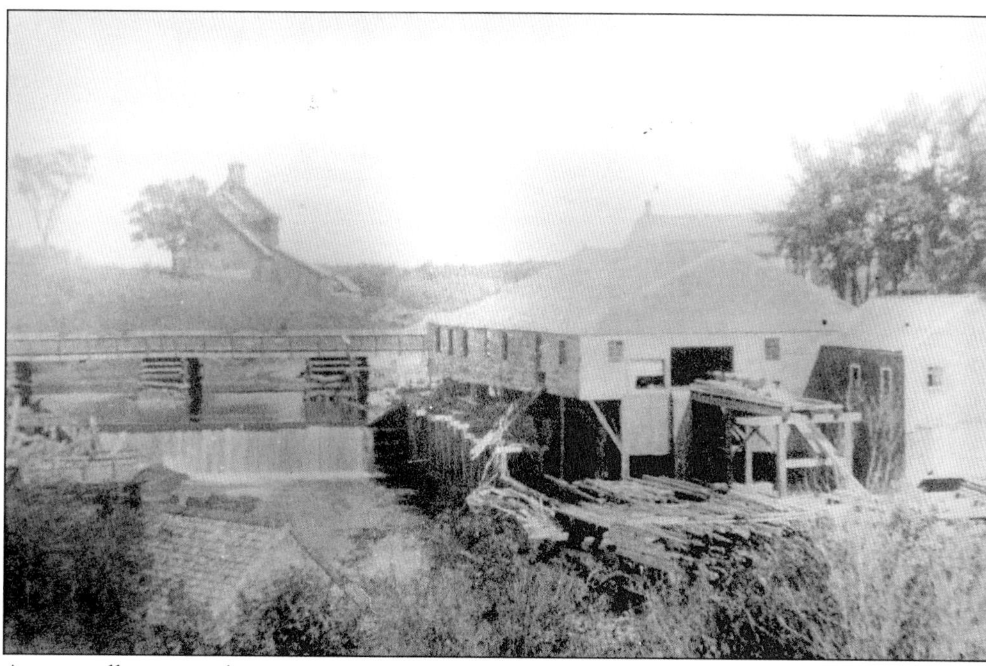

A new mill came on line in East Machias, *c.* 1920s.

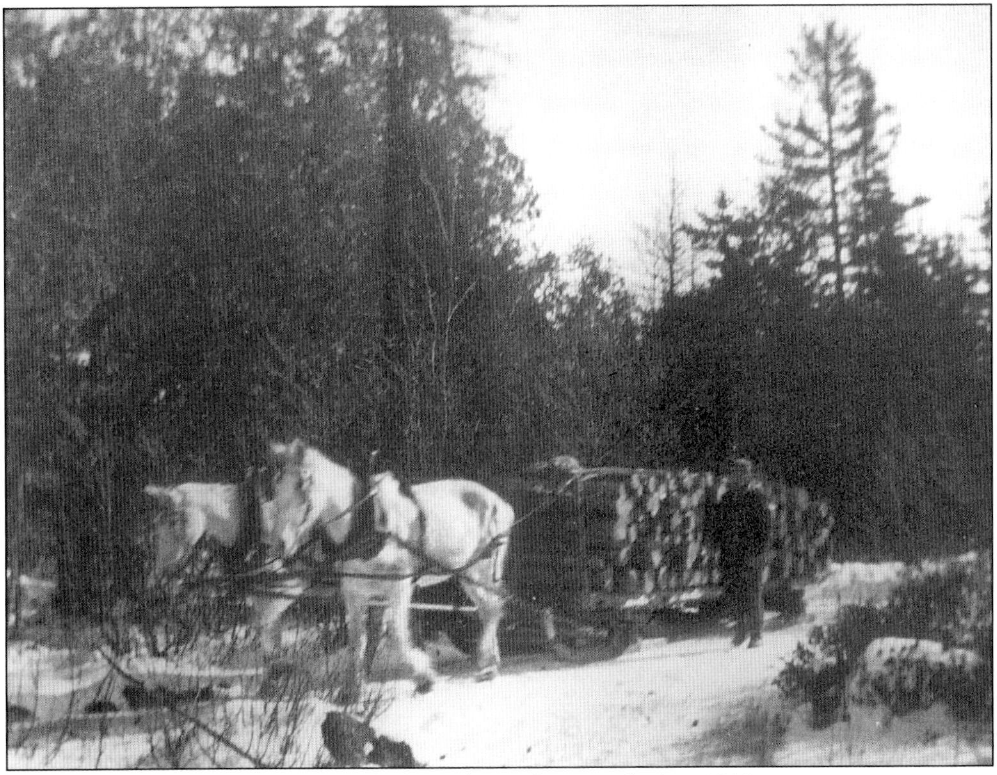

This double-runner sled with a load of wood was photographed in 1910.

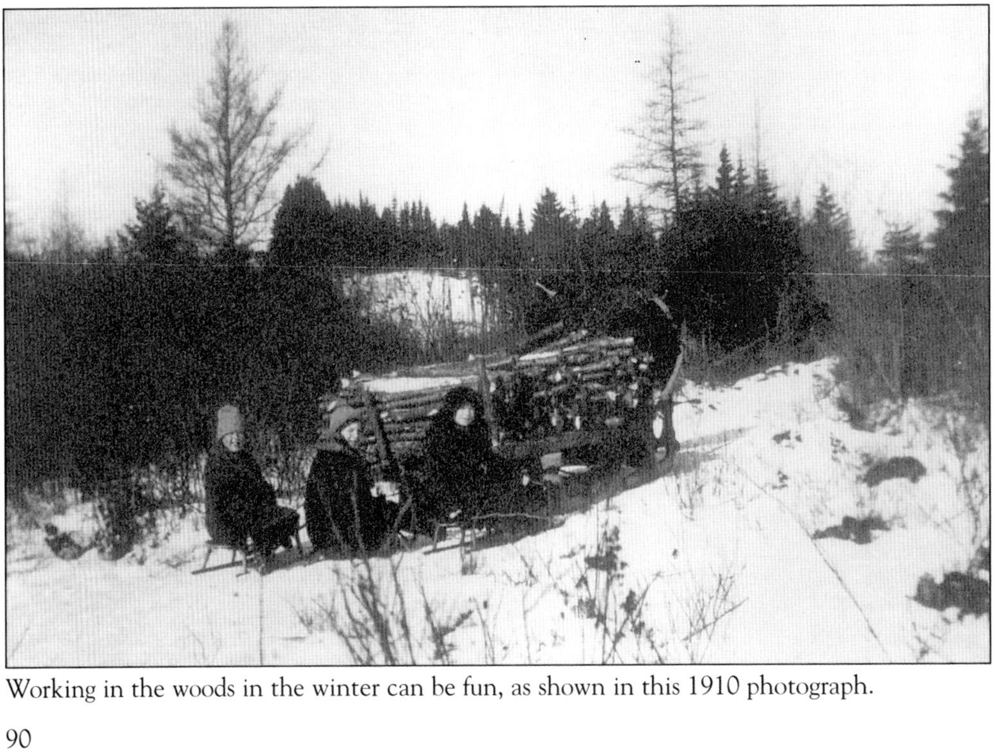

Working in the woods in the winter can be fun, as shown in this 1910 photograph.

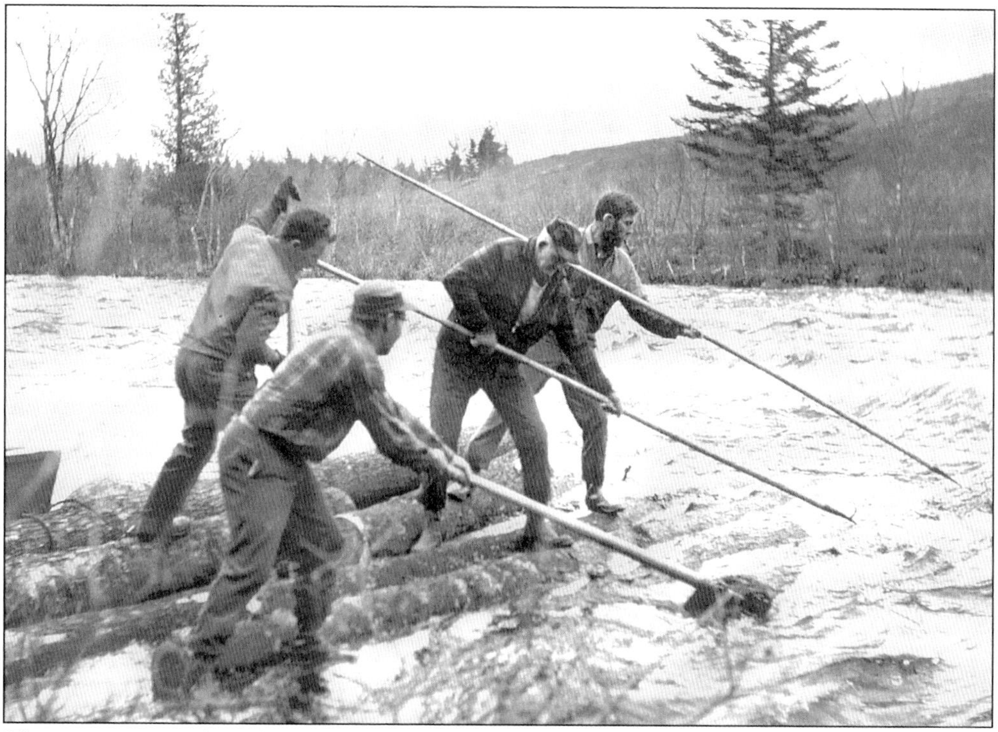
These men are working logs at Wigwam on the Machias River.

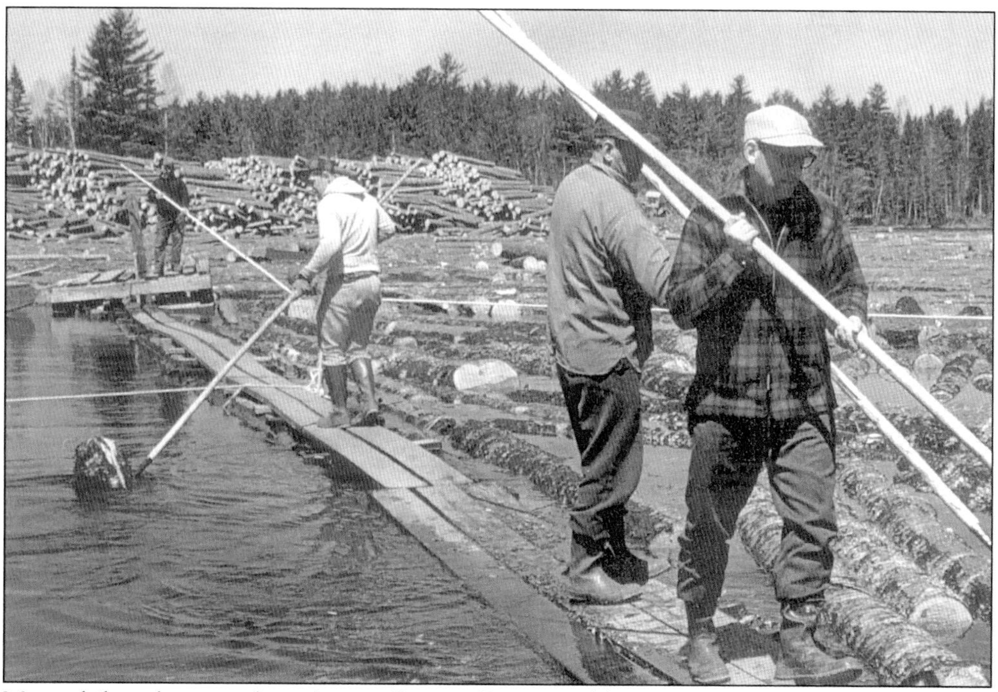
Meanwhile, others are sluing logs at Canaan Dam on Old Stream.

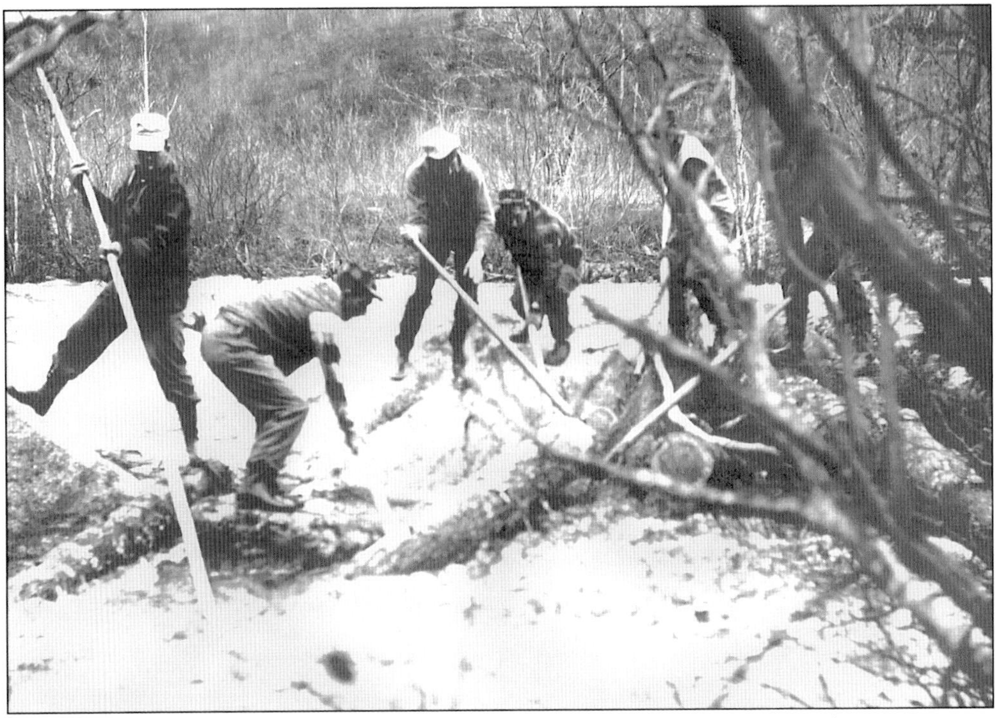

Bud Holmes, Guy Cox, Crow Catcomb, and Dick Albee are freeing logs at the Wigwam on the Machias River.

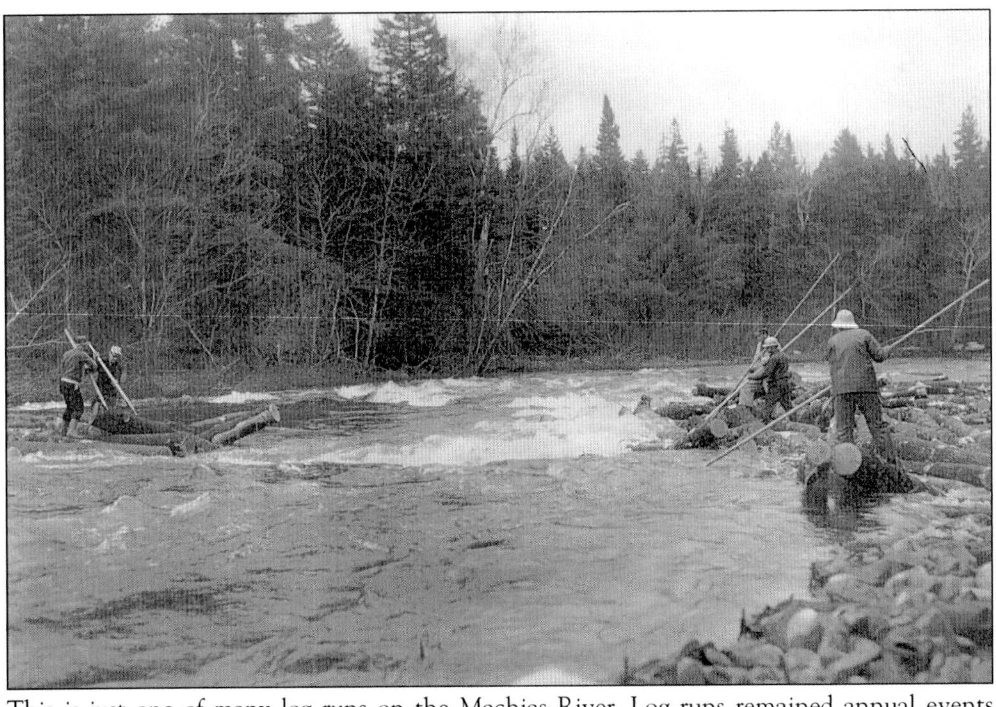

This is just one of many log runs on the Machias River. Log runs remained annual events into the 1960s.

Seven

Hometown Life

Technical innovation did not impact life in the Machias Bay Region until just before the communities celebrated their centennial in 1863. The soft breeze of change arrived with the introduction of a steam railroad that allowed lumber to be hauled from the mills in Whitneyville to the docks in Machiasport for shipment. Up to that time, all work was done by hand with the help of teams of horses. Technological changes continued to arrive through the 19th and 20th centuries at an increasing rate. This changed the way people live and work. The telecommunications industry has also had a profound effect on hometown life. Yet, at the same time, little has changed in terms of values, traditions, and the appreciation for the tranquility that makes each town and village within the Machias Bay Region so special. By understanding how hometown life has made the transition through time, one can better understand the strong New England character that is firmly rooted in the people of the region.

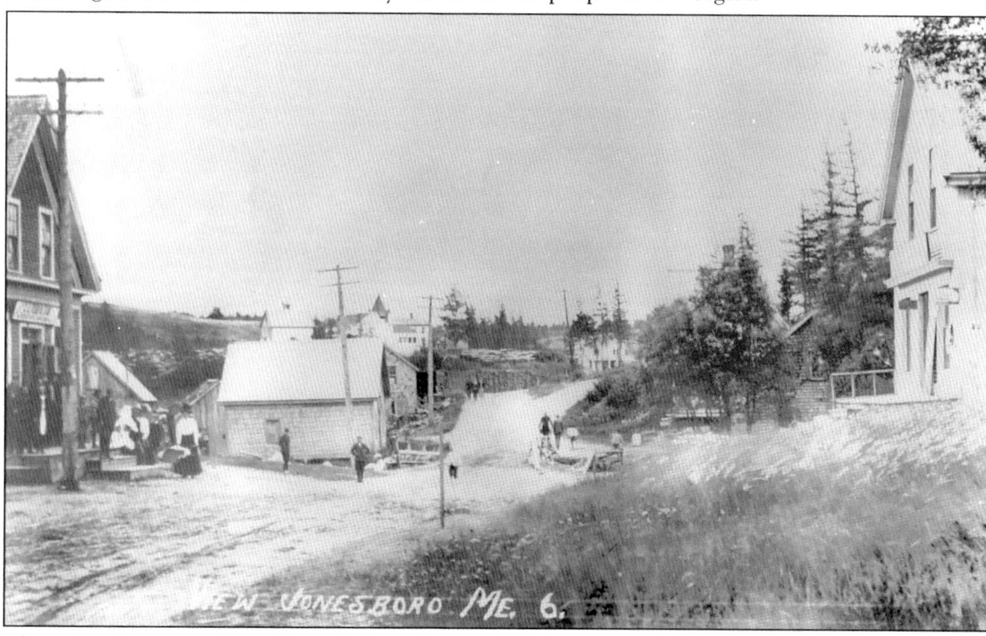

These locals are strolling through Jonesboro c. 1890.

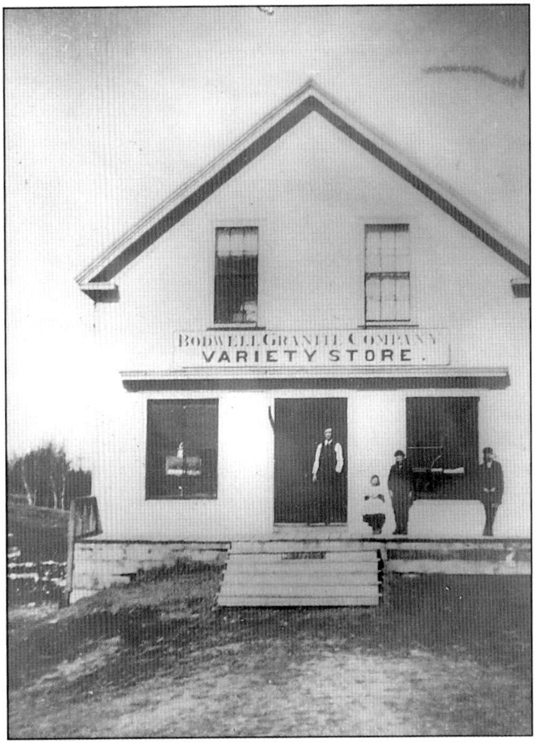

William F. West, store manager, stands in the doorway of the Bodwell Granite Company Store in Joneboro c. 1900.

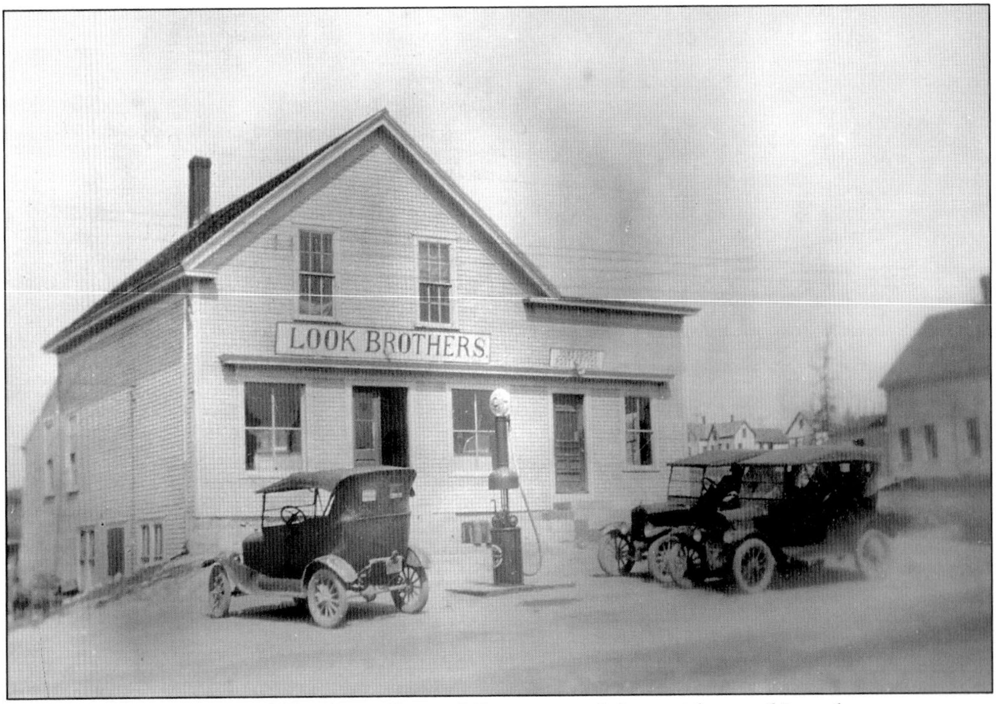

Shown here c. 1930, Look Brothers General Store served the residents of Jonesboro.

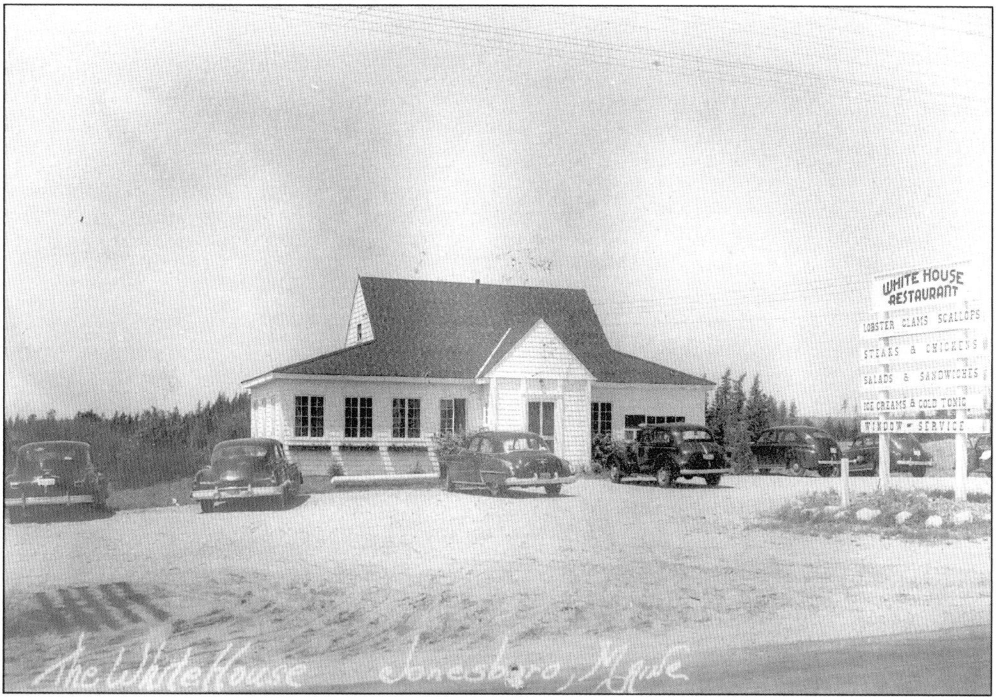

Some may remember Jonesboro's original White House Restaurant, shown here c. 1948.

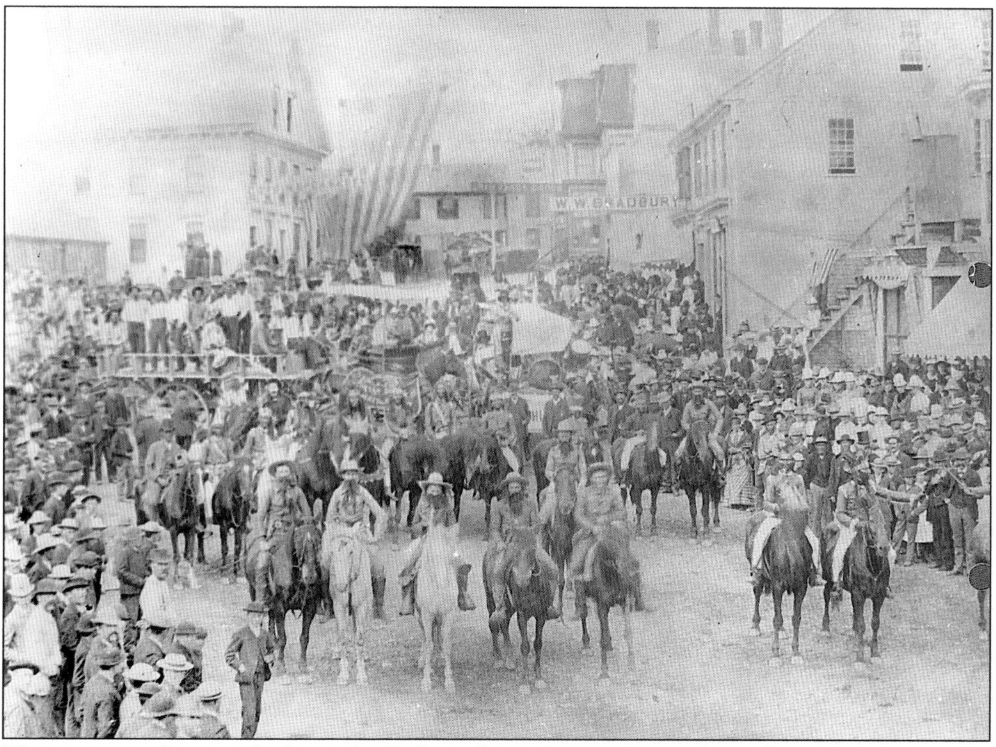
This exciting photograph shows the Independence Day 1883 parade in downtown Machias.

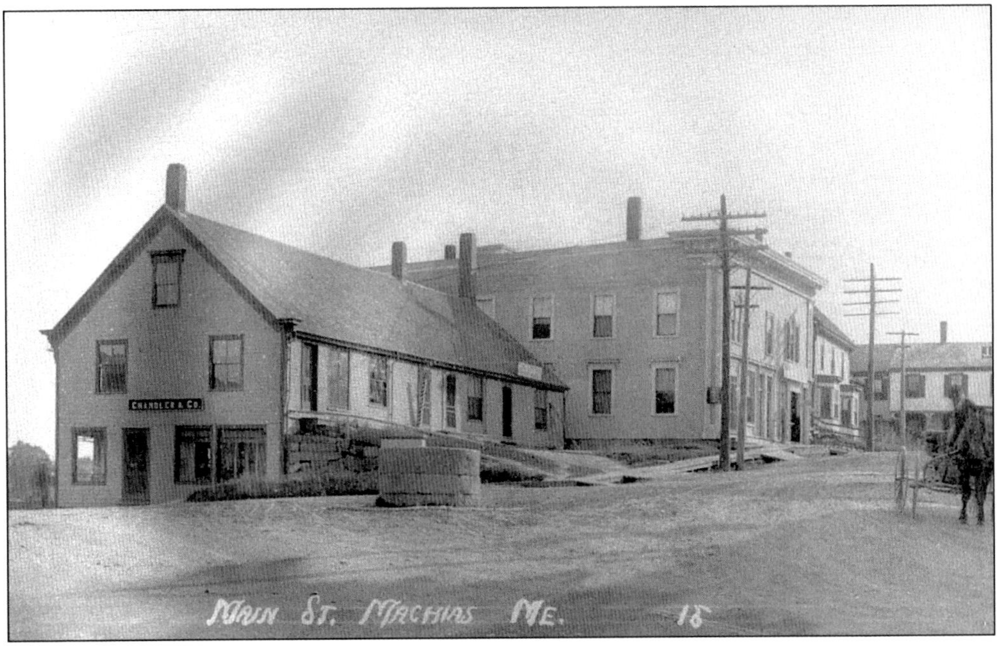

Main Street Machias looked like this c. 1890s.

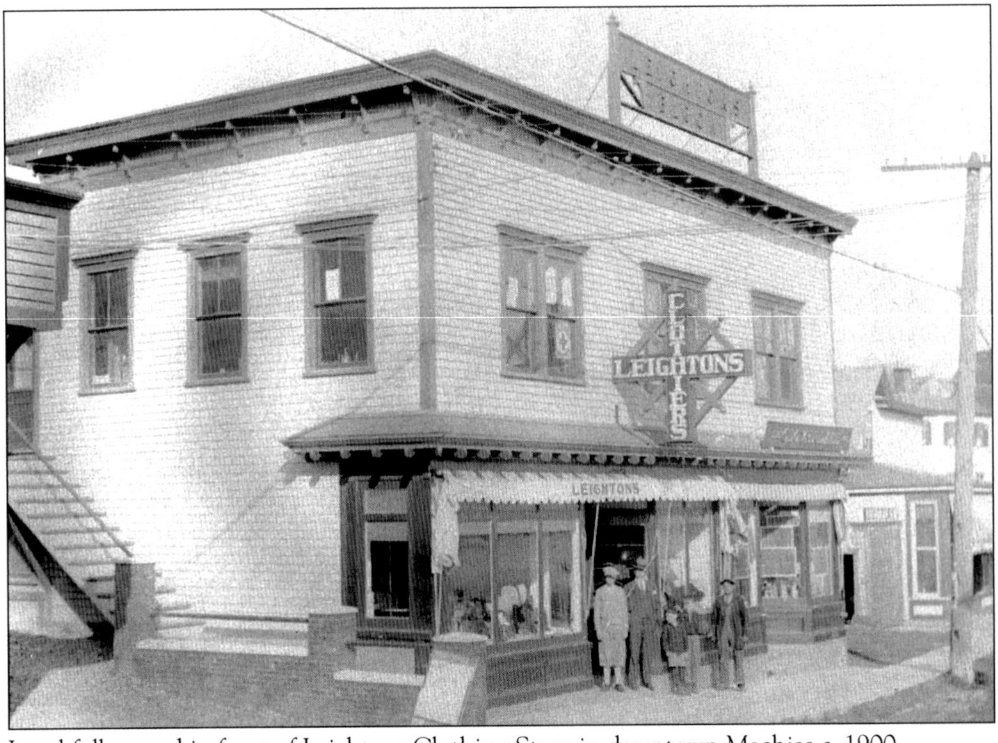

Local folks stand in front of Leightons Clothing Store in downtown Machias c. 1900.

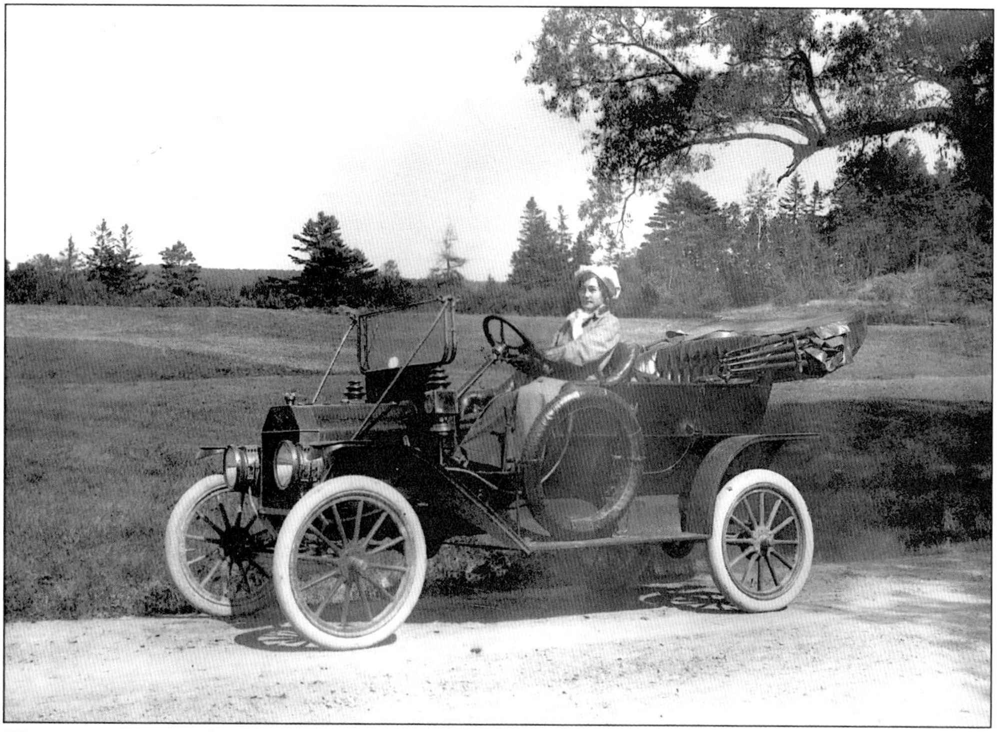

This woman is out for a summer's day ride in Machias, *c.* 1920s.

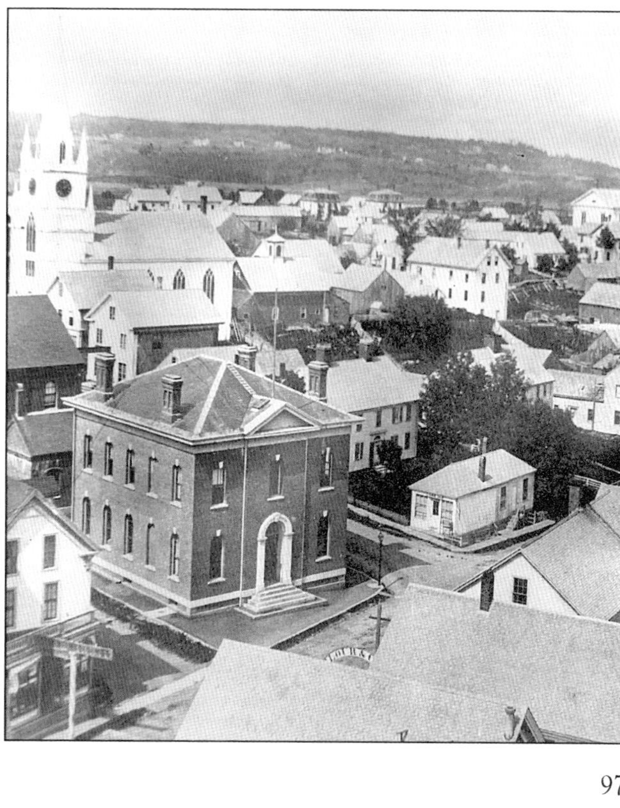

This view shows downtown Machias in the 1920s.

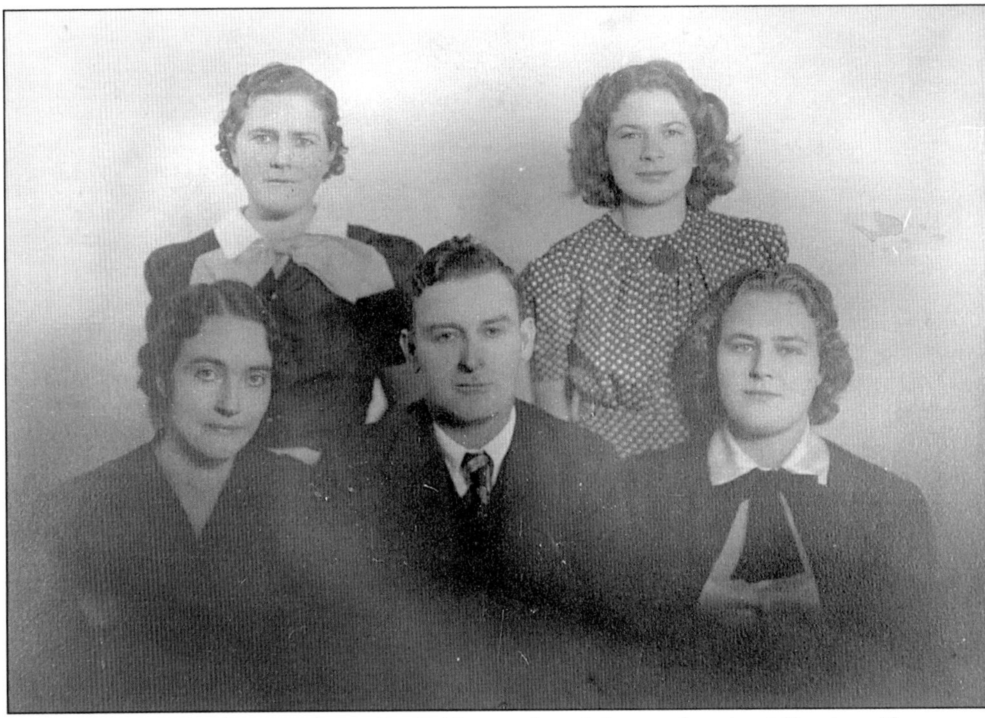

Posing for a family photograph in the 1940s are, from left to right, the following: (front row) Bertha Hill, Allan Hill, and Annie Hanscom; (back row) Mary Stevens and Clara Dow.

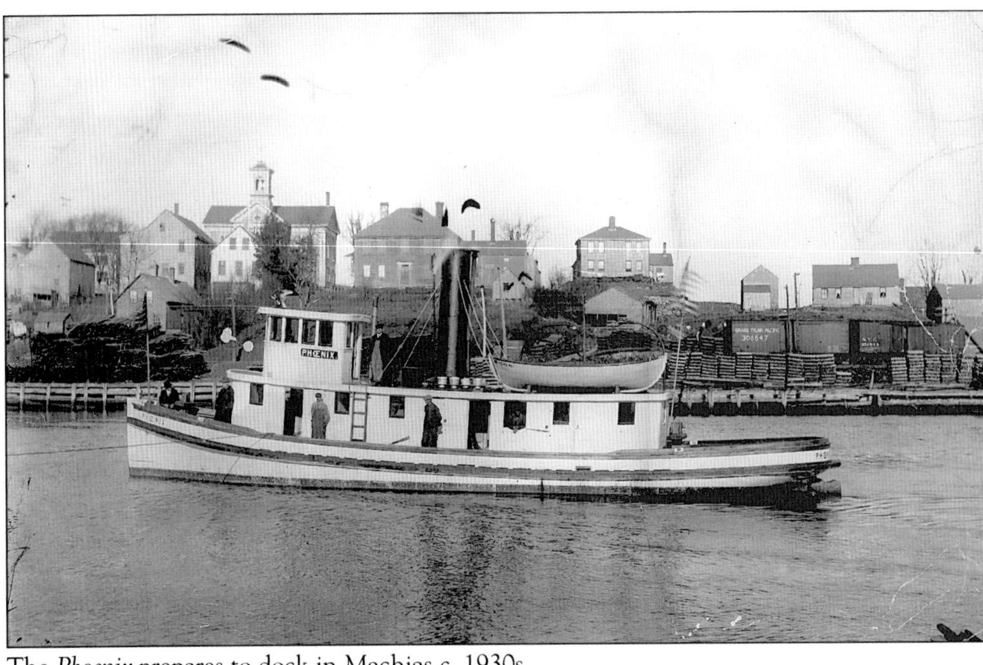

The *Phoenix* prepares to dock in Machias c. 1930s.

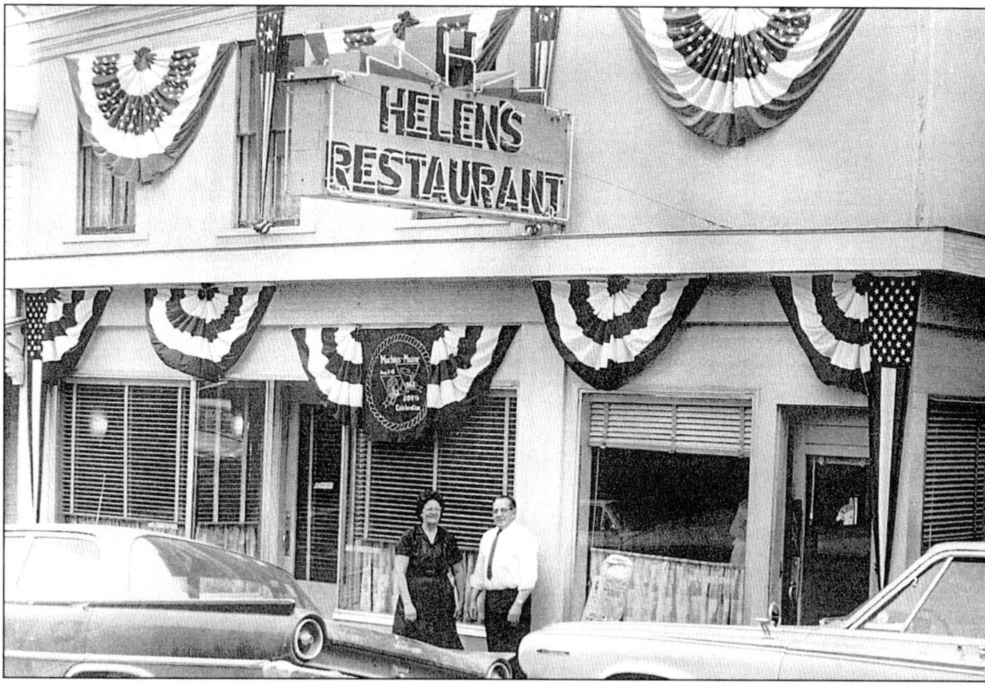

Standing in front of Helen's Restaurant on Main Street in Machias are the first proprietors, Helen and Lawrence Mugnai. Helene's Restaurant is all decked out to help celebrate the bicentennial in August 1963. The Mugnais started their operation as Helen's Ice Cream Take Out in 1950. Next came a 12-stool counter and then a 20-stool counter. For more than half a century, the restaurant has been a Down East landmark.

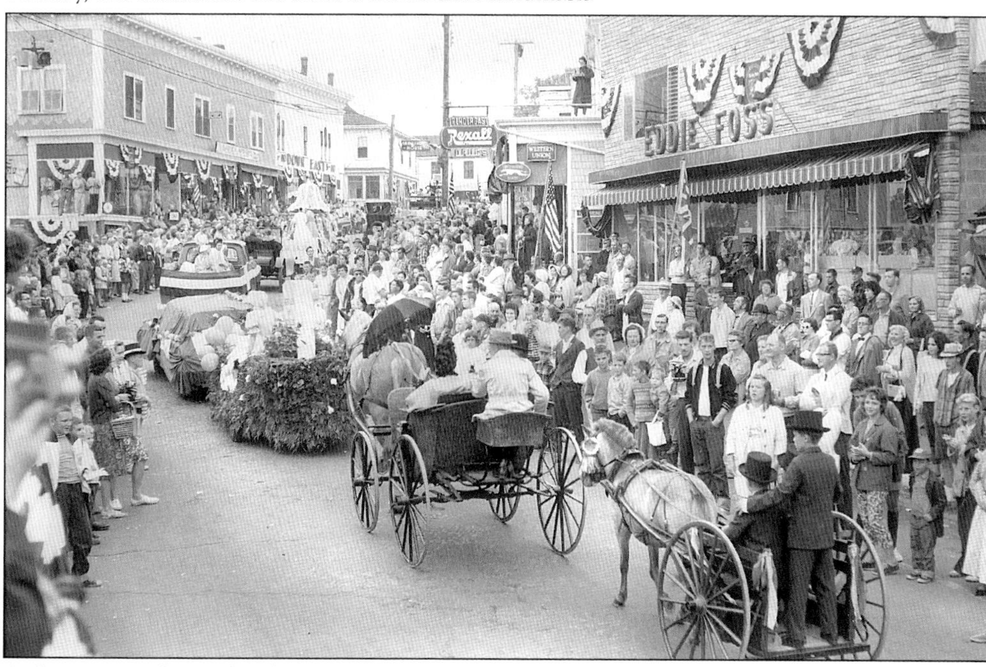

A large crowd stands along Main Street in Machias to watch the bicentennial parade in August 1963.

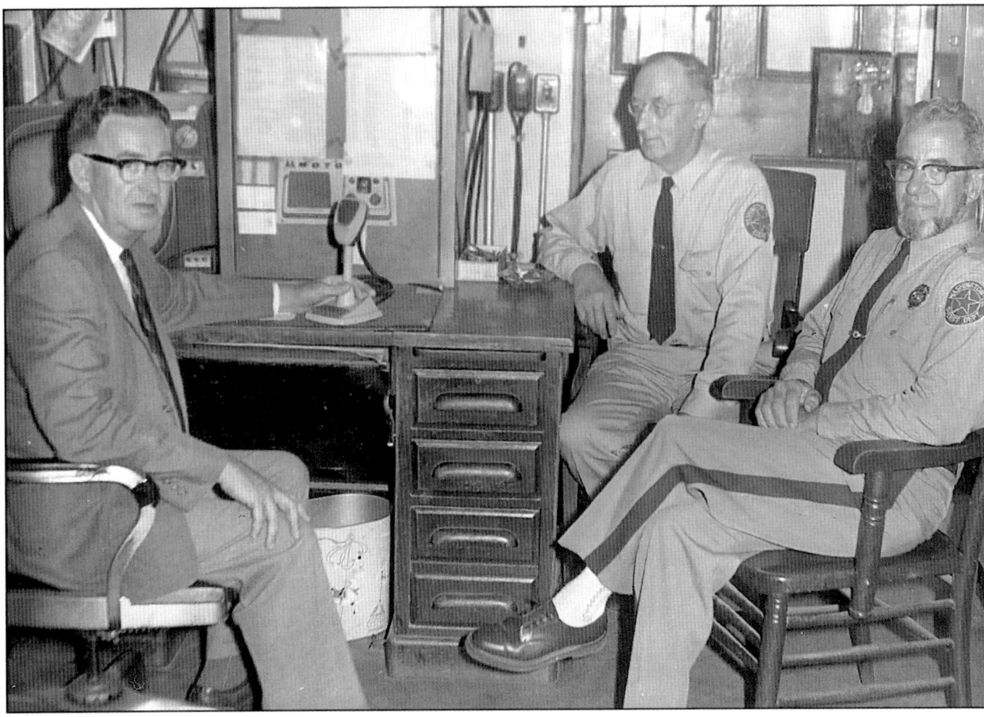

The Washington County Sheriff's Department office staff in 1963 included, from left to right, Sheriff Raymond Tracy, Ralph Berry, and David Clemons. Turnkey Maurice Worcester was absent.

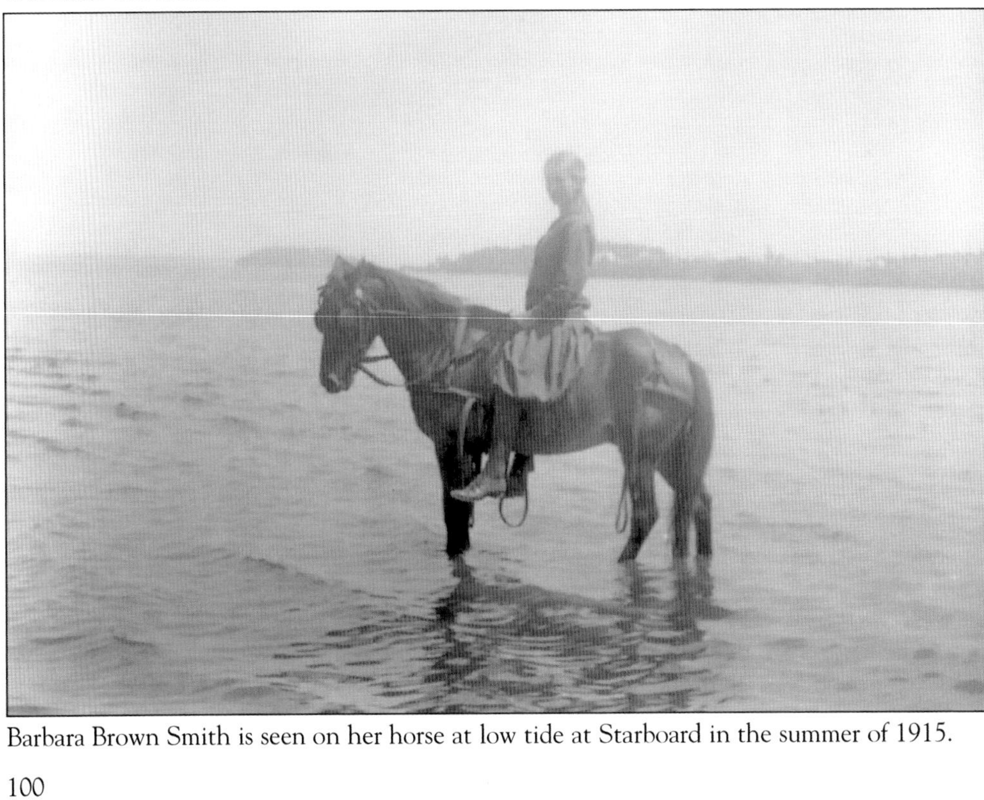

Barbara Brown Smith is seen on her horse at low tide at Starboard in the summer of 1915.

"Uncle" Charlie Johnson sits on the stoop of his Bucks Harbor home in 1949. Charlie was a beloved figure in Bucks Harbor. He operated a local variety store and kept a dairy cow and a horse. The authors live in the home that Charlie Johnson built at the close of the 19th century.

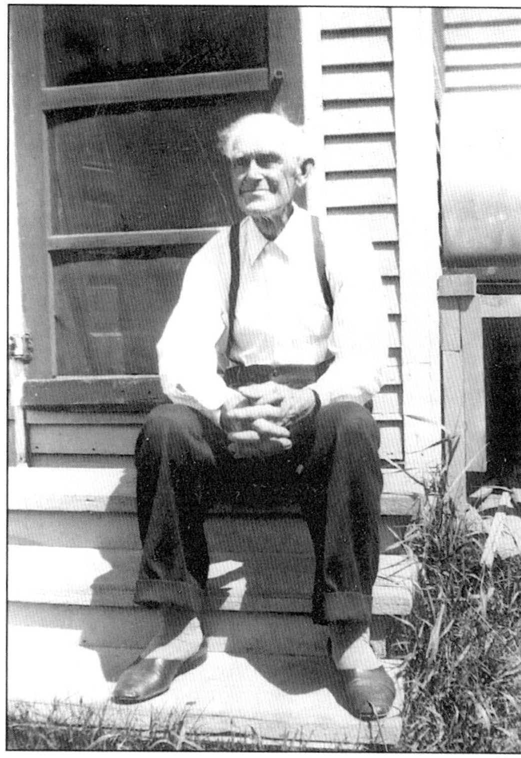

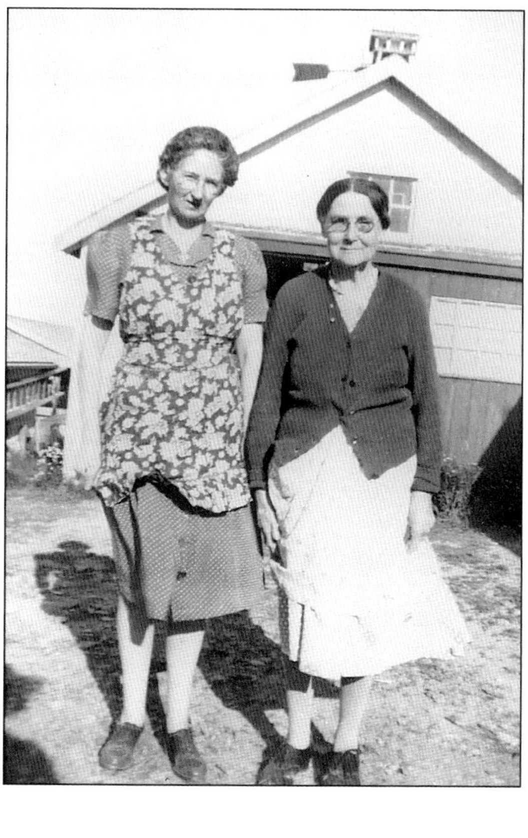

Agnes and Aubine Colbeth are shown in front of the Bucks Harbor store in 1949. The store was converted back into a home and is now the home of attorney Norman Toffolon and his wife, Cathy.

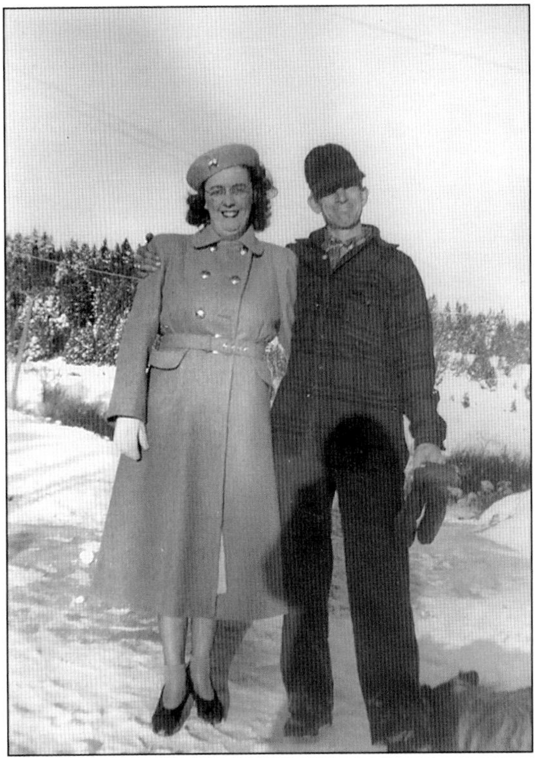

Irene and Duke Quinn are shown in Bucks Harbor in 1949.

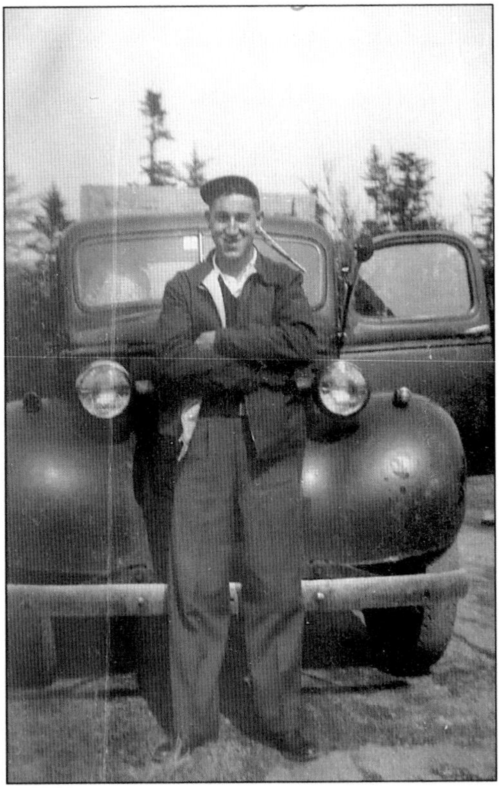

Vernon Wood stands proudly in front of his new truck in Bucks Harbor in 1949.

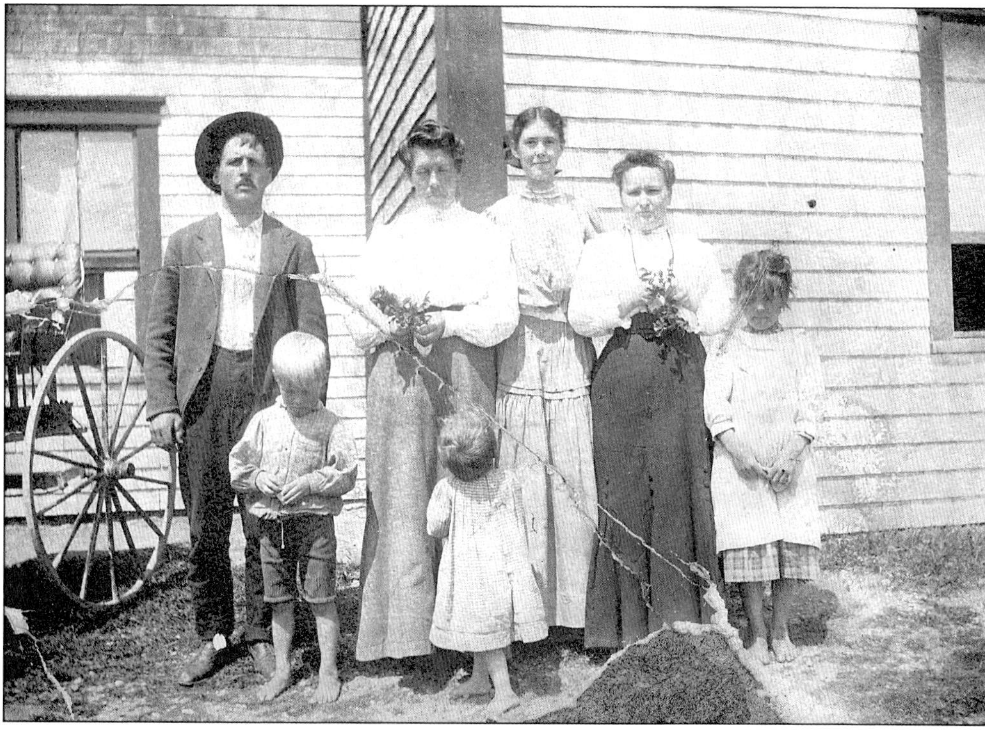

Shown at the Berrys' Jacksonville home in the summer of 1906 are, from left to right, Gilbert L. Berry, Cara Edwina, Minnie Hodgton, Hattie Graham, and Agnes. Children Albert and Alvin are the little ones in front of the group.

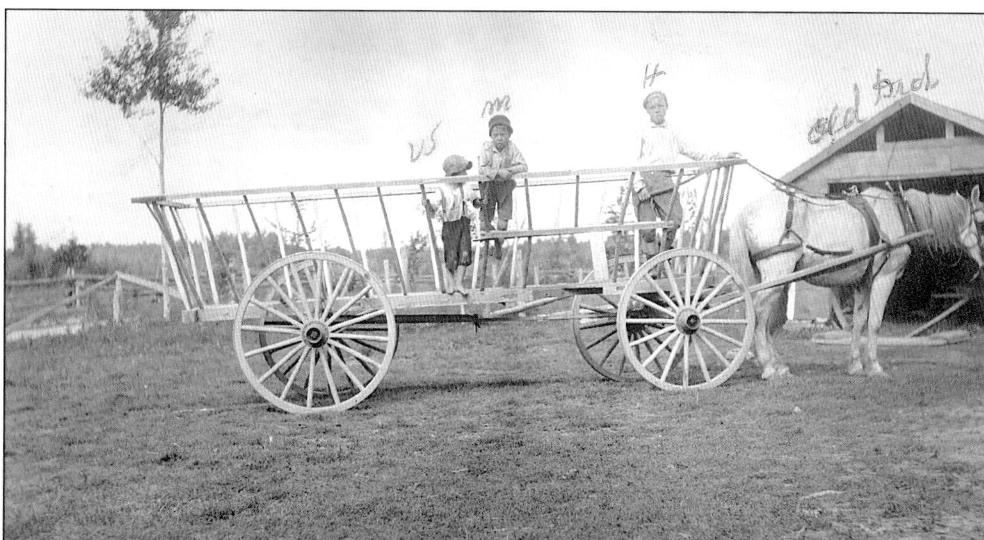

Standing in the hay wagon are, from left to right, Warren Berry, Maurice Berry, and Heber Berry with their horse Old Dick on the Berry farm in Jacksonville in the 1920s.

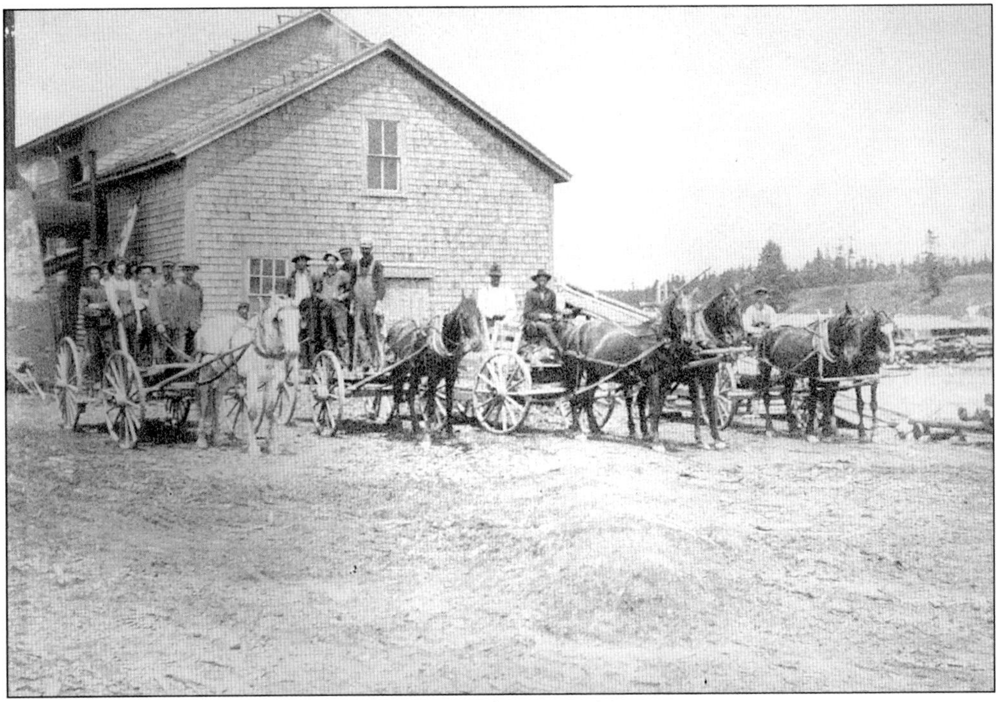

Horse and carriage teams lined up in East Machias *c.* 1900.

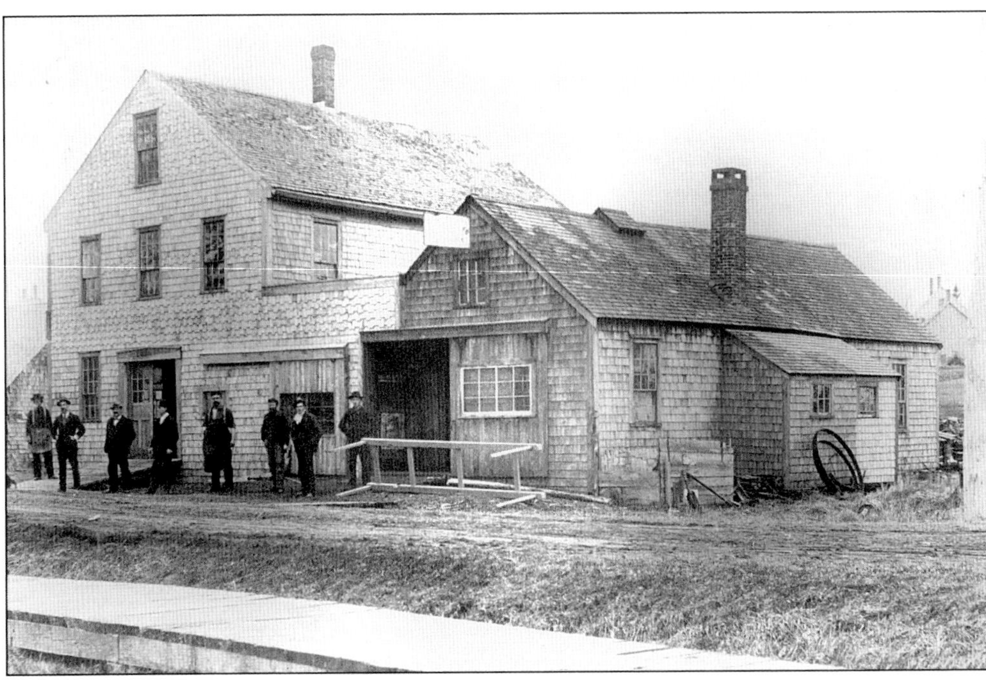

Some local men stand in front the Carriage House and Blacksmith Shop in East Machias *c.* 1900.

James Look rests in front of the home of his son Willard Look in Whiting, c. 1930.

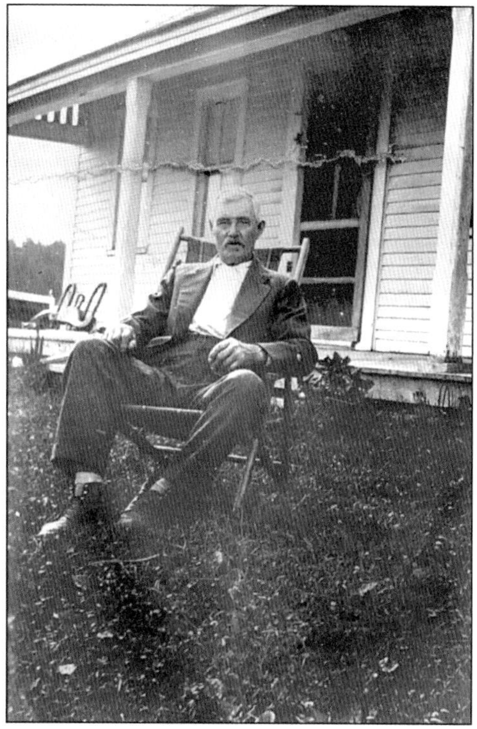

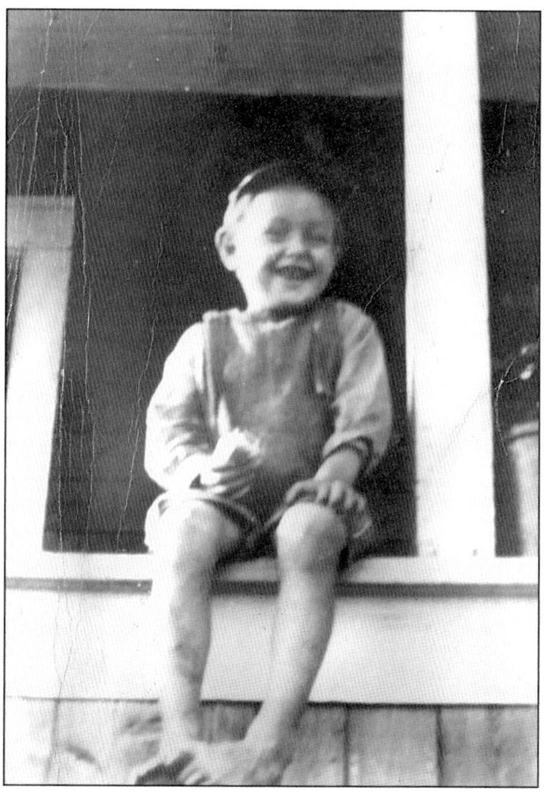

Don Look is enjoying a summer day on his porch in Whiting in 1928.

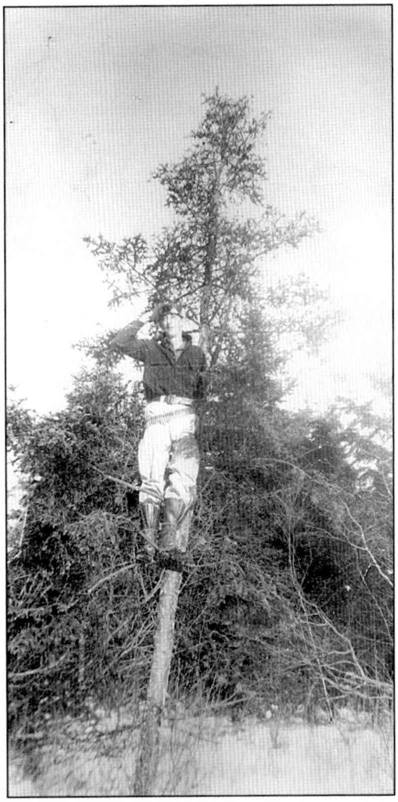

Don Look, home on Christmas leave from the navy in 1944, climbs a tree in his yard as a joke on his navy buddies.

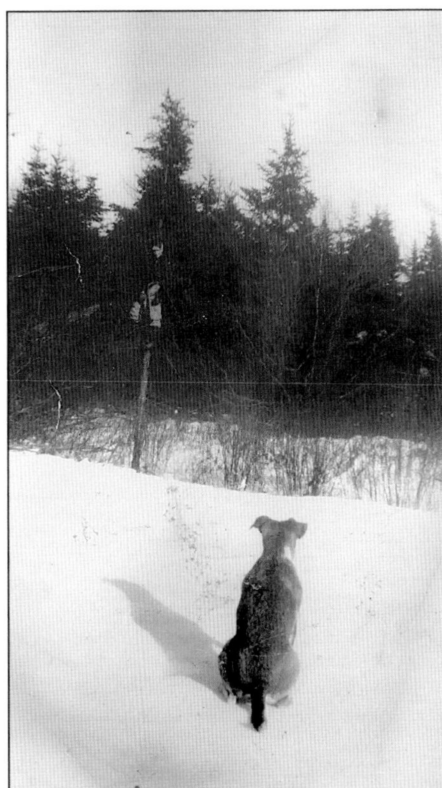

Don Look's dog Sandy watches Don up in the tree during the Christmas season in 1944.

Don Look, his father, and a navy buddy got together at the home of Don's aunt in Brookline, Massachusetts, while on a weekend pass in 1943.

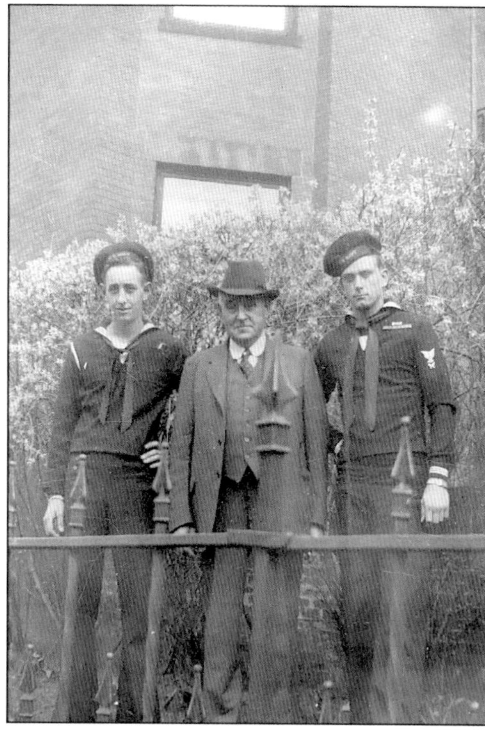

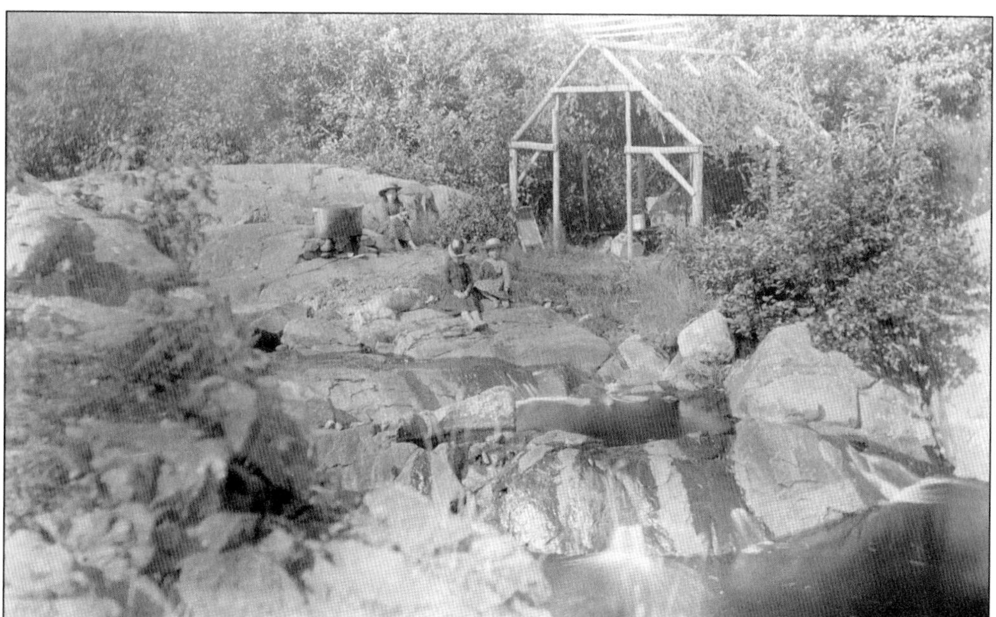

These folks are doing the weekly laundry at the Schooner Brook Wash House in Cutler in 1885.

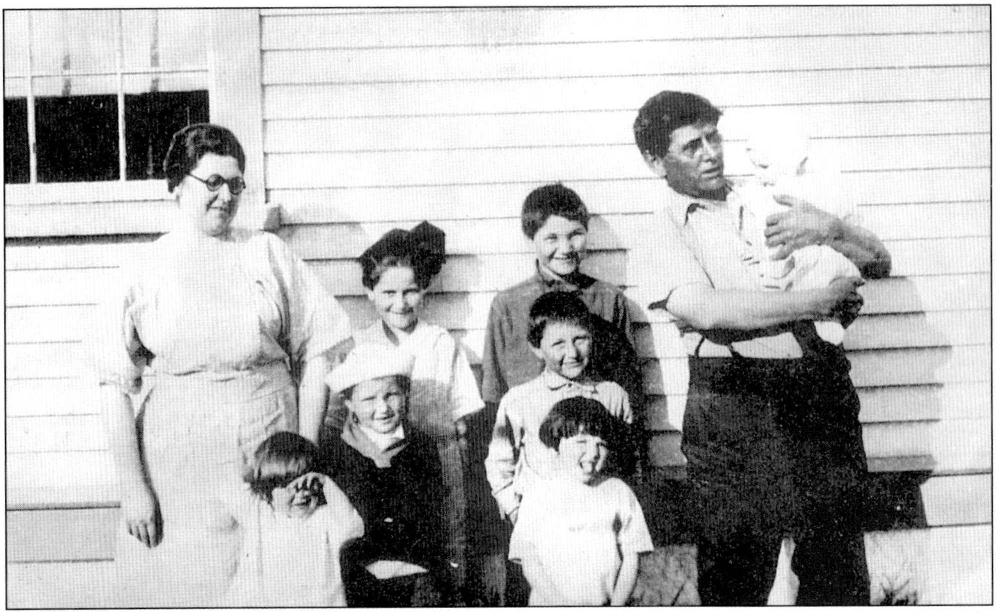

The Corbett family of Little River included, from left to right, the following: (front row) Emily and Ruth Corbett; (middle row) Purcell and Neil Corbett; (back row) Velma, Florence, Myron, and Willie Corbett (with baby Kathleen in his arms). This photograph was taken in 1924.

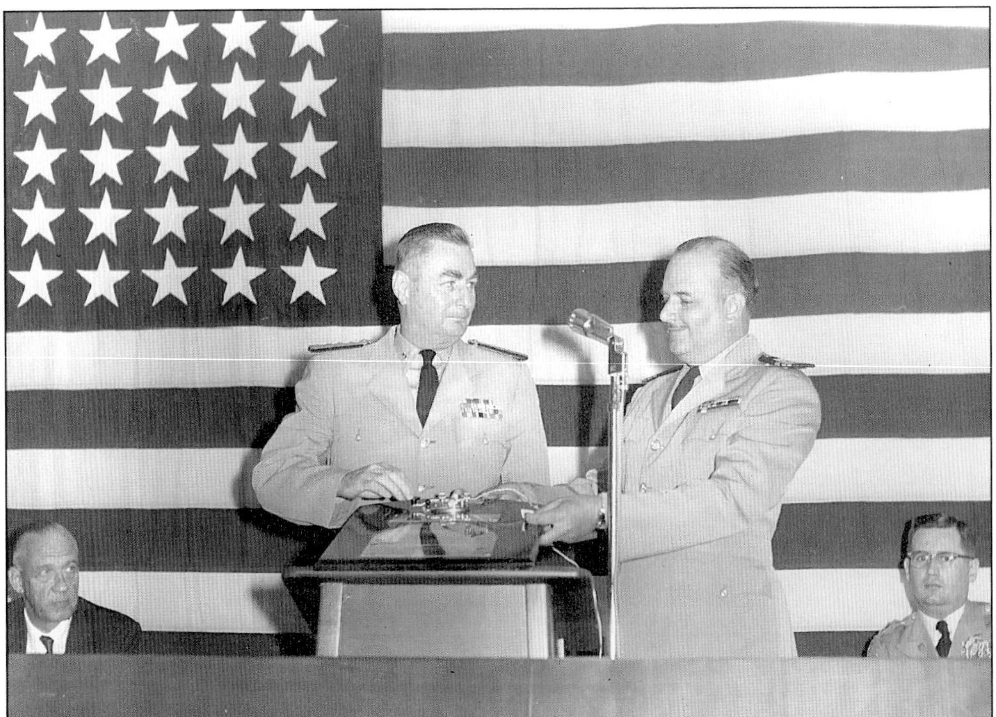

This photograph was taken during the commissioning ceremony at the U.S. Navy's newest and most powerful low-frequency radio transmitting station in Cutler in April 1961.

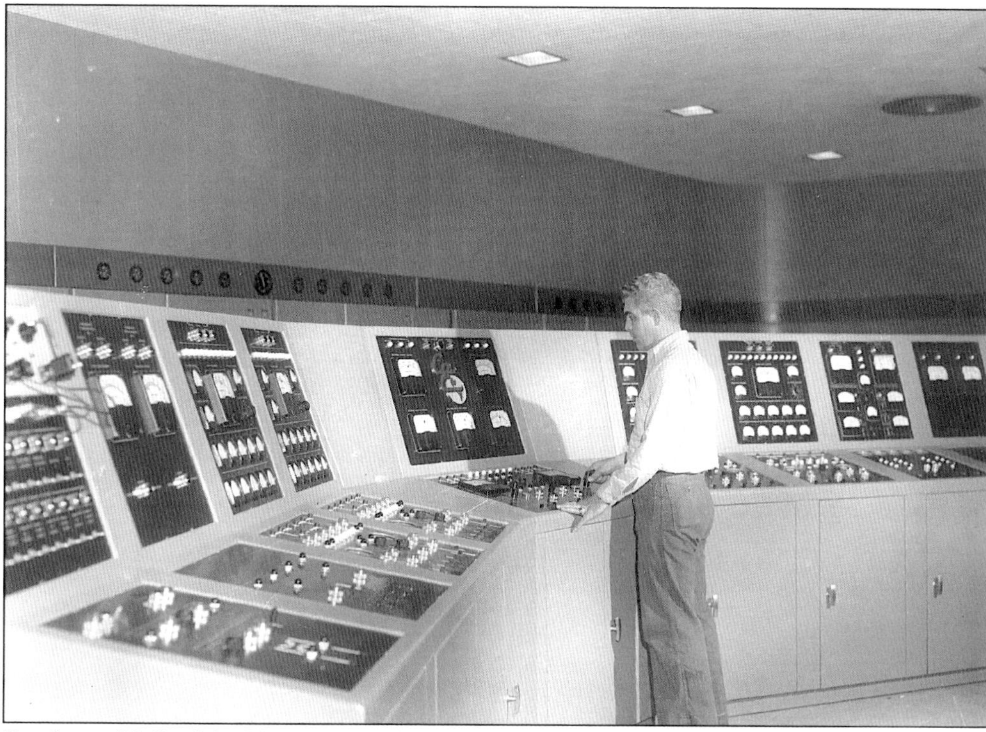

Smithson, RMI, of the U.S. Navy makes an adjustment at the console of the new transmitting station at Cutler on April 4, 1961.

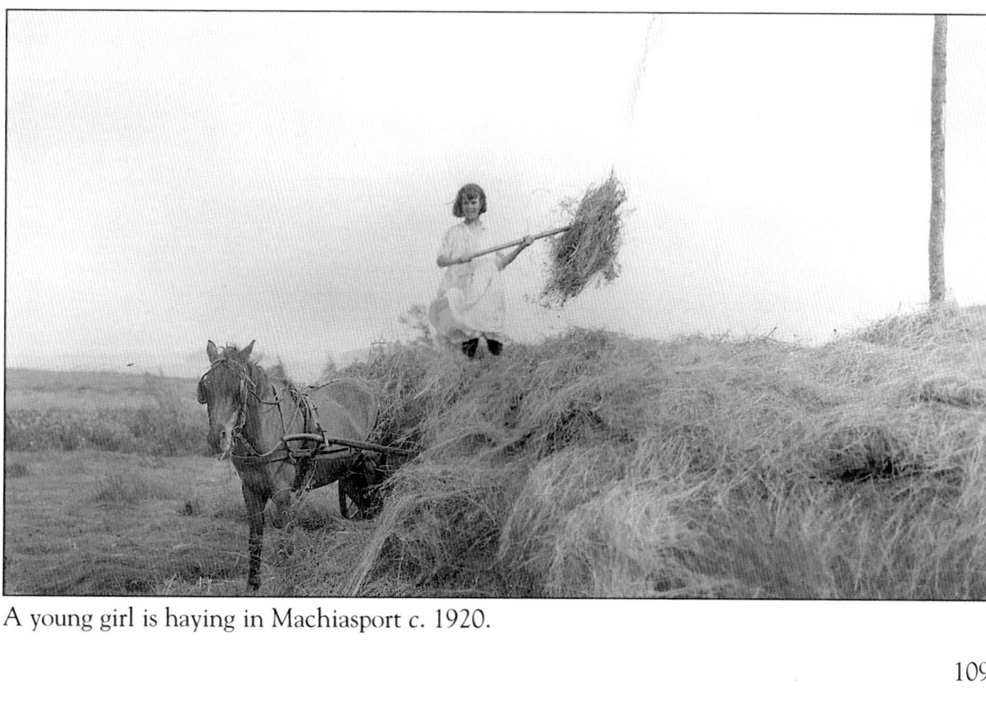

A young girl is haying in Machiasport *c.* 1920.

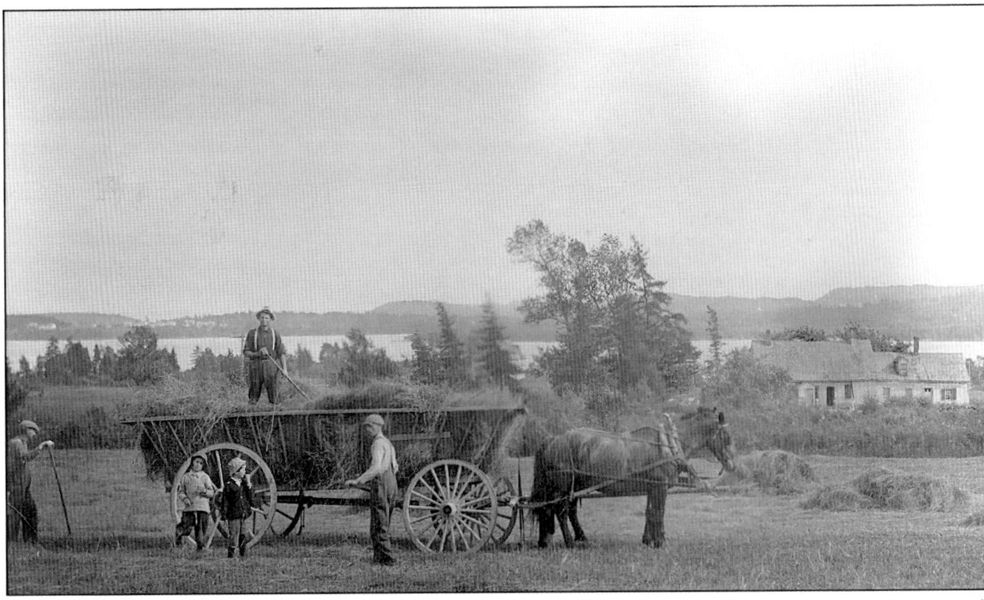

Everyone was involved in bringing in the hay, as shown in this *c.* 1920 photograph taken in Machiasport.

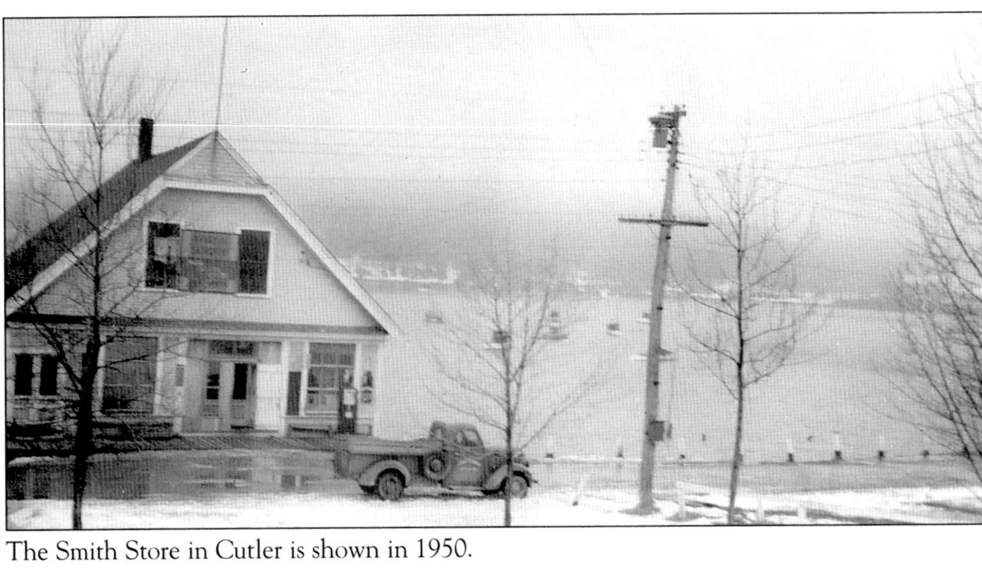

The Smith Store in Cutler is shown in 1950.

Eight

HOUSES OF WORSHIP

Churches have always played an important role in the lives of people in the Machias Bay Region. Fifteen months after the General Court of Massachusetts granted permission to the citizens of Machias to become an organized township, interested members of the community met and voted to hire a minister. In December 1771, Rev. James Lyon came to Machias to preach. There was no church building for services at that time, so services were initially conducted in a barn. In 1774, the first church and meetinghouse was built on the knoll overlooking the river. It was known as "the Little Brown Church on the Hill." This church became the Down East Church of the Revolutionary War. As the years passed, many different denominations built houses of worship to serve the spiritual needs of the growing community.

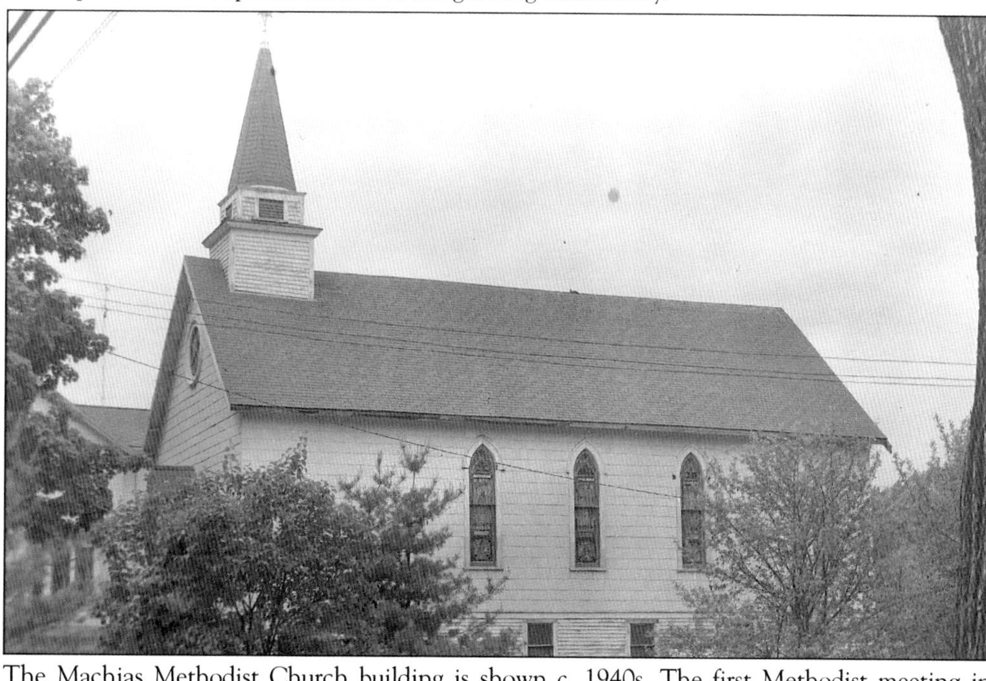

The Machias Methodist Church building is shown c. 1940s. The first Methodist meeting in Machias took place in the winter of 1838 when some citizens met and formed a Methodist class.

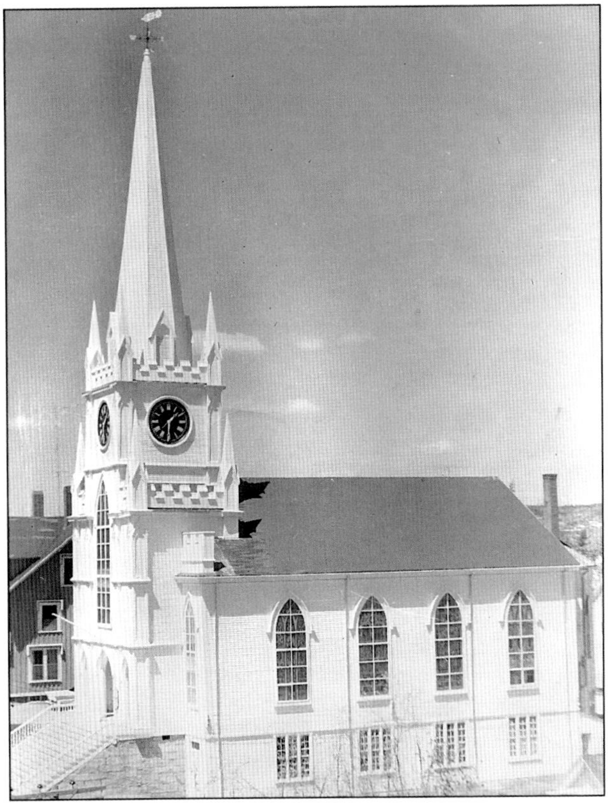

The Centre Street Congregational Church was built in 1836 and is considered one of the finest framed church edifices in Maine. The church is fortunate to have a Paul Revere bell as well as beautiful memorial windows. It was placed on the National Register of Historic Places in 1975. This photograph of the church was taken in the 1940s.

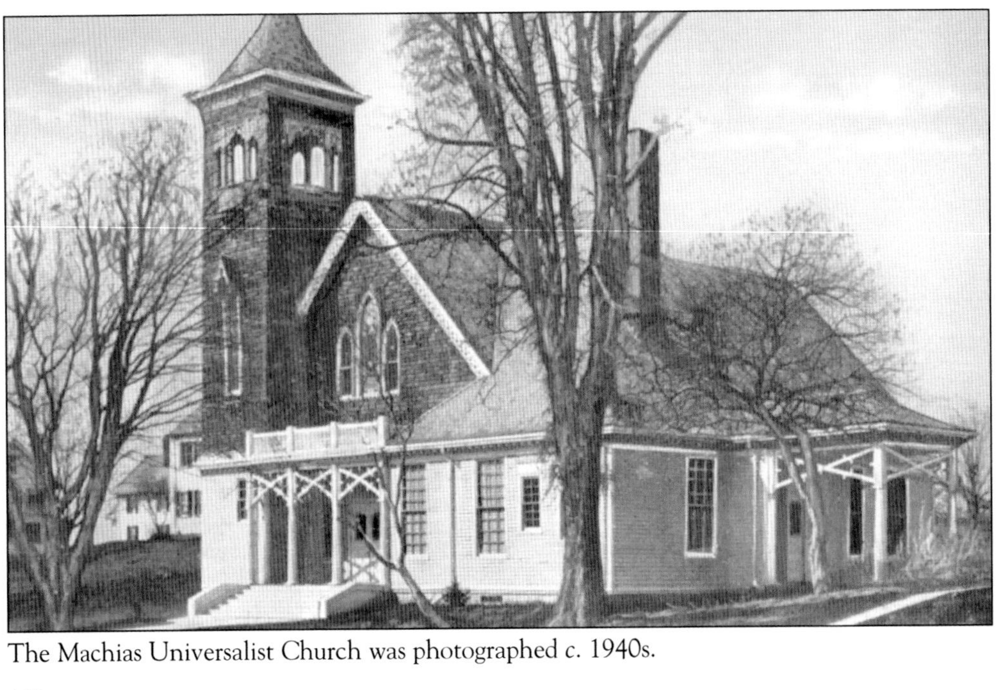

The Machias Universalist Church was photographed *c.* 1940s.

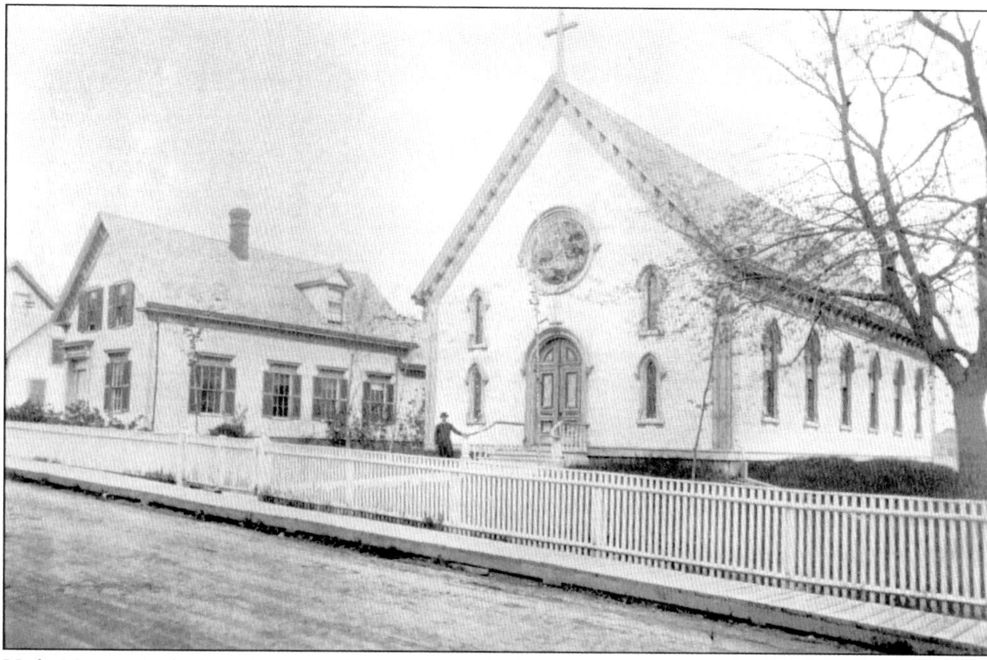

Holy Name Catholic Church in Machias was built in 1845. Prior to this, services were held in homes by priests who made missionary trips to the region. In 1875, the first church building was destroyed by fire. The present church, shown in this photograph before the steeple was added, was built in 1875–1876. This photograph of the church was most likely taken in the late 1880s or early 1890s.

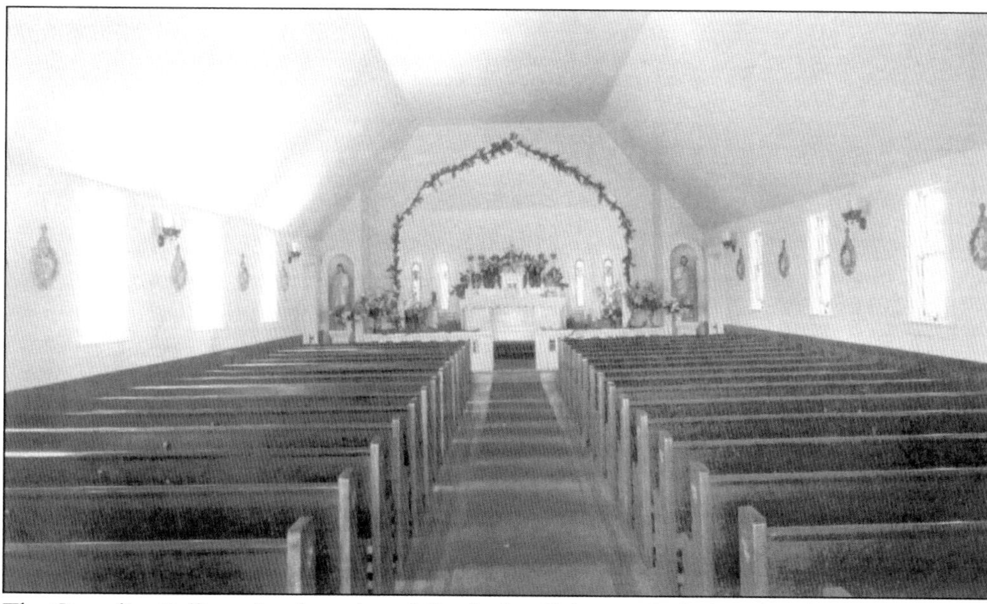

The Cornelius Sullivan family endowed Our Lady of Mercies Catholic Church in Whitneyville in 1936. The church was built in the shape of a cross, using all local wood milled at the Whitneyville lumbermills. The church served the Catholic parishioners of Whitneyville for 36 years until it was decommissioned by the Diocese of Portland in 1969. The building was destroyed by fire in 1996.

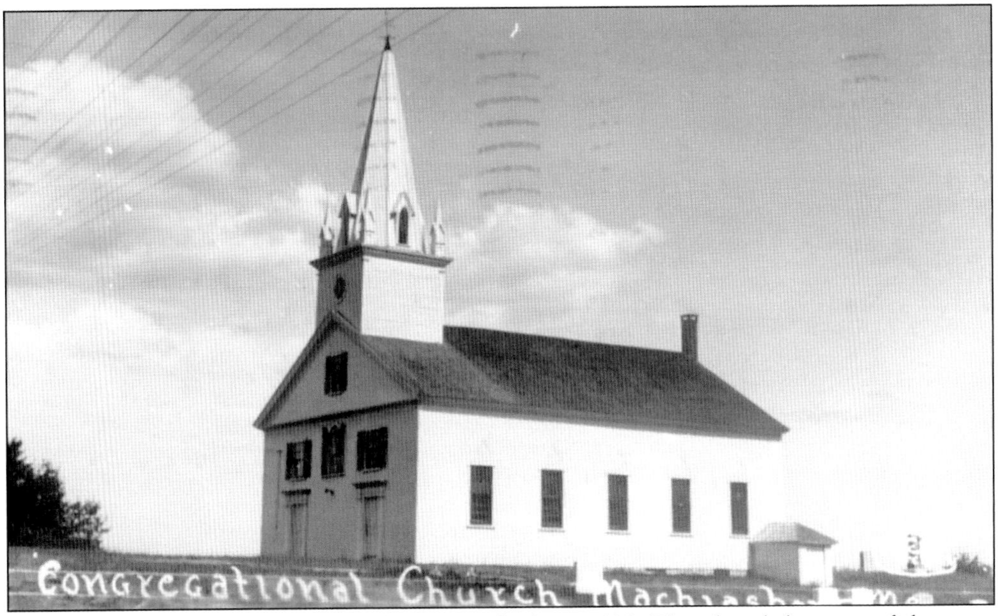

The Machiasport Congregational Church was built in 1828. The church has one of the most picturesque settings of any church in New England. Sitting atop a steep bluff, it possesses a commanding view of Machias Bay.

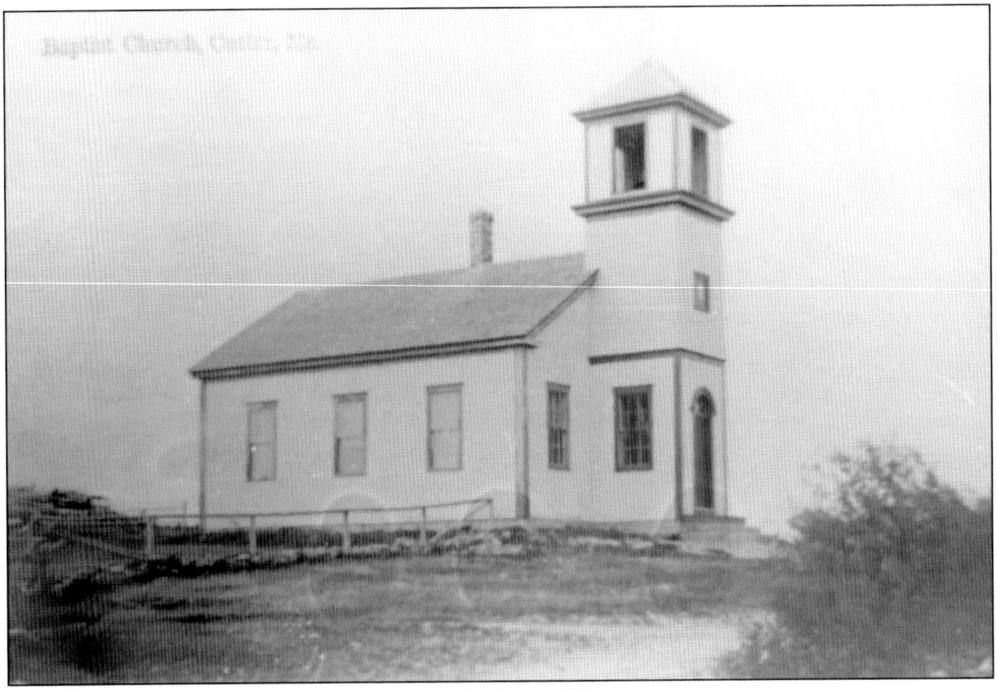

The Baptist church in Cutler was photographed *c.* 1920s.

Nine

The Holiday Season

For years, holiday decorating has been synonymous with products from the Machias Bay Region. Christmas trees, wreaths, garland, centerpieces, and other specialty holiday creations have been produced by the creative hands of local Down East folks and shipped to customers across the United States as well as overseas.

In early November, the traditional process of harvesting the finest tip ends of the balsam fir branches begins. Freezing nights are needed so that the sap will slow, providing the needles a chance to form a strong bond to their branches. Daily deliveries of the harvested tips are brought to the waiting creative hands that will turn the balsam fir into quality decorations. The intense fragrance of the balsam fir and the beauty of the finished product continues year after year to make the holiday season special in homes of families across the country.

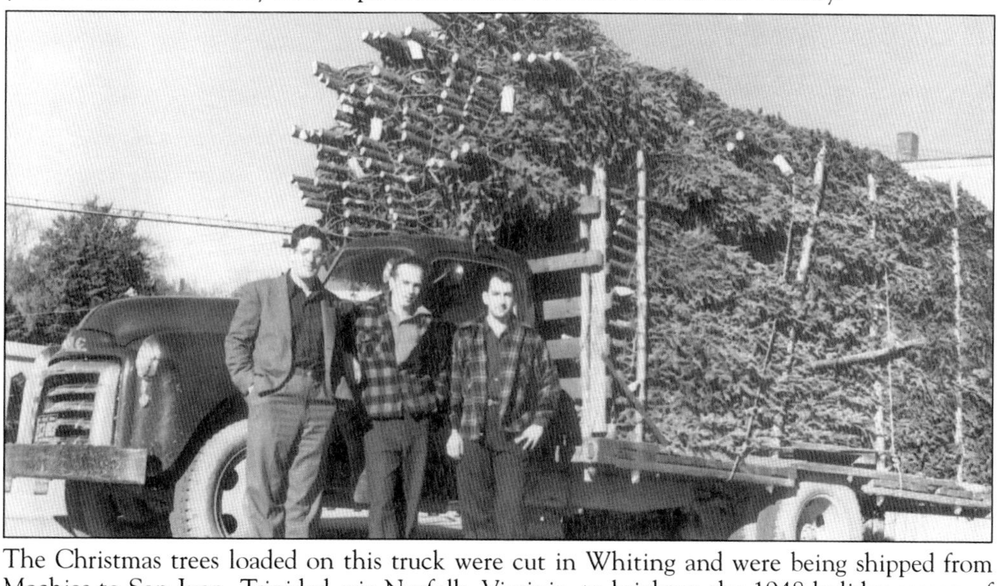

The Christmas trees loaded on this truck were cut in Whiting and were being shipped from Machias to San Juan, Trinidad, via Norfolk, Virginia, to brighten the 1948 holiday season of service families. Joseph Alessi (left), a tree broker from Pennsylvania, Herbert Hanscom Jr., and Mike Kopcha stand in front of their load. The truck left Machias in early November and was one of the first vehicles to drive on the newly finished Maine Turnpike.

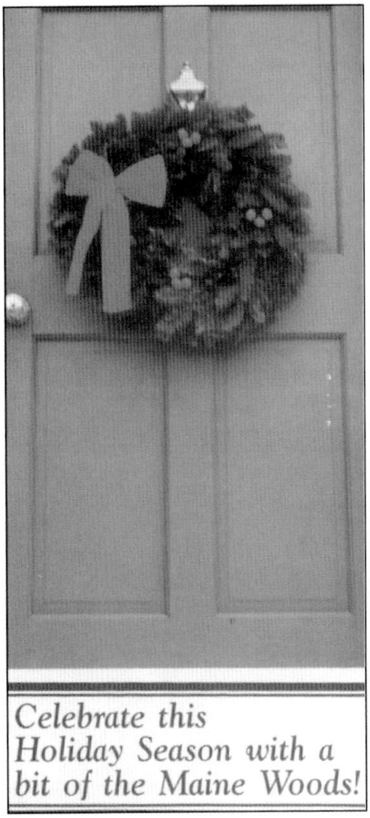

A Machias Bay Region invitation to celebrate the holiday season with some of our great balsam fir decorations.

Richard Hayward is tipping some high-quality balsam fir tips. The tipping process is always conducted in a very thoughtful manner. Local tippers take pride in being good stewards of the environment.

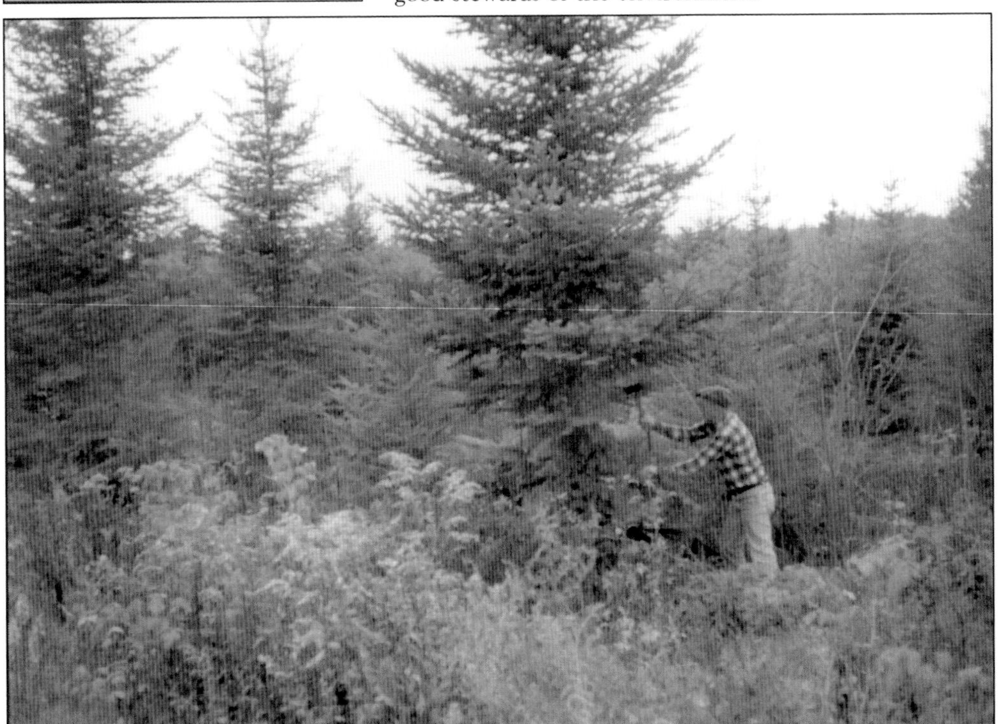

Work is in progress at Flo's Wreaths in Machias.

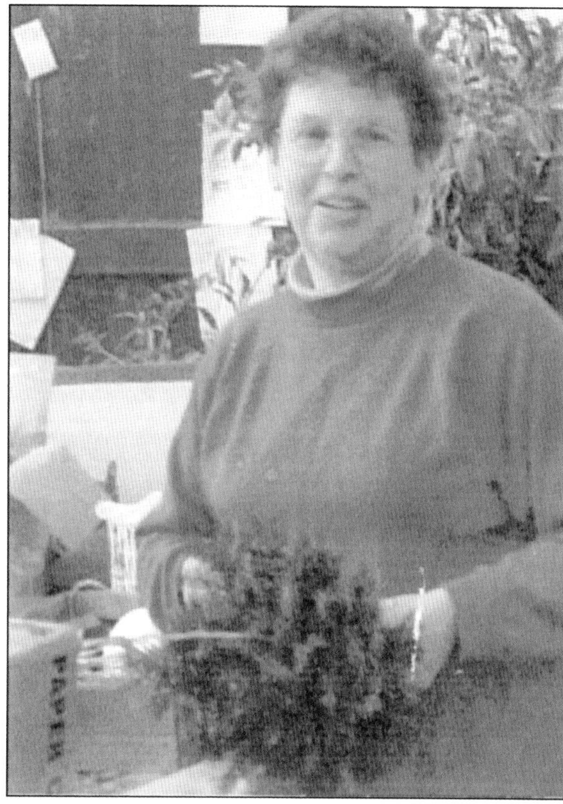

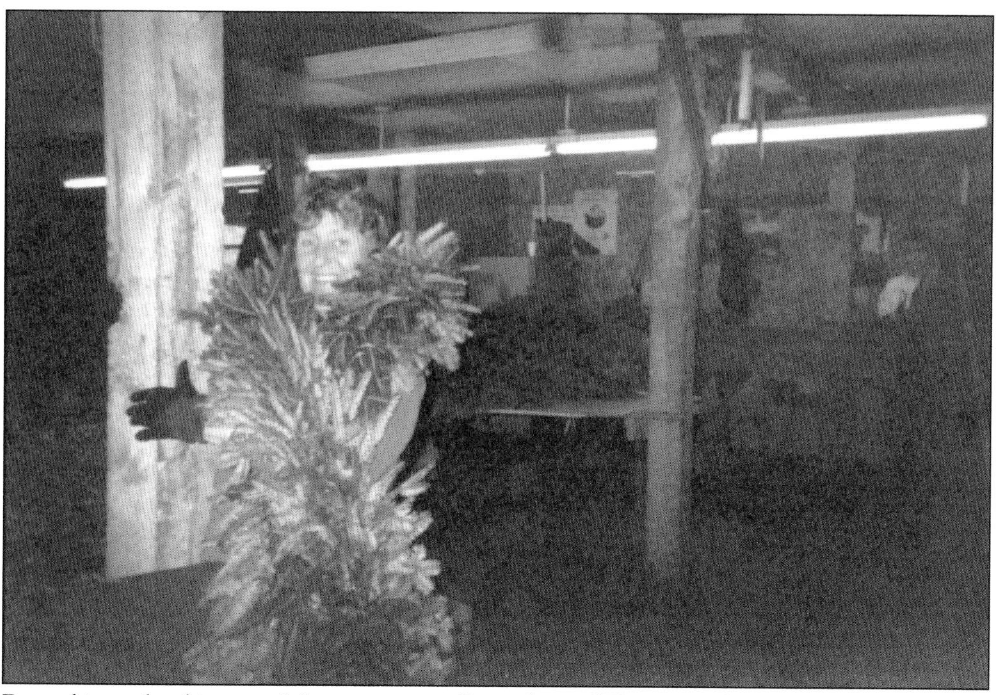

Draped in garland is one of the creative staff members of Flo's Wreaths in Machias.

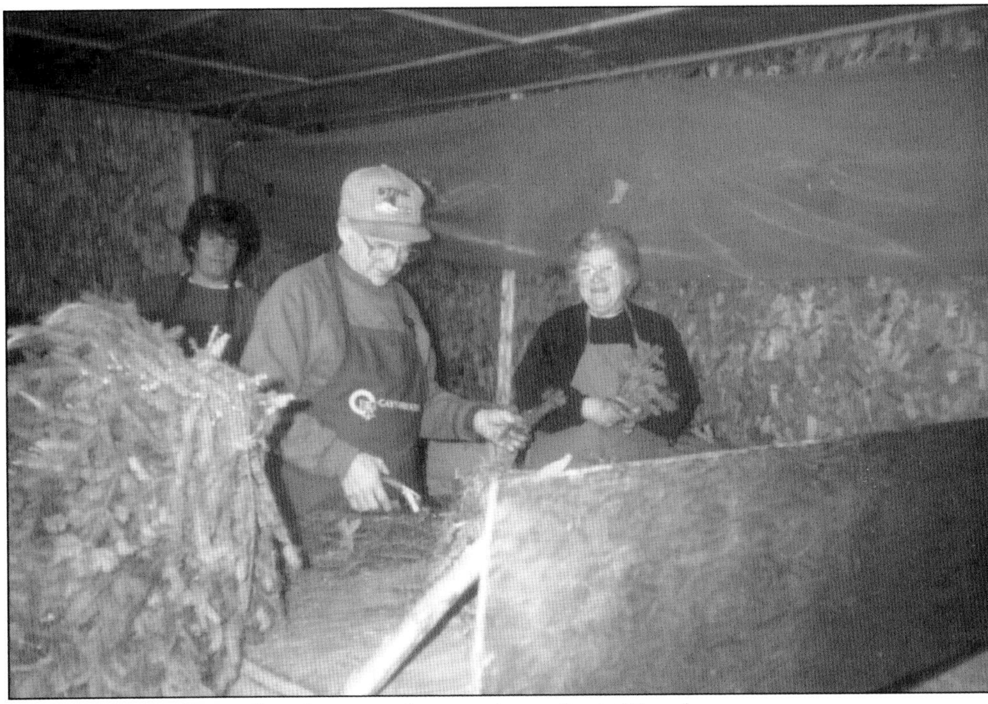

Ralph and Mary Pennell and team make wreaths at Gay's Wreaths.

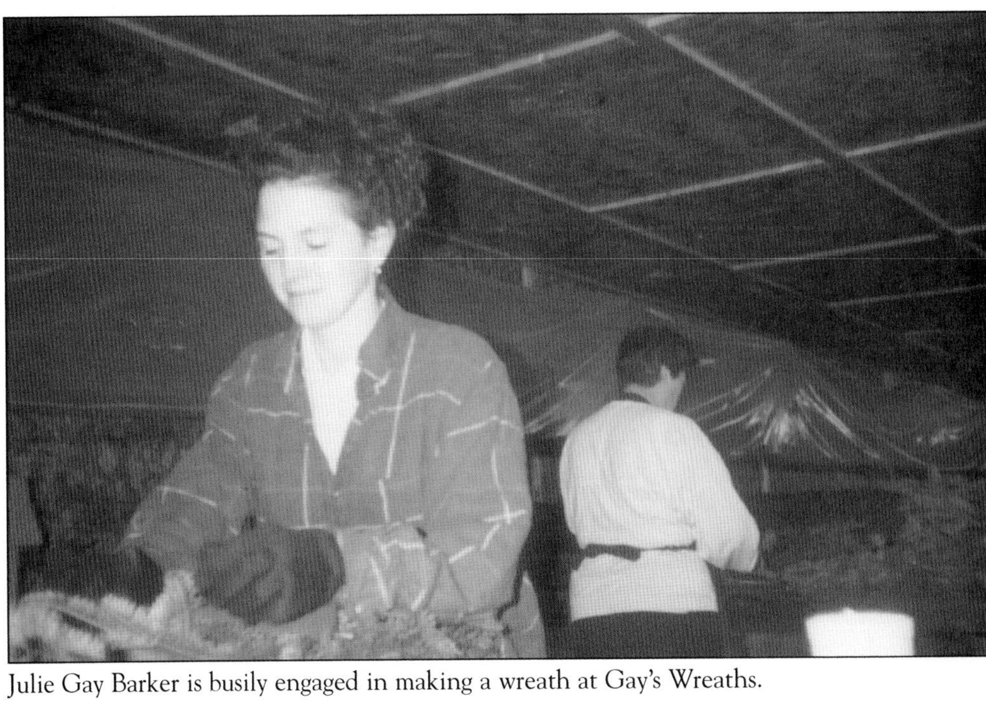

Julie Gay Barker is busily engaged in making a wreath at Gay's Wreaths.

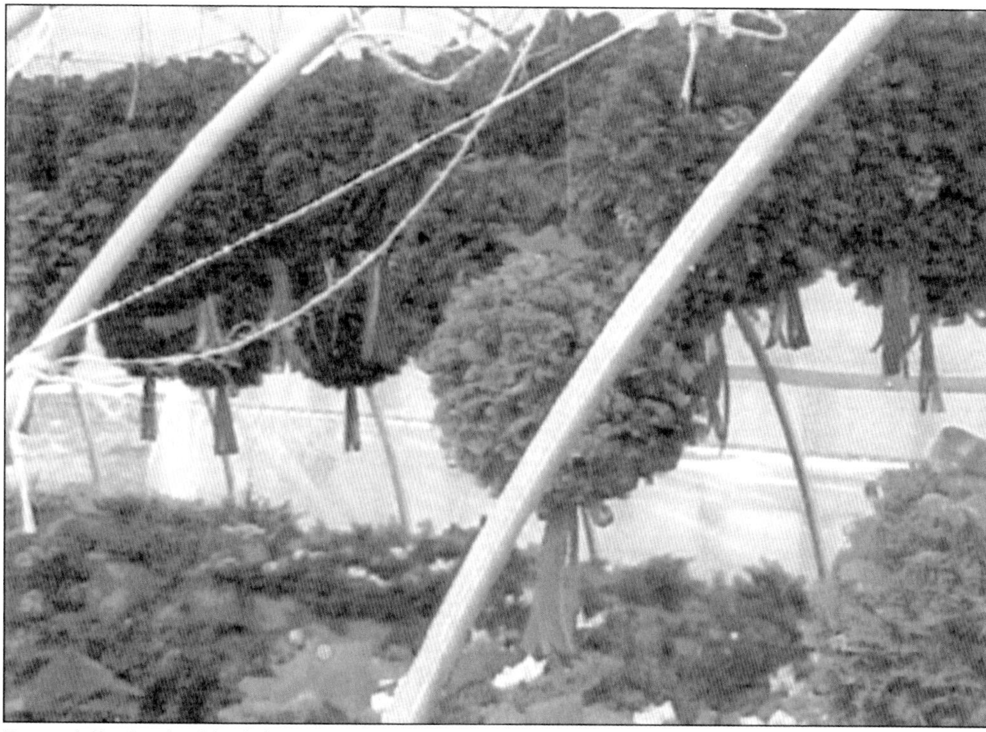

Beautifully finished holiday creations await shipment from Flo's Wreaths in Machias.

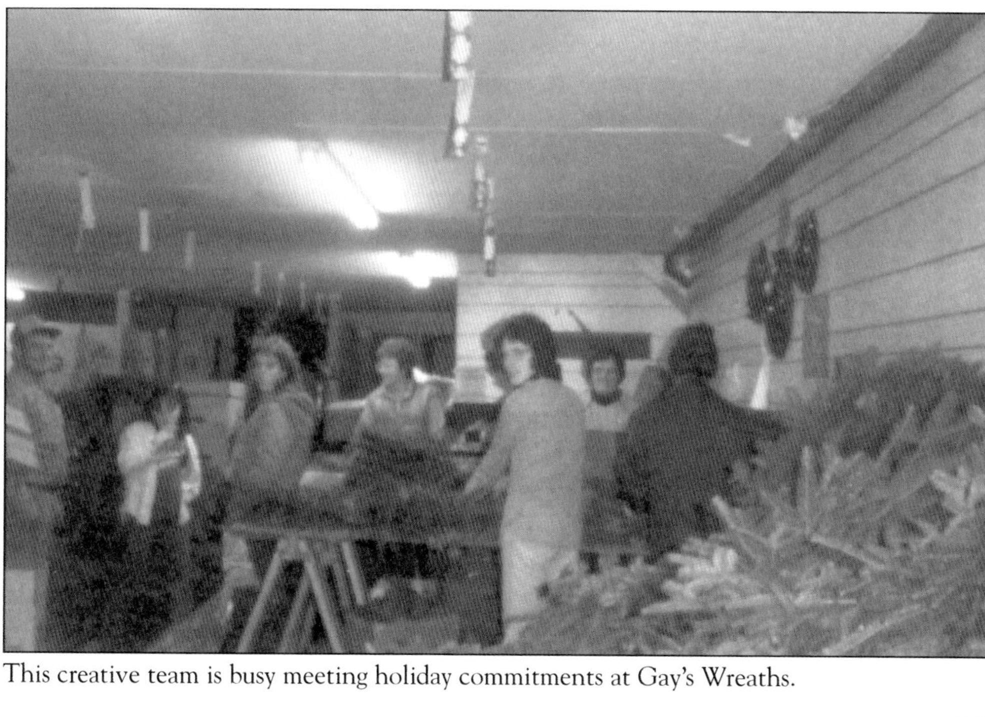

This creative team is busy meeting holiday commitments at Gay's Wreaths.

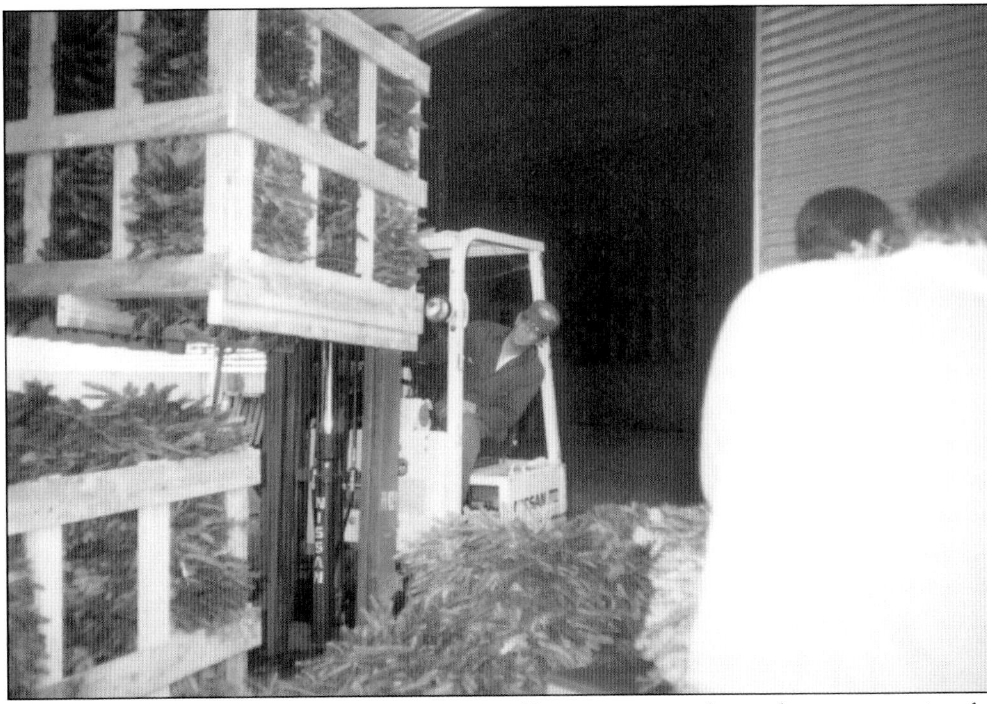

Irwin Reynolds is on the forklift moving crates of large commercial wreaths in preparation for shipment at Gay's Wreaths.

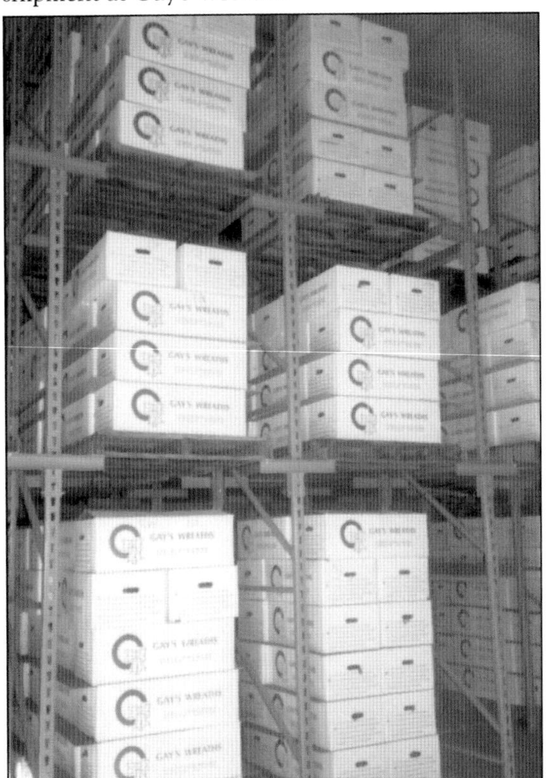

Boxed wreaths are stacked and ready for shipment from Gay's Wreaths. Gay's Wreaths was the first in the region to individually box wreaths.

Ten

Fun Times

In simpler times, a summer's day on the beach, a family picnic, a pony cart ride, a fall day hunting, a sleighride after the first snow, and the crack of the bat heard when the boys of summer would meet on the diamond would intoxicate the heart with joy and satisfy all one's desires. Some do not seem to find this same satisfaction with life today, but we have the memories of those glorious days past.

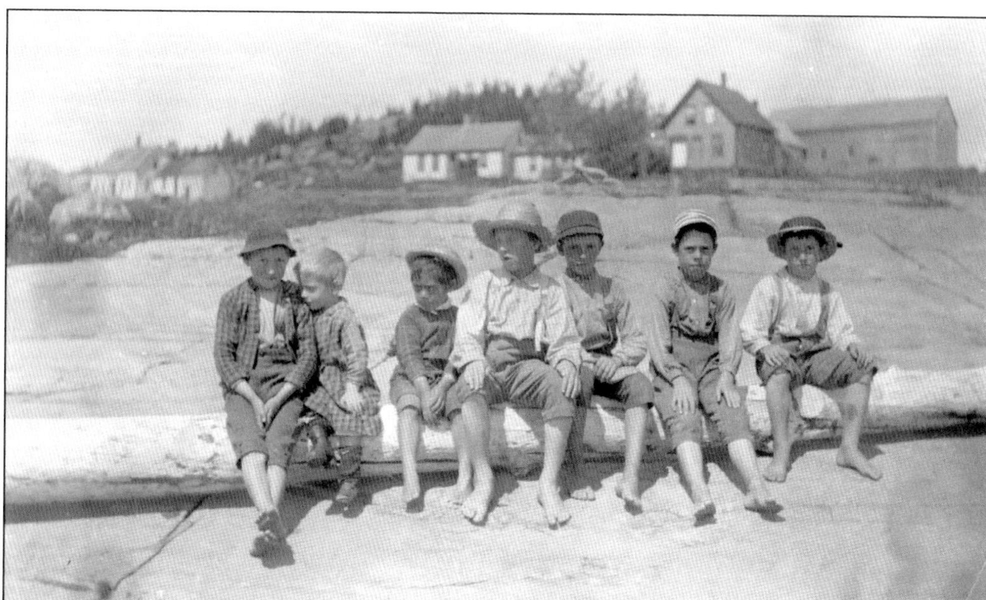

These Cutler boys were photographed in the summer of 1885.

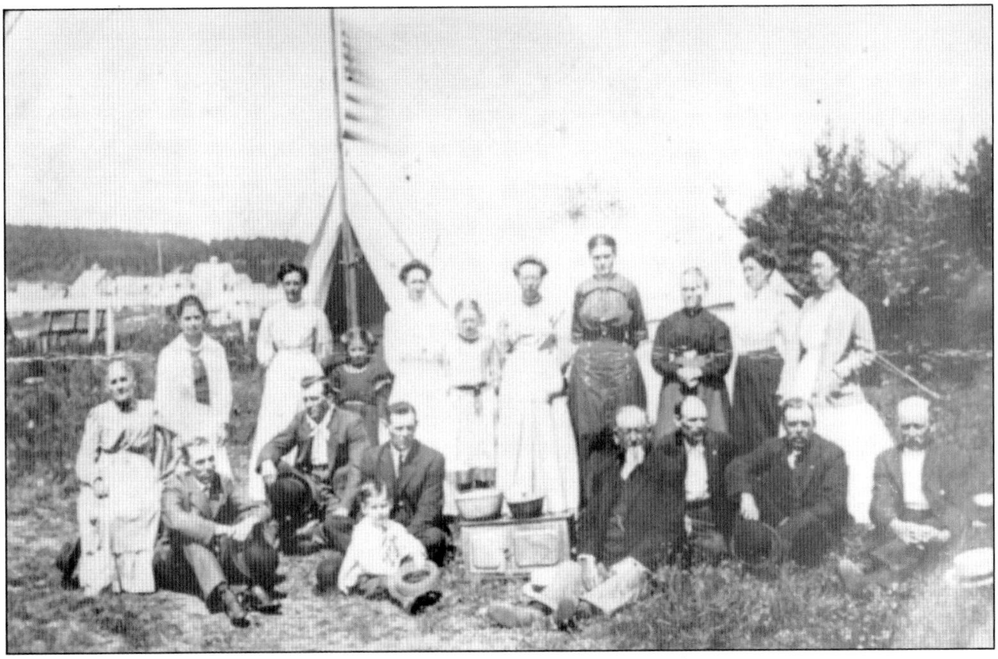

The Maker family's picnic took place in Cutler in the summer of 1906.

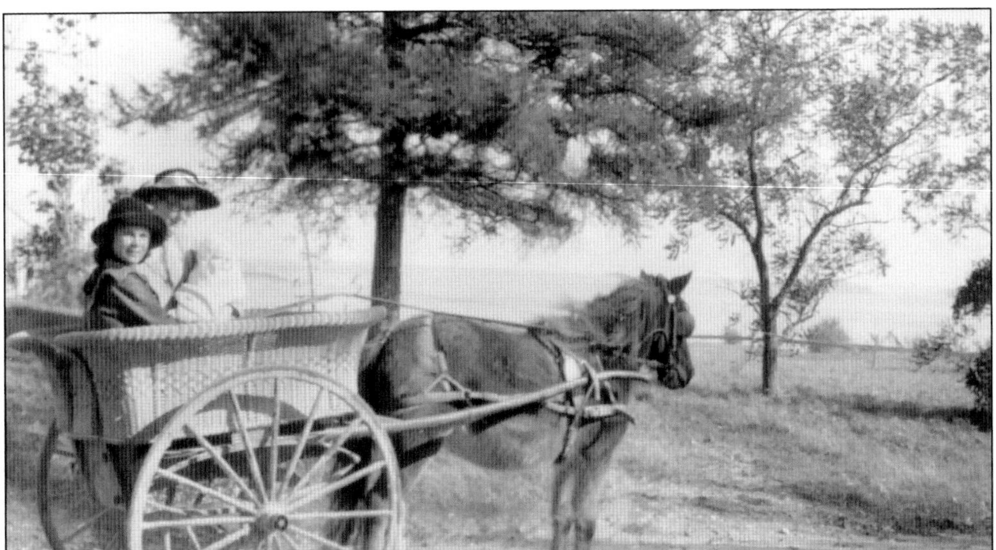

Barbara and Aulette Brown are out for a ride in Machiasport, *c.* 1910.

Gwenie Hooper enjoys a lovely summer day in Bucks Harbor in July 1948.

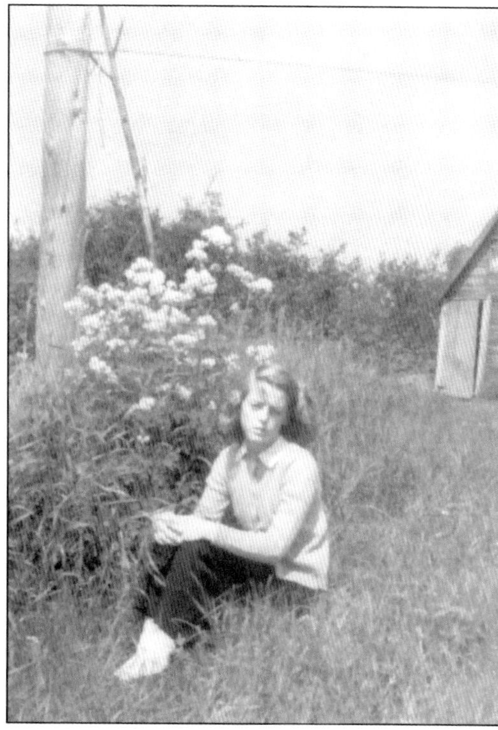

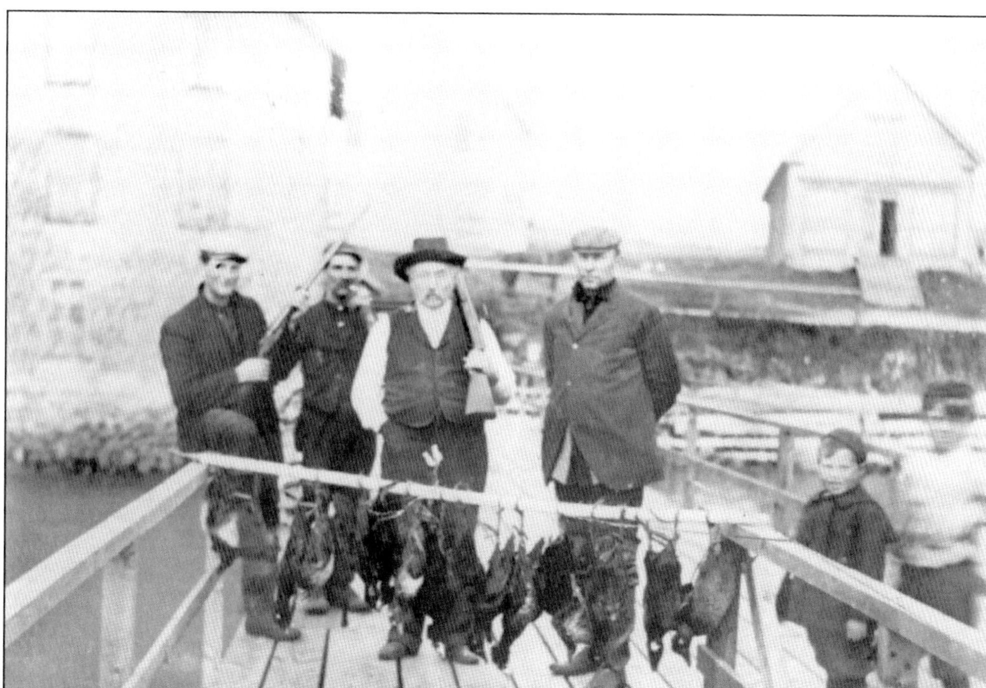

This c. 1910 photograph was taken after a duck hunt.

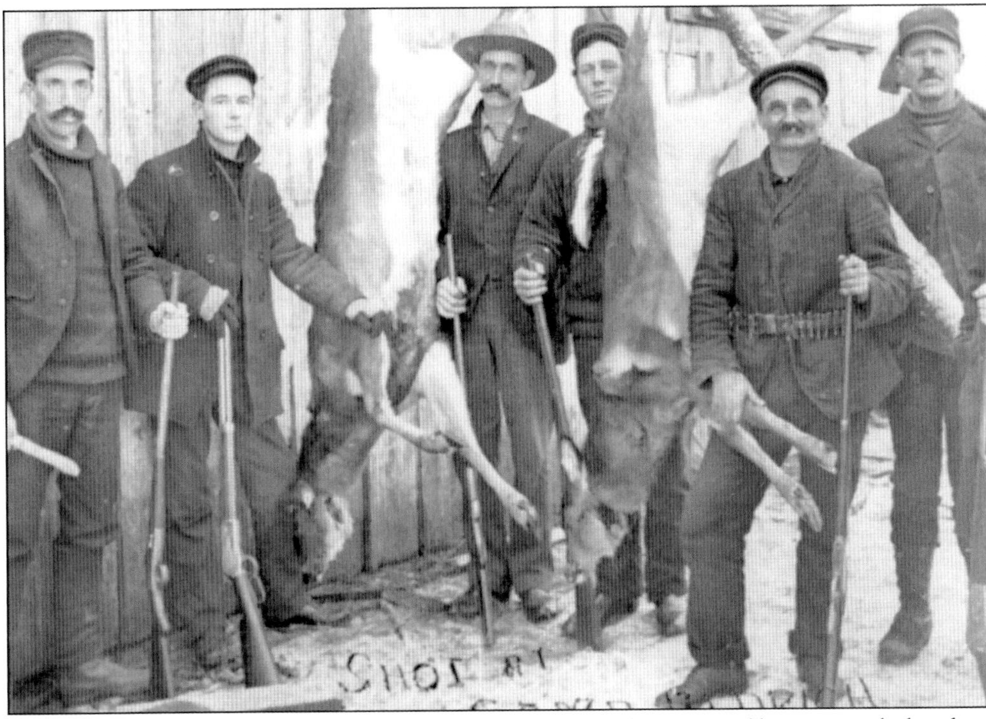

A good day's bag is shown at the Aldrich camp, *c.* 1910. The group of hunters includes, from left to right, Lee Maker, Lucius Gardner, Forest Stevens, Charlie Dennison, Westbrook Sparin, Caleb Aldrich, and Rosco Ackley

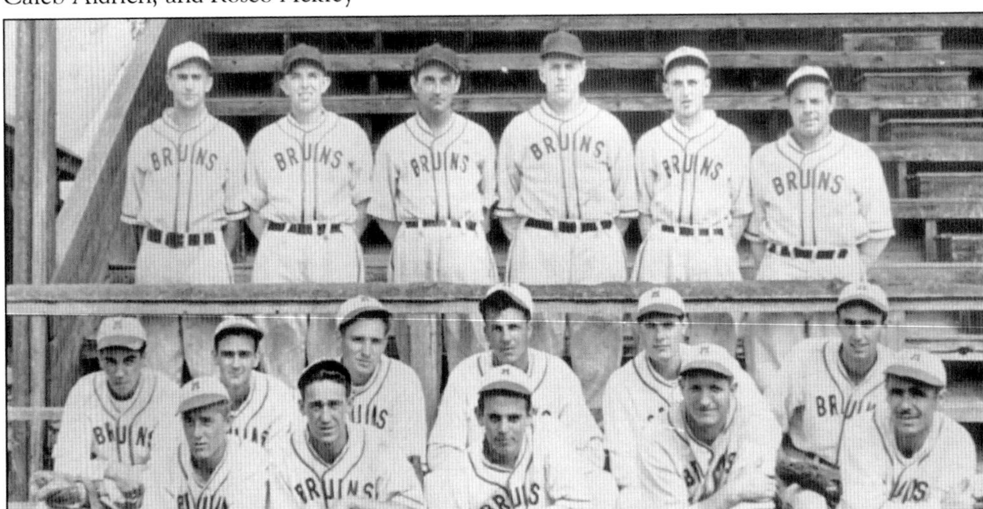

The Machias Bruins of 1948 included, from left to right, the following: (front row) Nonnie Johnson, Hank Browne, Rod McDonald, Bob Mealy, and Maron Ezzy; (middle row) Gary Chadwick, Harvey Armstrong, Ivan Graham, Bob Hudson, Mac MacFadyen, and Jim Haley; (back row) Tom Longfellow, Bill Parker, Al Bridgham (manager), Bob Gardner, Chet McDonald, and Julie Mugnai.

Eleven

WINTER DOWN EAST

Short days and frigid nights come with living Down East in winter. So does driving snow and icy winds. However, on a bright sunlit morning when the landscape has turned into a glittering wonderland, we know that this change by nature is part of the glue that binds each of us to this place we call home. Children out enjoying the opportunities that our winters provide brings smiles to our faces and thoughts of how we loved the snow in our youthful days.

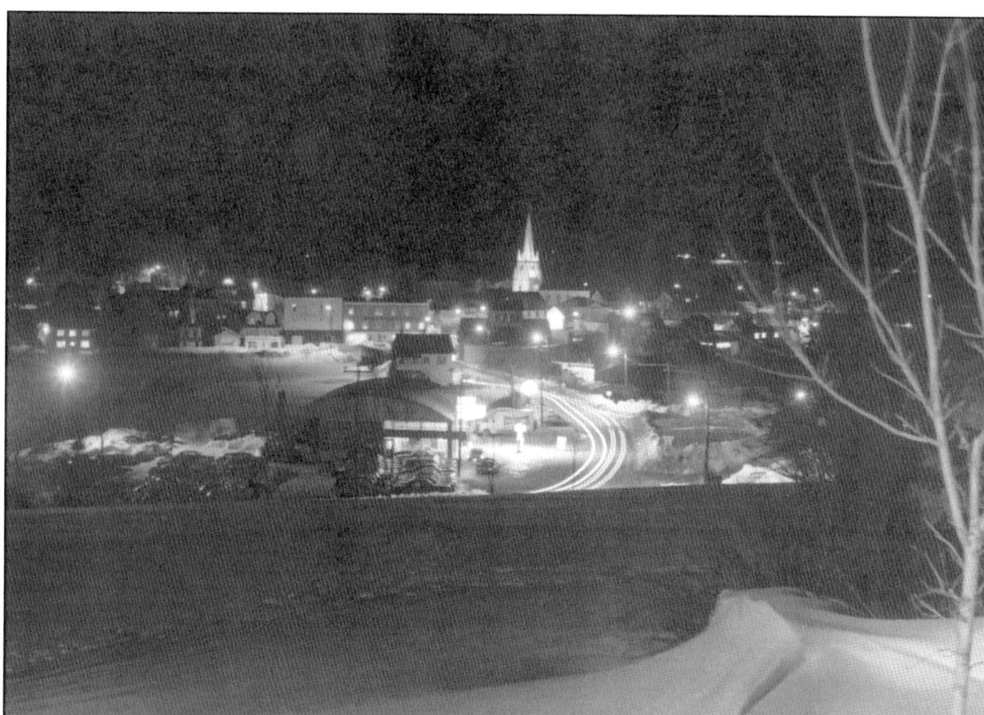

Shown is downtown Machias during a 1960s winter.

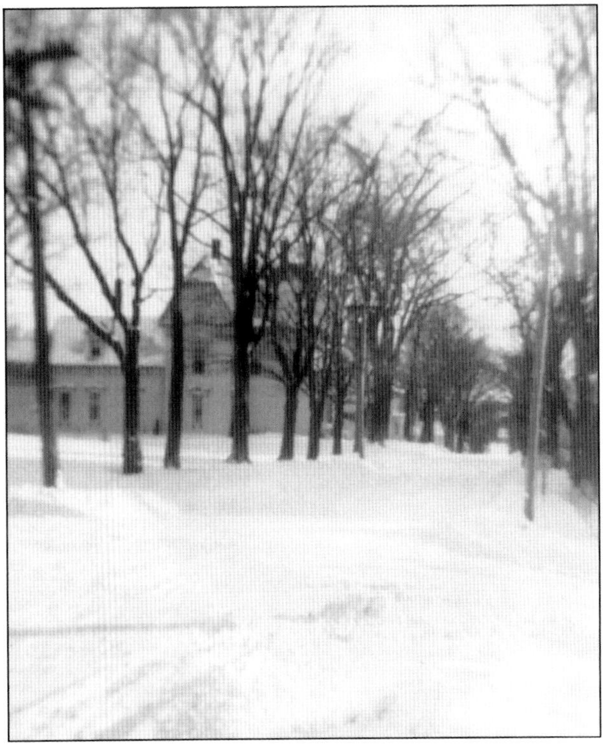

The corner of Free and Court Streets, Machias, was photographed in the winter, *c.* 1940.

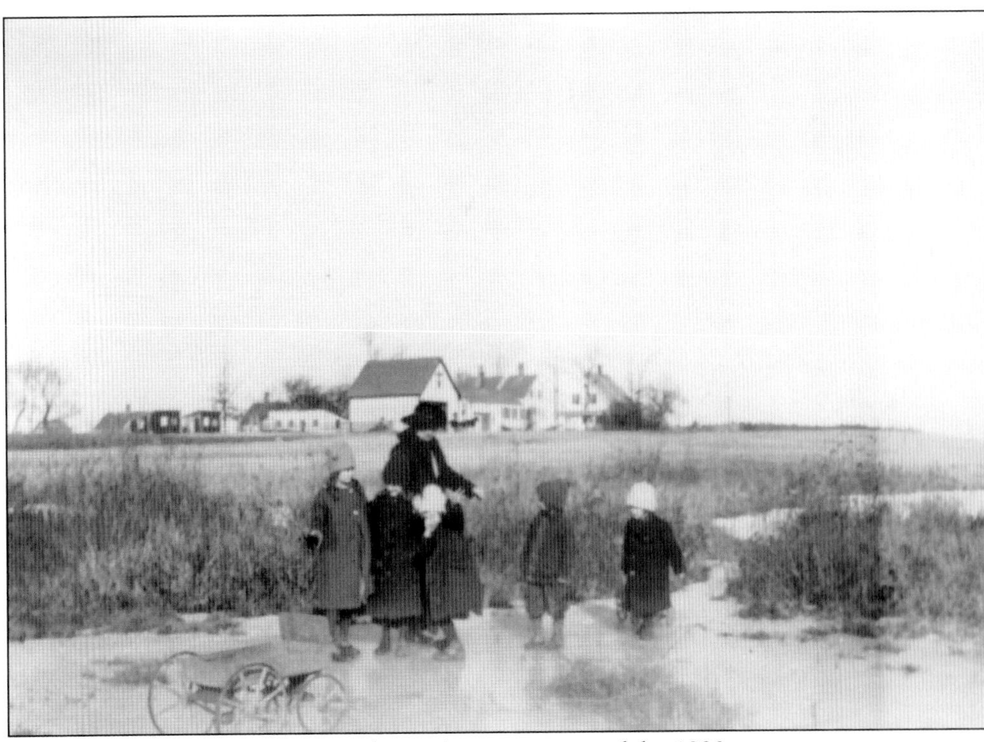

A skating party in Machiasport is shown during a winter of the 1920s.

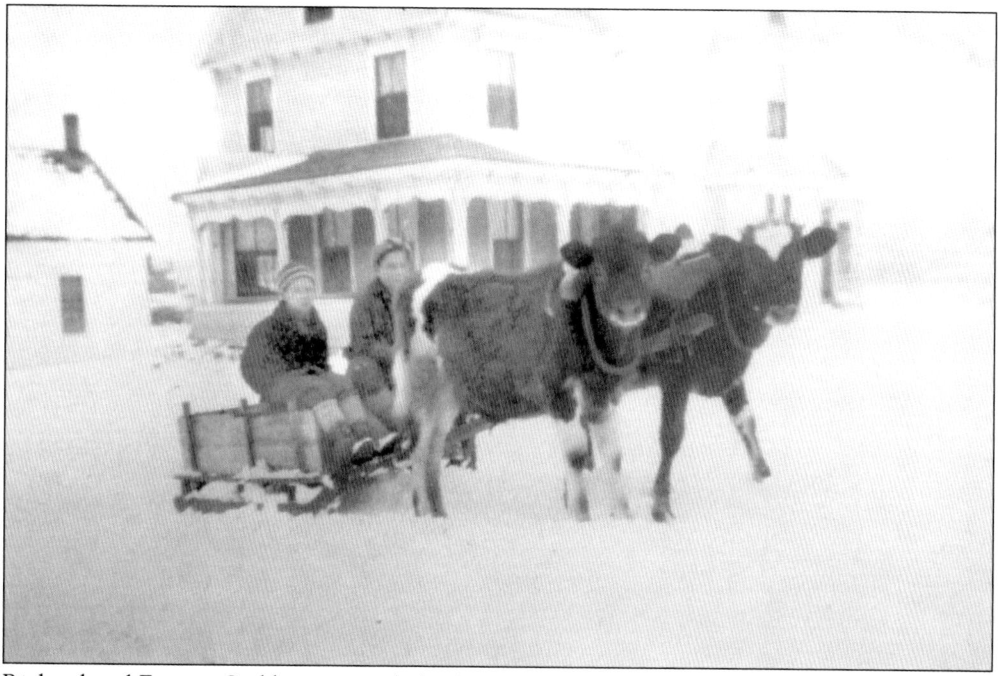

Richard and Francis Gaddis enjoy a sled ride in East Machias *c.* 1920.

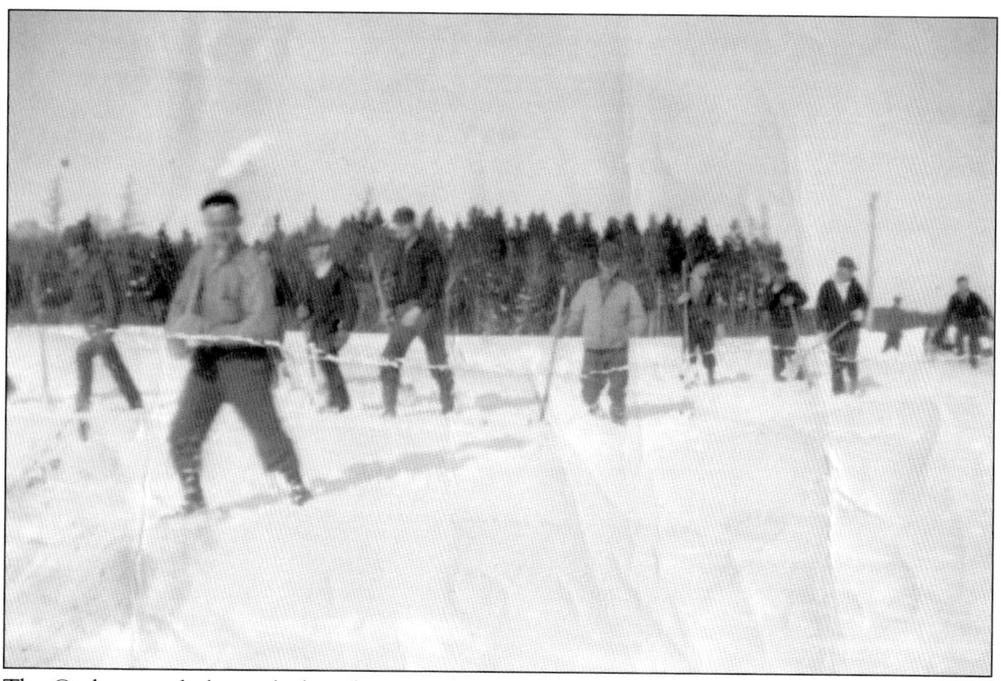

The Cutler crew helps with shoveling in Whiting after a snowstorm during the winter of 1940.

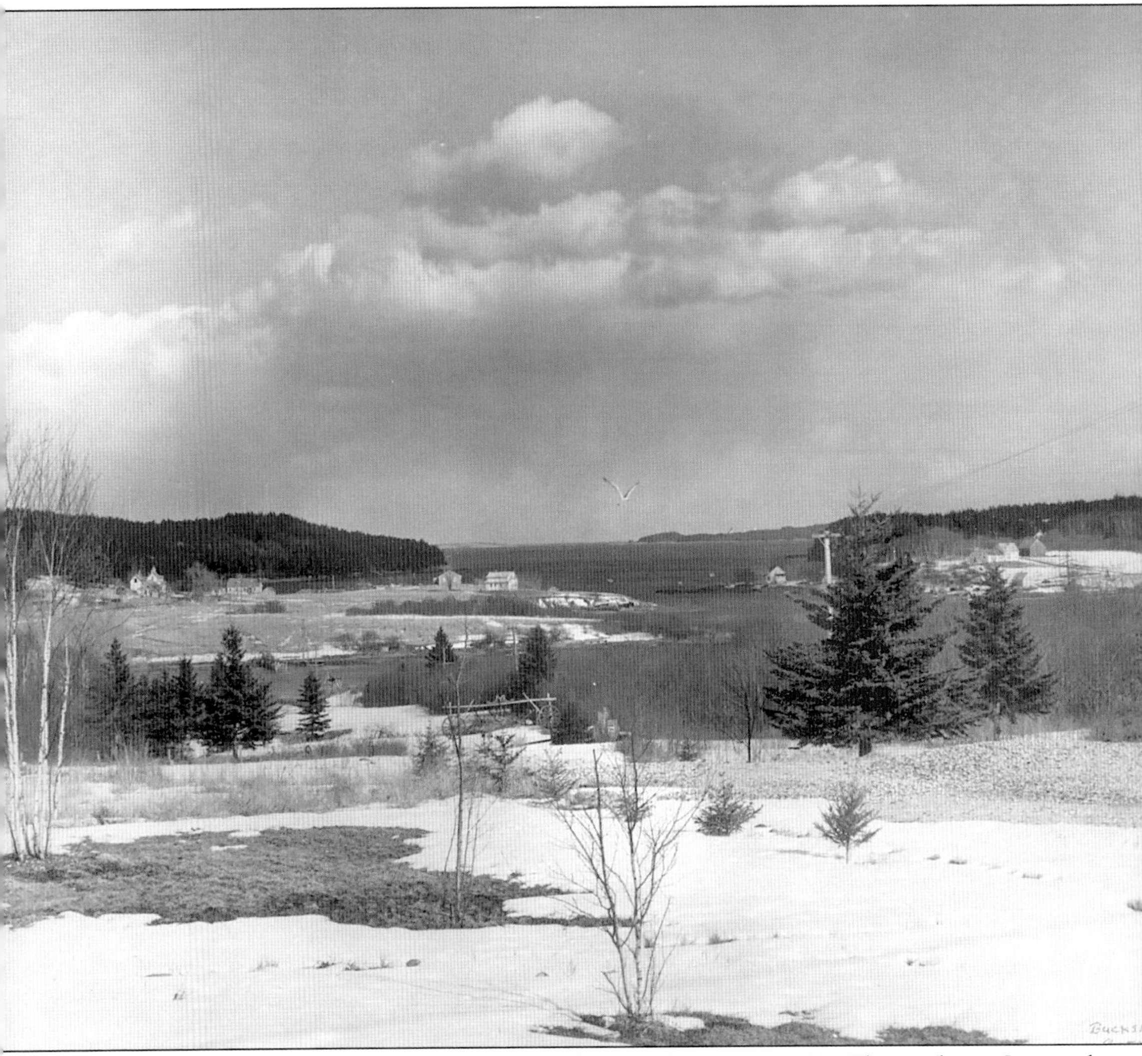

A picturesque winter scene of Bucks Harbor is shown c. 1960. The authors, Jim and Jane Harnedy, view this same winterscape as they are completing the process of compiling this book in January 2001.